Refugeehood and the Postconflict Subject

SUNY series in National Identities
_____

Thomas M. Wilson, editor

REFUGEEHOOD AND THE POSTCONFLICT SUBJECT

RECONSIDERING MINOR LOSSES

Olga Maya Demetriou

SUNY PRESS

Cover image: © 2018 Natalie Demetriou

Published by State University of New York Press, Albany

© 2018 State University of New York

For information, contact State University of New York Press, Albany, NY
www.sunypress.edu

Library of Congress Cataloging-in-Publication Data

Names: Demetriou, Olga Maya, author
Title: Refugeehood and the postconflict subject : reconsidering minor losses / Olga Maya
    Demetriou, author.
Description: Albany : State University of New York Press, [2018] | Series: SUNY series in
    national identities | Includes bibliographical references and index.
Identifiers: ISBN 9781438471174 (hardcover : alk. paper) | ISBN 9781438471181 (pbk. : alk.
    paper) | ISBN 9781438471198 (e-book)
Further information is available at the Library of Congress.

10 9 8 7 6 5 4 3 2 1

To Livia; as ever

CONTENTS

ILLUSTRATIONS

ACKNOWLEDGMENTS

"Cyprus is UN recognized country in Europe. It shares a border with Akrotiri and Dhekelia." This is how a virtual assistant we received as a Christmas present in 2017 answered my test question, meant to check the manufacturer's geographic biases: where is Cyprus? For the uninitiated, naming two British military bases as border-sharing entities would be the equivalent of describing Cuba as the territory extending north of Guantanamo. More ludicrous appeared the emphasis on these two borders by comparison to the line that divides the island into a UN-recognized state and one that is not. Over the course of a decade, I have received innumerable answers to ontological questions about Cyprus, and they have never failed to astonish me, putting into question what I thought I knew about where I come from.

In the course of that questioning, this book has incurred debts to all those who have provided answers and those who have opened up further questions, debts that are impossible to enumerate here. The people at the center of this book are owed the most: they have shared thoughts under difficult circumstances in many cases, answered prying queries, and walked me through their worlds patiently showing me aspects of postconflict life in Cyprus that I would probably not have fathomed otherwise. Many of them are represented here under ethnographic pseudonyms. To those whom, because their roles have been so public, I could never hope to anonymize effectively, I owe a special thanks for allowing their words to appear in public.

For unwavering support and encouragement over many years, I thank Yael Navaro, Elizabeth Anne Davis, Maria Hajipavlou, Jane Cowan, Louiza Odysseos, Effi Voutira, and Gisela Welz. For discussing themes of interest to the book (borders, refugeehood, displacement, citizenship) in ways that made the insights sharper, I thank Sarah Green, Hastings Donnan, Rozita Dimova, Cindy Horst, Engin Isin, and Jackie Stevens. And for commenting on different parts Fionnuala Ní Aolain, Julian Reid, Toula Liasi, Antonis Ellinas, Eleni Meleagrou, Costas Constantinou, and Theodoros Rakopoulos. Other colleagues engaged with the realities of Cyprus, many through kindly accepting invitations to speak to local audiences, in ways that opened new understandings of the relationships across geographical and disciplinary fields: Veena Das, Costas Douzinas, Kerem Öktem, Sossie Kasbarian, Alexandra Zavos, and Liza Schuster. I hope we continue to construct such bridges across fields, and to places as yet unfathomable.

For collaborations that contributed to the exploration of borders, I thank the contributors to *The Political Materialities of Borders* volume: Lenio Myrivili, Stef Jansen, Tuija Pulkkinen, and Chiara de Cesari. This, and other projects I have been involved in were the places where I originally posed many of the questions in the book: the CRIC project funded by the EU's FP7 program (#SSH–217411), COST's EastBordNet action (#IS0803), the PCC's projects on loss and refugeehood, PRIO's Aftermath of Hotspots project (#802495). And of course, the project that started it all many years ago, the Wenner Gren's postdoctoral project on Insecure Minorities.

At the other end, for seeing the book into production, I want to thank the team at SUNY Press: Tom Wilson, for his encouragement right from our first exchange; Michael Rinella and Rafael Chaiken, for patience and support in the initial stages; my two thoughtful and discerning reviewers; Jenn Bennett, for accommodating timing and formatting requests; and Fran Keneston, for making sure the presentation reflected what I wanted to say. And not least, Therese Parent for thoughtful copy editing that left just enough scare quotes to reassure me in dispensing with the rest.

Writing the book has been an exercise in reflection: on theory and practice, on the home and the field, on experience and analysis. On all those counts, my exploration of gender would not have been the same without the Gender Advisory Team, among them Doğuş Derya, Eleni Apeyitou, Nayia Kamenou, and Umut Bozkurt. The insights of Neshe Yashin, Gregory Ioannou, Marios Sarris, Murat Kanatli, Lisa Dikomitis, Vassos Argyrou, and Pafsanias Karathanassis aided further this reflection. And the connecting threads across themes and between knowledge and communication would not have been as clear without the help of my students at the University of Cyprus and many of my colleagues there—the support of the late Ceasar Mavratsas has been invaluable and his absence keenly felt. For welcoming me into a new beginning at Durham, I thank Elisabeth Kirtsoglou, Jutta Bakonyi, Stephanie Kappler, Shaun Gregory, and John Williams.

As ever, family debts are difficult for their sheer inevitability. The lives of my grandparents and those most close to them, spent in Cyprus as subjects of various regimes—from the dimming Ottoman Empire, through British colonial administration, to Cypriot statehood and its punishing conflict, the war of 1974, and the long process of restoration into which I grew up—kept reminding me that citizenship is a matter of time as well as, or even rather than, geography. Their stories have been catalytic to the shaping of the questions I ended up asking. From younger relatives I learnt to grapple with that legacy in public, in performance, and in silence. I especially thank Yiannos Economou for allowing use of his father's art, and Natalie Demetriou for the wonderful work on the cover, and Nicolas Demetriou for assisting. Discussions with Erdal Ilican have offered a wealth of insight on formal and informal perspectives from the other side, and their at times strange confluence. I owe a debt to my parents for what they said and didn't say that shaped this book over decades. And to Tania, for being around whenever. To Murat for many of the ideas explored, many careful readings, and for insisting on the matters at stake. The discussion of enemy subjects in particular condenses much of his insight and work. To Livia, for great patience—yet again, and for pushing me to reconsider, everything and always.

ONE

THE IMBRICATED STRUCTURES OF REFUGEEHOOD

DISPLACEMENTS

It is summer 2003, a little after Turkish-Cypriot authorities announced they would no longer prevent people from crossing in and out of a self-declared state in northern Cyprus, across the island's Green Line boundary. Masses have been flocking to checkpoints since that late April declaration, venturing into places they had not visited since the bloody period of the 1960s and the war of 1974. A restaurant in the old commercial center of northern Nicosia is preparing for the evening's clientele. As we sit down, a friend joins our table for drinks. There is excitement over the opening of the border. We reminisce at how the last time we met some months ago we had to drive for an hour to meet outside Pyla village, in the east of the island, the only location reachable from both sides and closely watched. We keep repeating to ourselves and each other, through a myriad of examples, how just a couple of months ago, what we are doing tonight was unimaginable.

There is a mood of playfulness even as we criticize societal structures that endure. There is still need for change, we agree, and walls of prejudice to be broken. The South Asian waiter serving us, we assume, is exemplary of the problems of discrimination and integration still existing. So we ask about his living conditions and, not surprisingly, hear they are not great. But he also expresses a different concern, since after his visa had expired, he crossed from the south to escape arrest and continue making a living in the north: "Every day I wake up and look across to the other side and remember the house where I used to live, and the place where I worked. It's so near and yet I can't go."

These words prompted a long reflexive pause that inspired the writing of this book. At that moment in 2003, those words sounded strangely familiar; and as I continued to reflect on their possible meanings, I became aware of how deeply imbricated "the Cyprus problem" is with the experience of being in Cyprus—no matter where one is placed and what position one occupies. This book is the outcome of those reflections and the ten years of research that they have informed. It is a study that looks at all those minor losses that have been engulfed by the Cyprus problem for the last half-century and treated as insignificant, or at least secondary, to that other big question and the questions that attend it: how the Cyprus problem came to be, how the two sides interpret things, what the political future might hold, how we (academics, activists, citizens, internationals, mediators) can help realize that future. Those were the questions that occupied many of us in that jubilant mood of 2003 when this comment of tangential loss brought home to me the expanse of all those questions that major losses foreclose. Those minor losses, I came to realize, have not been incidental to the conflict—they have been shaped by it, and they have shaped subjectivities within and beyond it. And just like in other long-lasting conflict situations (Ireland, the Basque and Catalan regions of Spain, Israel/Palestine), those subjectivities are now informing everyday "normal" relations. They service the jubilant and other affective socialities forming around newfound postconflict freedoms—as these develop across the now loosely monitored border and take the form of movement, work, and consumption. It is to these processes that we must now attend if we are to understand the afterlife of conflict.

Physical separation in Cyprus today is no longer a vitally urgent concern for many locals, even though political division is the cornerstone of official rhetoric (see figure 1.1). But the echo of the waiter's words, which communicate this vital urgency in a surprisingly slanted way, continues to inform my understanding of the border in Cyprus. Those words were strangely familiar in multiple senses. On the one hand, they condensed the hegemonic Greek-Cypriot discourse of displacement in Cyprus: that "our" lands, having been snatched unjustly by Turkey after its invasion in 1974, are just over there, so near and yet so far, waiting for us to liberate them. The motif of the Greek-Cypriot refugee seeing her house but not being able to touch it appears in all kinds of literature from elementary-school books, where short stories depict children sending kites across the Green Line, to poems, fiction, and film, which show envy of stray animals crossing—something people cannot do. Before the opening of the central crossing point in Nicosia, binoculars were handed to tourists by Greek-Cypriot soldiers on guard, so they could see across the other side; dignitaries are still often bussed to the easternmost border point in the village of Deryneia to peer through a viewing machine turned towards the abandoned beach resort of Varosha, outside the Turkish-military-controlled town of Famagusta (see figure 1.2). There is a dwelling on division that has come to define Greek-Cypriot subjectivity. The tragedy of Greek-Cypriot refugees, the rhetoric goes, is that they are "refugees in their own country." The impossibility of crossing the border "to go home" was for many years packaged as a corporeal experience for foreigners who, having felt it, are encouraged to become ambassadors for the cause of return. For the Greek-Cypriot-schooled public, the effect was to cultivate a sense of generalized refugeehood. This is a notion I explore in later chapters. To Greek-Cypriots growing up after 1974, the definition of "refugee" seemed obvious and the sentiments of loss that were expected to attend it were perceived as a structure of feeling that the whole population should share. The affective register was, and largely remains, central to the governmentality of conflict subjectivities.

KEY

1 Kontemenos / Skylloura area	8 Pyla
2 Gonyeli	9 Achna
3 Aloa, Maratha, Sandallar	10 Karpasia enclave villages
4 Kofinou	11 Kormakitis enclave villages
5 Ay Theodoros	12 Tillyria area enclave
6 Tochni	13 Akrotiri SBA
7 Dali, Potamya	14 Dhekelia SBA

FIGURE 1.1. Map of Cyprus, showing areas mentioned in the book.

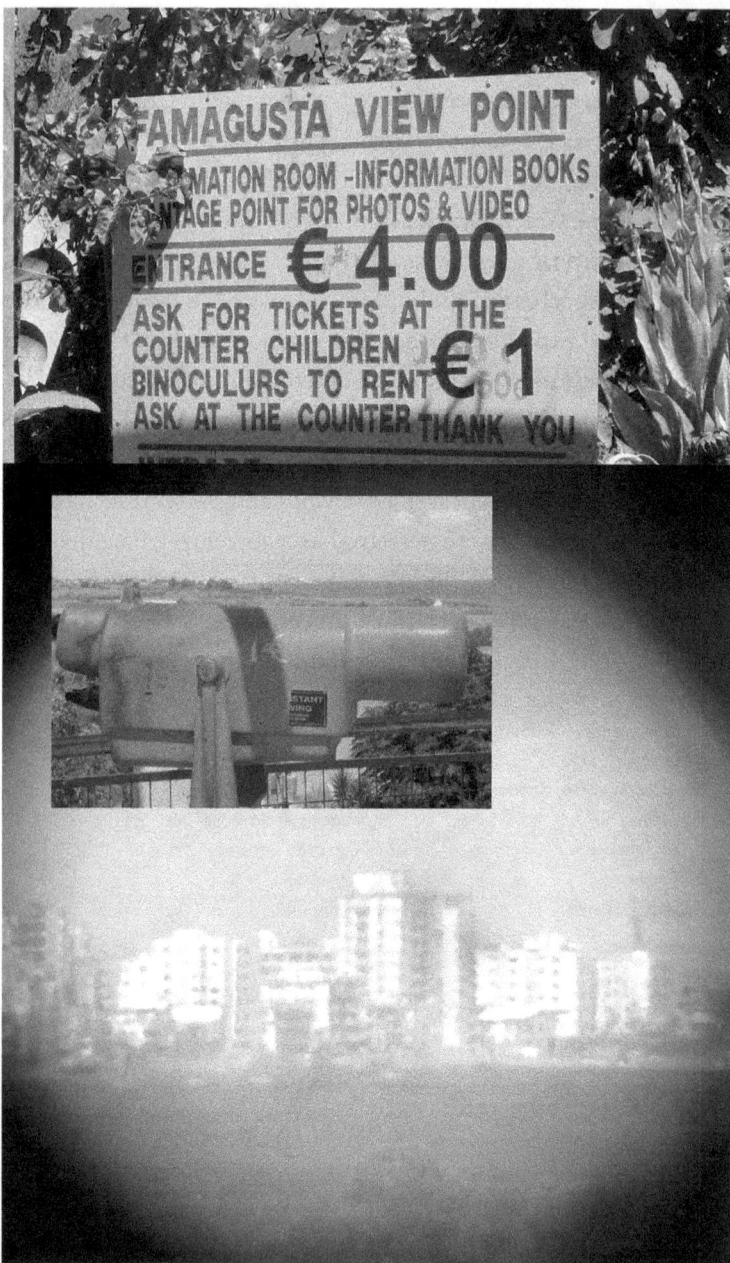

FIGURE 1.2. Deryneia viewpoint: Entrance sign (top); coin-operated viewing machine (center); Varosha ruins outside Famagusta town through the view finder (bottom).

So to hear this discourse articulated on the opposite side of the divide seemed strange—it was not quite refugeehood. First, the unreachable other side was now the south, not the north. This was only partly strange. Since 1963, Turkish-Cypriots have often articulated longing for homes left in the south, and this has been well researched.[1] This longing is well known, and it is also opposed to the official rhetoric that, since the war of 1974, has emphasized forgetting the homes in the south and looking forward to a brighter future in new homes in the north.[2] Even when not explicitly opposed to official discourse, articulations of longing are positioned against this background, making the desire for return and lament for lost homes complexly ambivalent.[3] What seemed strange, in this sense, was a kind of geographic dislocation of affect. It is not that people in northern Cyprus don't pine for homes in the south, but that they pine for them in *this* way.

Second, the time of this affective expression seemed strange. The inability to go home, which produced this longing, was not in response to the solidity of the border. It took shape precisely at the moment the border opened up, and when it seemed that in fact it was about to be dissolved altogether. Turkish-Cypriot authorities decided to allow crossings over the Green Line in April 2003, during a period (2002–2004) of intense political negotiations. At the end of these, a plan for reunification (the Annan Plan) was put to a referendum in April 2004 and rejected by Greek-Cypriots, while Turkish-Cypriots supported it. This deferred the dissolution of the border; but this referendum was still to come in that summer evening of 2003, and the atmosphere of excitement was not conducive to such predictions, as I explain in later chapters. The waiter's comment exemplified what much of border-studies literature has recently been documenting: that changes in the operations of bordering (the materialities of borders, the apparatus that govern them, and the practices that develop around them) are not evenly distributed across populations. Instead, the easing of some movement might imply, or in this case accentuate, the restriction of other movements (Aas 2011; Rygiel 2010; Brown 2010; Bigo 2006).

The radical change in the operation of the border in Cyprus in 2003 saw thousands streaming across it. Going home was one of the primary activities Greek-Cypriots with ties to the north had been engaging in, *en masse*, and on a daily basis throughout the previous months. Middle-aged men and women visited homes they remembered from childhood; elderly parents were driven to meet neighbors and friends, collect agricultural produce from fields, and retrieve movables saved and collected by those now living in their former homes; youngsters were guided through houses that suddenly seemed much smaller and through landscapes less grand than they had remembered or imagined. There was ambivalence here too in the encounters between different owners and in the performance of return. But there was a definite sense that the main barrier to whatever return might ensue, was slowly being lifted. So on that evening, the emblematic articulation of Greek-Cypriot refugeehood seemed misplaced, in both place and time. This was not the time to pine for lost homes, but to celebrate their imminent recovery—for Cypriots.

And ultimately, the cause of that misplacement was the strangeness of a specific subjectivity. It seemed strange to hear what I had come to recognize as a Greek-Cypriot discourse on loss, articulated by a stranger—an immigrant with no apparent familial ties to Cyprus. There was an uncomfortable realization of the presumptuousness with which I, and others, had approached the Cyprus conflict up to then, which guided much of my questioning since. So what did its strangeness mean? Is the so-near-yet-so-far discourse actually the articulation of something banally self-evident, perhaps, and not the epitome of Greek-Cypriot politics at all? And does this banality point to something universally applicable rather than a feature of a specific political culture? What is the affect that a sealed border exudes and how does it come to surpass the conflict that sealed it in the first place? How do ethnic divides exceed the binaries that define them? At the time, the waiter's comment seemed a spontaneous attempt to relate the excitement of meeting someone coming from the side that had become inaccessible. I since wondered whether it might have also been mediated by the experience of having lived in the south and among the Greek-Cypriot refugee discourse (likely to have been expressed by people above him in the class hierarchy). But it is the questions about the excesses of conflict imaginaries and the losses they foreclose that I have repeatedly returned to, and which I want to highlight as inroads to reconsidering the subjectivity of refugeehood in general.

To recognize that the waiter's discourse is misplaced is to recognize the misplacement of subjectivity too. And to reflect theoretically on the validity of these analytics of misplacement requires that we ask where it is that subjectivity is "correctly" placed in Cyprus. Who are Cypriots, and who are the proper subjects of Cypriot refugeehood? To probe this question requires examination of several layers of discourses about refugeehood, displacement, and loss, which I engage in later on. And most importantly, I argue, it requires engagement with the ways in which all these layers are connected to each other—examined under the metaphor of imbrication.

Such imbrication is not unique to Cyprus. To return to the long-standing conflicts previously mentioned, the discursive structures developed in Palestine, Ireland, and Spain govern and affect the experience and policy of migration today. After the Good Friday Agreement in Northern Ireland, where a border has undergone a similarly radical shift as in Cyprus, the legacy of the conflict has created an all too familiar "grim reality for people of colour, refugees, and migrants" (McVeigh and Rolston 2007, 11) where the "politics of identification . . . position migrants and minority ethnic communities within dominant sectarian discourse" (Geoghegan 2008,174). In Ireland, narratives of immigration and the legitimacy of refugees entail "unresolved Irish memories of colonisation, the Famine, and emigration" (Moriarty 2005, 6.7). The politics of occupation and international recognition in which the Israeli/Palestinian conflict is embedded is also familiar to Cyprus. International migration in Palestine arises through these politics as a question on which "Israel demands the last word," and this results in limited and patchy regulation by the Palestinian Authority, as exemplified by failure to link regular work with regular stay (Khalil 2008,12). And on the other side of the wall, "Israel's labor migration policy reflects the state's continuous anxiety over a changing ethnoscape" (Raijman, Schammah-Gesser, and Kemp 2003,733), an anxiety stemming directly from the history of the conflict there, and resulting in the placement of irregular women migrants at the bottom of the scale. This arises because the citizenship regime, ethnically determined through and through, leaves no prospects of integration, assigns foreign workers to a category "with a biblical connotation of profanity" (ibid., 747) and conceptualizes domestic work within the patriarchal-military imaginary that societies emerging from conflict, like Israel and Cyprus, know so well. And in Spain, conflicts over autonomy and secession in the Basque region and Catalonia have differentiated both areas in their immigration policies. Catalonian parties have articulated opposition to centralizing attempts from Madrid on the point of immigration policy resulting in sometimes more progressive and at other times more restrictive approaches. In the referendum of 2017, which solicited independence from Madrid, both pro- and anti-immigration arguments propped the separatist position: independence could ensure more autonomy to improve integration structures, and more autonomy to stem migration policies too. The strong emphasis on Catalan identity and language, which is currently a cornerstone of integration policies, can easily be adapted to opposing perspectives that drive the secessionist argument. In the Basque region, on the other hand, Basque parties have built on "the link between the promotion of internal diversity and Basque values" (Jeram 2013). The legacy of conflict in Spain means, in short, that "immigration is not so much a component of diversity as it is a vehicle through which existing diversities are brought to the fore" (Zapata-Barerro 2010,171). These complex situations are in different ways reflected in the themes I examine in Cyprus.

A major claim of this book is that the entrenchment of conflict structures in society and government implicates—and most importantly imbricates—forms of classification and exclusion, as well as the experiences that go with them, that stretch far beyond the conflict. And it is out of these imbrications that postconflict subjects of multiple positionings emerge. In Cyprus, the framing of such imbrications is refugeehood.

REFUGEEHOOD, POWER, AND CONFLICT

Wisdom has it that refugees flee war. Much less is said about what they find after they do so, not in terms of the reception they receive, but in terms of the conflicted societies they land in. At the same time, much of the literature on forced displacement grapples with this seemingly simple link between conflict and refugeehood. One example is the debate that persists over the appropriateness of the term "environmental refugees" to describe people who are forced out of unlivable habitats. And while environmental degradation could have been tied to wars and conflict in the past (El-Hinnawi 1985; Kibreab 1997), it now more often results from natural disasters and rising sea levels (Bates 2002; Keane 2003; Hartmann 2010). This only confirms a basic tenet of refugee studies: that refugeehood is not an objective but a political category. As McNamara puts it, "[The assertion] that environmental refugees do not exist is still a social construction of environmental refugees, a subject identity reliant on an absence or negation of a particular characteristic or condition" (2007, 15).

In the same way, the assertion that political and economic adversities can be separated out as producing refugees in the first instance and economic migrants in the second is also a social construction of refugees and economic migrants. This second debate, the most enduring in the field of forced migration studies, manifests the predicament of using legal standards to square politics and ethics. Many scholars have insisted for some time now on the need for policy makers to extend the interpretation of "refugee" from the two categories (political refugees/economic migrants) to account for the fact that most irregular migrants fall somewhere in the vast gray area between them. Scholars have convincingly argued that the insistence of states on this erroneously sharp distinction is a political tool that enables them to deny refugee protection to great numbers of people who might otherwise qualify for it (Gibney 2004). They have also shown that the legal basis of labeling refugees is a shifting field itself: over the last two decades, argues Zetter,

> the refugee label has become politicized, on the one hand, by the process of bureaucratic fractioning which reproduces itself in populist and largely pejorative labels whilst, on the other, by legitimizing and presenting a wider political discourse of resistance to refugees and migrants as merely an apolitical set of bureaucratic categories. (2007, 174)

At the heart of this regime, Andersson has more recently argued (2014), is a vast industry that relies on security and surveillance apparatus and employs humanitarianism and development discourses to meet out profits on everyone but irregular migrants. And even though Andersson brackets out the legal debate and the terminology of "refugeehood" from his study, he makes it clear that this is the performative stake in the entire operation of what he instead terms the "illegality industry." This use and abuse of the legal concept (Schuster 2003) also elicits differentiated practices of migration, we now know—far from being docile victims, asylum seekers make choices, often based on considerations of these shifting legal apparatus (Schuster 2005). But for precisely these reasons, others have argued, it is vital to insist on maintaining refugee status as a special category requiring protection irrespective of political priorities (Hathaway 2007). The discussion over the categories "refugee" and "internally displaced person" (henceforth IDP), developed on the back of two opposing perspectives on refugee assistance, is particularly interesting in this respect.

Described by Brun (2010) as the "UN-Brookings" and "ICRC" approaches, one focused on the tailoring of specialized assistance, the other on prioritizing needs. Like the categories previously discussed, both of these

are also political. Brun shows how in Sri Lanka IDPs are provided humanitarian assistance and initial hospitality, but never fully integrated into the
societies they flee too. The question is therefore both moral and political:
it concerns the "responsibilities of institutions in dealing with internal displacement, the general responsibility we all have towards others, and how
these two forms of responsibility should interact" (ibid., 351). Ironically, this
debate about the correctness of classifying "convention refugees" as different
from others (e.g., refugees, internally displaced persons, individuals in need
of humanitarian protection) hinges on the interpretation of the parameters of
the 1951 Convention Relating to the Status of Refugees (henceforth the 1951
Convention) as if these clauses could be objectively upheld. Yet, at the same
time all sides agree that their implementation in practice is political.

  This book looks at these politics in an expansive way that stretches
beyond the legal frame of the 1951 Convention application. It traces how
legal parameters produce political subjects who are oriented in specific ways
vis-à-vis refugeehood, explicitly or unbeknown to themselves. An economic
migrant who pines for a home in southern Nicosia but not a home in south
Asia; asylum seekers whose claims may be judged on whether they have
crossed a ceasefire line in Cyprus but not multiple lines before getting there;
foreign women who suffer violence normalized by a militarist structure sustained through concepts of refugeehood; Cypriots who engage in litigation
battles because their losses are not properly scripted into the calibrations of
refugeehood by the powers that be. All these subjects fall out of the strict definition of 1951 Convention refugees. And yet, their subjectivity is determined
by how that definition is understood and diverges from the multiple local uses
of the term "refugee." Attention to these subjectivities and their (re)productions
provides a clearer sense of the tensions and contestations in the foundational
concepts of refugee studies, forced migration, and displacement.

  In the pages that follow, I explain how, in Cyprus, the label "refugee"
has come to denote the victimized condition of the national self in remarkable
divergence from the script of the 1951 Convention; how that subjective positioning can be internalized by others who do not belong to the national group
but who are remarkably fluent in the idiom of longing for the other side; and
also how it has constructed a solid basis for excluding a number of people who
feel they too have legitimate claims to refugeehood. Taking the situation in
Cyprus as exemplary of the governmentalities that inform applications of the

1951 Convention elsewhere, I argue that it is from these exclusions, and the claims of loss that they deprioritize, that we have to begin constructing the political field within which the "refugee" label comes to create refugee subjects. And it is precisely that political subjectivity that the term "refugeehood," as I use it here, is meant to convey. Those losses that officialdom classifies as minor in Cyprus and discounts from the hegemonic imaginary of loss constitute fields of experience, modes of being, affective dispositions, reflections on the legal, orientations within the political. They are not descriptors of identities that we might take for granted (refugee, nonrefugee). Refugee*hood*, and not refugee*ness*, is not an identity but a subject position that is in this case thoroughly invested in the Cyprus conflict. And it is one that determines not only the status and position of refugees on the island (however we define them) but of everyone living on one or the other side.

In Cyprus, refugees (in the 1951 Convention sense, but arguably beyond it too) do not *just* flee conflict. They also land in it, whether they arrived here having fled other conflicts, or whether they have fled their homes on the island years ago. Whether consciously or unbeknown to them, people on the island live with a conflict that determines their everyday lives in significant ways. The temporal connections between conflict and refugeehood exist here in the multiple. They orient political subjectivity towards transition by fostering a rhetoric of return at the same time as they solidify this rhetoric, making such political subjective orientation permanent. Refugeehood in this sense is not only shaped by specific national discourses, which Malkki suggests are incredibly pervasive even beyond national and territorial boundaries (1995, 4–6)—it is also a key factor of the "national order of things" (ibid.). So a central point of analysis in this book is about the way displacement comes to displace other displacements—as when, for example, people are made to feel they are less refugee than others, or where their refugee identity is questioned or denied altogether. For if refugee subjectivity hinges on the conditions of empowerment, as Malkki's study shows, the Cypriot case prompts us to rethink the temporal manifestations of governing refugeehood. Malkki argues that Hutu refugees in the Mishamo refugee camp were less empowered than those settled in Kigoma town because of their attachment to the refugee identity (ibid., 8–17). This attachment shares similarities with Greek-Cypriot refugee discourses, giving pause for rethinking how the temporal governmentalities of refugeehood might produce diachronically disempowered political subjects.

Part of the problem is that in Cyprus, as in other protracted conflicts such as Palestine (Chatty 2010a), refugee identity endures across generations. At the point of writing in 2017, third-generation Cypriot refugees would themselves be young adults. It is also a matter of the quality of "durable solutions" (Harrell-Bond 1986) and the fact that the solutions provided by the state at various phases of the conflict were embedded in a logic of temporariness. Those grandchildren of 1974 refugees have come to expect different things from their displacement-certification documents—their "refugee cards," as they call them—than their parents did. And it is also that while repatriation did not materialize for many refugees in Cyprus, the rebuilding of lives that renders "refugee return" always a misnomer (Hammond 2004) began shortly after that crisis point. Refugee settlements comprising tents made of canvas might loom large in the imagery of refugeehood in Cyprus, but their actual existence was relatively short in the Greek-Cypriot case (they were dissolved by 1976). So even though temporality is a crucial factor in the multiple layering of refugeehood in Cyprus, it is not the passage of time per se, or the views on history and the nation, or even the infrastructures that mark continuity and belonging that are at stake. It is the way time is governed that makes the difference and the way time is used to distinguish some refugees from others who are officially excluded from that category. And that time refers not only to the temporality of waiting, which has recently been pointed out in migration studies as a predicament of irregular mobility (Andersson 2014; Griffiths 2014; Conlon 2011b, Brun, 2010). It refers also to historical time, which marks out major events that created "proper" refugees and other events that created other forms of displacement—in the language of law and policy. It is that governmentality of time that places people, infrastructures, law, and affect within and outside refugeehood.

Cyprus has served as an important example in understanding conflict and development. Even in early studies, there was a concern to look beyond the moment of flight to the ways in which refugees manage lives and uncertainty (Loizos 1981; 2008; Volkan 1980; Zetter 1991). Nearly four decades after that seminal study of Greek-Cypriot war refugees (Loizos 1981), the question today is not about development but the detrimental effects of those policies and logics that had initially appeared successful. The refugees at the focus of this book are not the coherent groups that make up classic ethnographic case studies. They are the marginal groups that the "refugee" label keeps out. In this sense, it could be said that the book departs from mainstream research on displacement. It examines refugee subjectivity as a structural aspect of citizenship regimes. It looks at specific but multiple refugee groups differently integrated in the same location. Analyzing their battle with integration, it recasts "refugee" as the foundational concept for establishing structures of exclusion. It is a study of what refugeehood does on an everyday basis across society.

Refugee studies have for good reason argued for a need to view refugees as more than victims. It is a call, as Nyers (2013) shows in a careful examination of UNHCR, activist and other refugee-focused discourse, that is easily expounded, but nearly impossible to achieve in a context where the proof of refugee status is so intimately tied to victimization (also Fassin and Rechtman 2009). What I present here brings the argument full circle. I revisit the image of the *sans papiers* as an iconic political figure to argue that multiple exclusions and possibilities arise within the evolving structures of displacement and accommodation. I want to recast the relationship between refugees and conflict, as a relation of power in a Foucauldian sense, meaning that the question we should be asking is not about a property that is or is not (power, conflict, refugee), but qualities that morph and change.

It is incredibly apt that since 2015, faced with a purported refugee crisis—which is rather a crisis of refugee reception in Europe—citizenship scholars are turning to one of Foucault's shortest texts to speak about the confrontation of people and governments.[4] In it, Foucault speaks of a division of labor between people on one side who are indignant and talk and on the other governments who deliberate and act.[5] This is immensely instructive for the work of scholars who have thus far argued that citizenship is not a binary (in or out, passport holding or not), but a matter of gradation (native, minority, migrant, naturalized).[6] The destitute Vietnamese boat people, who prompted the writing of Foucault's Geneva address, may be the extreme of victimhood, but power morphs through them in the international scene in the call for accountability demanded by a new regime of international citizenship that Foucault proposes on their behalf. Loss, through their absolute destitution, remains a key theme here.

Images of destitution in the iconic refugee figure are prominent in other philosophies. Derrida's notion of "hostipitality" (2000) where the space between hostility and hospitality is explored, focuses on the lack of knowledge invoked by the image of the stranger in the history of philosophy. But when this aporetic concept is folded into a call to practice, to create cities of refuge that do not prefigure mutuality as a condition of care, the central image invoked is concrete: "[a]sylum-seekers knock[ing] successively on each of the doors of the European Union states and end up being repelled by them"; an image that becomes even more specific in the image of a Kurdish refugee unlawfully deported to Turkey (2001, 13). Destitution drives the specific critique of Schengen Treaty politics. The same image is also present in the figure of the person who remains unaccounted for by government mechanisms in Badiou's vision of Evental (revolutionary) Sites existing outside the "situation" (2005). It is from this unaccounted person the one who "is not registered and remains clandestine" that the Event begins (ibid., 174). This divestment of subjectivity (regained either by these figures themselves or by others speaking on their behalf or giving them refuge) is power laden and political. It is as if the refugee is the ground zero from which philosophy can become political. Agamben's insistence on the process by which encamped Jews were molded into bare life figures after being denationalized by the Nazi regime (2004; Arendt 1951) is precisely about that process both as analytical tool and a philosophical question. Agamben's answer on both counts is to insist that being a *sans papiers* is not a condition but a political process. But if it is today a fact that refugees have agency and that the stripping of life to its bare form is no simple task (even in the face of proliferating camps across European spaces), we must now reconsider how and why we have come to think of refugees as totally lacking that agency in the first place.

Arendt, the foremost theorist of the *sans papiers* subject brings us back to the political underpinnings of refugee terminology:

> The term "stateless" at least acknowledged the fact that these persons had lost the protection of their government and required international agreements for safeguarding their legal status. The postwar term "displaced persons" was invented during the war for the express purpose of liquidating statelessness once and for all by ignoring its existence. (1948, 355)

It is often remarked that Arendt's and Foucault's analysis of the refugee situation are prescient of what we are witnessing today. It is vitally important, in making such remarks, however, to clarify that what is current in their analyses is not some chance characteristics of a situation but the parameters within which the links between refugees, conflict, and power emerge. What sounds hauntingly familiar today is the realization that the "more the number of rightless people increased, the greater became the temptation to pay less attention to the deeds of the persecuting governments than to the status of the persecuted" (ibid., 374). It is not random things, actions, situations, that we see today that resemble what Foucault and Arendt saw, but deliberate practices that have endured their criticisms. In practice, cities of refuge may be configured by ambivalence as Derrida predicted, but that ambivalence comes to look very different when it becomes imbricated in specific national discourses and politics of locality. The affective ambivalence articulated in "hostipitality" could easily be read alongside Papataxiarchis's analysis (2016) of native responses to the arrival of refugees (estimated at three to five thousand a day) on the island of Lesvos in the summer of 2015. Papataxiarchis frames the response within a discourse of "patriotism of solidarity" (2016), a conditional kind of humanitarianism that sets up cities of refuge open to everyone "unconditionally," but which succeeds in doing so only in the knowledge that such lifting of conditions is temporary. Such solidarity ultimately falls back on well-established connections between hospitality and national identity: refugees (no matter under whose say) are welcome, but so long as they remain refugees, and on the move (albeit slow) to an elsewhere. And so long, I would add, that they remain destitute, and in dire need—Lesvos, and Greece in general, is a shining example of first response, but by the time of writing in 2017, the lack of durable structures and integration planning seems to be developing into yet another crisis situation. In Cyprus, as we shall see, mass displacement established the conditions of refugeehood that still guide reception today, as conditions premised on temporality, ethnicity, and gender.

In the following pages, I argue that it is by examining the politics that produce the status of the persecuted between scales of legal and political priorities that we can put the attention back to the practices of persecution. And when we do that, we also see that the persecuting governments are not only the ones from whom refugees flee, but those to whom they appeal for refuge too. A careful and critical calibration of loss is required, I argue, that pushes the debate past the binary either/or approach and examines how the evaluation of loss operates; who and what it subjects; what actions and agency it elicits; what it produces, and what it forecloses.

IMBRICATIONS

Refugeehood is about the intricacies of citizenship. In this book, it does not signify the lack of citizenship. If anything, in Cyprus, refugeehood could be thought of as a privileged position in civic subjectivity. What it shares with mainstream accounts of refugeehood, however, is that either through presence or absence, it defines citizenship. These links are not simple or stable; they are uncertain, shifting, unexpected. But they nevertheless emanate from firm structures that exist and are maintained by daily work on the governmental, legal, and affective planes. As a way of maintaining this double focus on the structural aspects that need to be questioned, and the shifting aspects of what actually happens at the intersections of individual and governmental practice, I use the idiom of "imbrication."

In the wake of well-rehearsed poststructural critiques, a call for such double focus might seem tired. Yet it is in the context of an increasingly obvious need to account for structure that much of the current theory seeking to understand the neoliberal order is emerging. And yet, that structure can no longer be a simple question in the way that middle-way theories such as structuration (Giddens 1984) might have suggested earlier. The questioning of what exceeds materiality in the most tangible of objects that actor-network theory asks is exemplary (Latour 2005). The emergence of geography as a key domain for understanding complex capital shifts (Harvey 2001; Sassen 2011; Thrift 2008) is equally indicative. Structure is important to seminal poststructuralist texts exactly because it bears the possibility of deconstruction (Derrida 1976) and the dissolution of single-order signification (Baudrillard 1975). It is from this perspective that I keep returning in this book to structures, metaphorically in the image of a roof, and analytically in the case of governmentality apparatus.

Foucauldian governmentality—the full force of which emerged in Anglophone analysis after the translation of his *Collège de France* lectures (2004; 2007; 2010, 2011)—hinges on exactly this centrality of structure even in the most counter-conductive formation of self.[7] Central to Foucault's concept is the double facet of discipline and care, working not in separate domains (as for example in the repressive and ideological apparatus of Althusser [1971]) but arising within the same field. The workings of power in governmentality is about the subscription and reproduction of ways of being governed from within. And this "within" is again, a double ground when we are dealing with biopower: working on the level of the body as well as on the level of population, both of which are produced by biopolitical governmentality. Thus, a body of citizens is posited as the "population" and defined by particular characteristics down to the individual body level, but then (or rather so that) governmental apparatus can be put in place to ensure the congruence between the putative population and the actual bodies being governed. In my earlier work, I examined such practices in depth with reference to the rendering of minority populations in Greece (2013). I am here developing a much more encompassing concept of minoritization: I am talking not only of particular and generally targeted exclusions (such as the situation of Turkish speakers in northern Greece), but at the various forms of governing put in place that exclude or discount a much broader spectrum of experience—in fact the vast majority of the population who do not fit the ideal. And they do so not always, perhaps not even mostly, in a targeted way, but often inadvertently, as a by-product of other governmental conducts. That is the way *minor losses* arise. Minor losses are thus also a double concept because they are conducted through a central figure of the victim but found wanting, and lose out, with reference to that victimhood.

But that conduct through the ideal, is precisely what also elicits counter-conduct. For as soon as that ideal is recognized as such, it is recognized as a *dispositif* of government and not an actual body or population part. It is recognized for the incongruence between the "us", which "population" is meant to solidify, and the exclusion of "me" effected in the process. This is the workings of performativity that Butler's earlier work on Foucault tackles (1997b). For Butler, performativity emerges in the space between subjection and subjectivation as a destabilizing condition of selfhood—a real self, just as a totally performative persona recedes from view. And this allows space for critique and, I argue, the contemplation of being conducted otherwise. It is in this space that what earlier anthropological theory has termed "resistance" (Scott 1985) begins to emerge—but only in an uncertain form. In question is not only the way in which it will be actualized, as for example in everyday practices, but indeed, if it will be at all. So what I am interested in is the moment at which the disciplinary forms of subjectivation, so well described by ethnographies of colonialism (e.g., Mitchell 1991), morph into a more politically reflective disposition. In those moments, Das (1995) reminds us, critical events of past violence are reworked in the everyday and rupture the mundane. Whether and how they do so remains uncertain, however. Stevens speaks of "accidental citizenship" (2017, 17) and of "caprice" (a term I have also found useful in previous work) in articulating the uncertainty with which rights and rightlessness are bestowed and the line between them delineated in law and policy. I propose *imbrications* as an idiom that captures and exceeds these concepts to better reflect the tension between the unintentional and the structural. What I want to highlight through the idiom of imbrication then is a way of maintaining a focus on what is constraining, or enabling, in governmental practice and thinking, to the ways in which people interact with, internalize, or counter those structures. I am recasting, in this process, some of the major questions in this theoretical trajectory: what allows subjects or prompts them to "see like a state" (Scott 1998)? What excess of explicit knowledge is it that subjectivizes them in implicit ways (Mitchell 2002)? And how is the everyday crafted as a question of the state (Das 2007)?

The image I wish to evoke here is of a roofing structure where tiles overlap in specific arrangements, but only partly; and where these interstices allow processes to happen (rainwater to run off, soil and dust to build up, plants to sprout, animals to nest), while also serving the purpose of preventing other processes (water leaking or air gushing through). And while the structure itself has this purpose, it is characteristic of roofs to leak, tiles to break, gaps to allow wildlife in. The unexpected is embedded in the structure and not distinct from it. I therefore ask here how we might think these metaphors theoretically in ways that allow us to approach refugeehood in an expanded way. For if refugees in Cyprus appear difficult to recognize through current debates in refugee studies, we should resist the instinctive reaction of classifying them on the basis of the legal parameters of the 1951 Convention and infer that they "are not refugees" because they reside in their own country. Instead, we should look to the techniques by which refugeeness is conferred and denied and see in the subjects of refugeehood the continuities between international, national, and individual assumptions about what refugees are, what they should look like, and how they should behave. In those terms, refugeehood in Cyprus is about otherness. But it is so in surprising ways—a category punctuated by many crevices that entrap people they were not meant to. I speak here not of ethnic otherness, but an otherness that was not targeted in the first place, as an exclusion that the Green Line border was meant to effect. This surprising aspect of the border requires us, I want to argue, to employ similarly expansive metaphors. The conceptualization of the border as process (Green 2013; Demetriou and Dimova 2018) thus also requires a geometric metaphor that goes beyond the shift from line to area and two-dimensional area patterns (lattice, nodes, mesh). The visual metaphor of imbrication communicates this expansiveness.

References to imbrication have been used to describe how planes are entangled in one another (e.g., the political in the social, the local in the global).[8] The metaphor of imbrication seems to be taken in stride, without much discussion of what it might help us conceptualize. An imbricated arrangement, the definition goes, is one "composed of parts (leaves, scales, or the like) which overlap like tiles" (OED). Roof tiling is given in most dictionaries as the key image for this definition, and the Latin origin of the word points to gutter tiles (*imbrex*) that carry away the rainwater (*imber*). *Imbrex* roof tiles are differentiated in masonry from *tegula* roof tiles because of their curved form—*tegula* tiles being flat, and the two kinds are often used together for better drainage. Valpy's *Etymological Dictionary of the Latin Language* of 1828 associates the word *imbrex* to the Greek word for rain όμβρος [*ómvros*] (197), where, in classic etymological fashion, the tracing stops. There are, however, suggestions that this backward trajectory continues outside the Indo-European linguistic system (Beekes 2009). This etymological story can in fact be taken as exemplary of my point in using the word "imbrication" to refer to power complexities. I do not see etymology as holding some truth in itself, so that one can follow a route (e.g., down the gutter tiles) and arrive at some beginning of time located in Greek antiquity, but as offering interesting overlaps that can help us expand a conceptual tool—in this case a metaphor—which inevitably will hit upon its own limitations too.

Imagined as the effect of tiling a roof therefore (and not the original gutter tiling), imbrication speaks of an expansive layering and patterning that is different from three close alternatives: (1) stacking, where layers overlap completely; (2) alignment (as in gutter tiles) where there is no layer but a singular route; and (3) enmeshing, where layers are dissolved into one. Imbrication, furthermore, retains something of substantive differentiation (each tile) but in an arrangement that is neither fixed (as in that much problematized metaphor of coexistence, the mosaic) nor completely arbitrary. The unexpected arises in imbrication as the interaction of matter with process (tiles, water, soil, and animal droppings, with rain, wind, or nesting). Imbrication is expansive in that it goes beyond a single-layer mesh, beyond a single type of interaction as in the mosaic that is looked at and makes sense only in being looked at.

In the analysis I undertake in the book, imbrication describes the aspects of emplacement and displacement that give rise to interactions between individuals, practices, laws, policies, and patterns of thought. If the border in Nicosia exudes an aspect of trauma and loss for a migrant, a tourist, or a refugee (however and by whomever defined), this cannot happen without the process of politicization, in which the border is thoroughly embedded. While differently configured in each case, this politicization is neither anterior nor posterior to the ontology of the border; it is the effect of conflict, violence, and war, as well as policing and the continuous reenactment of forms of violence that policing entails. By seeing this relation between the border and politicization in terms of imbrication we could better analyze processes unfolding in time and space and influencing one another on legal, affective, and material registers. And we can begin to clearly see the fault lines between police, politics, and the political that according to Rancière (2010) mark out the terrain of democracy.

In Cyprus, access to rights relating to migrant and refugee protection, as well as its limitation, is mediated through the structure of the conflict. The words of the waiter with which I began this chapter are indicative of how work and residence, denied by migration law on one side of the divide, can materialize on the other while this denial can produce discourses that emulate political subjectivities of unlikely populations. The links between ethnic enemies and migrants are an important part of this layering. They form an imbricated infrastructural frame that shapes lives and subjectivity. This is not the Marxist infrastructure that underpins ideological (nonmaterial) superstructures. They merge the two to form the bedrock on which new structures (policing, political campaigning, and refugee and immigration procedures) are deposited. Imbrication is manifest here in its geological sense, as the formation arising from sediments deposited in an alluvial or other channel. Time is crucial to this layering, whereby governmentalities oriented at one kind of population at a particular point in time (Turks as ethnic enemies) come to subjectivize others (migrants) as the border develops into something else. These connections structure the chapters that follow.

THE LOSSES ENCOUNTERED

The metaphor of imbrication guides the book's organization as well as the methodology that informs its insights. The exploration is itself an effect of time. Since my first engagement in 2002 with the Cyprus conflict as an object of study, different questions have been asked within the different layers I examine here. How do refugees, individually and in organized ways, narrate, explain, and perform understandings of loss? How has the law interfaced with political rhetoric and people's needs in the postwar polity? What does the terrain of conflict, in the materiality of the Green Line, look like, and what is its heritage value? How do migrants experience the divided capital of Nicosia? What are women's priorities in a peace settlement? How are Turkish-Cyptiots governed within postwar structures in the south? These questions have guided my research through the years, asked separately under projects themed around displacement, human rights, conflict heritage, migration, gender, and insecurity. Some of the answers were partly to be found in sets of recorded interviews with refugees, litigants, civil-society representatives, and migrants. Others were formed in practice, through my involvement in reconciliation initiatives since the late 1990s, and my association with youth groups, peace activists, foreign trainers, local professionals, women's groups, and, more recently—as reconciliation was inserted into mainstream politics—policy makers too.

The coherent formulation of these answers, however, and the new questions it prompted, was the result of a primarily ethnographic approach, where daily encounters, chance conversations, class discussions, the rituals of public protest, and those of domestic protestation, were observed and noted—sometimes in writing, sometimes not. A native anthropology here prompted a particular emphasis on reflection taking shape as constant questioning of my positionings vis-à-vis interlocutors, of possible deeper meanings, and most importantly through awareness of the performative field of interactions. That awareness in turn was heightened through another, if fraught, resource of native anthropology—my situated past. In the context of research and writing, I often encountered memories of conversations held and conversations silenced, and of the moments when conflict violence appeared, flash-like, in familial exchanges. They left traces in the analysis, which I have tried on several occasions to render transparent. But the trace I have mostly tried to tackle is the very question of the appearance of those moments. An example: A few years ago my mother had a bougainvillea in front of the house pruned, exposing a hole in the sandstone, which I remarked was quite some damage for a support nail. "Oh no, that's not from a nail, it's from a bullet in 1974, when coupists came looking for your father; and we [herself and her parents] were standing right behind the wall"; she matter of factly, on the occasion, corrected a chance remark and switched back to the topic at hand—was the pruning overdone? Flash-like talk of the conflict, throwing the scripted narrative off course in the largely leftist environment in which I grew up, in the period immediately after the war—occasional jokes about family members who had been "a little bit coupist" in the past—popped up infrequently, unexpectedly, parenthetically; flashes difficult to follow-up as the conversation at hand moved on. It is the nature of these flashes that puzzled me over the years, and it is partly those flashing trails that my analysis tries to grasp.

Not accidentally then, my inquiry begins with violence. Chapter 2 is an attempt to illuminate events around those flashes, to retell the story of violence that frames the major losses within which the minor losses, which I discuss later, emerge. This is a reflexive and analytical exercise. It recounts those major losses but at the same time questions the counting done so far. Still uncertain, debated, and largely unavailable, this counting founds a govern-mentality of conflict that still determines how one becomes a political subject in Cyprus—it is an exercise of necropolitical demography.

These major losses construct the registers on which refugeehood is examined in the rest of the book: the affective, the legal, and the topological. The first section, *layers*, suggests that we see these registers as layers of tiling: affect (chapter 3), law (chapter 4), and space (chapter 5). Thus focused on the affective register, chapter 3 surveys differing descriptions of loss among Greek-Cypriot refugees and analyzes the ways in which differently situated discourses conform and confront the hegemonic narrative. This continues into chapter 4, which explores the extension of the affective register into the legal. Here I explore specifically the disjuncture between local and international law and the formation of "displaced person" as a legal category in Cyprus, the meaning of which is intimately attached to the everyday notion of refugee. It is this disjuncture that propels the working of performativity, I argue, in turn enabling forms of counter-conduct based on litigation. This form of counter-conduct is firmly anchored in systems of evaluation specifically around the notions of property and home. I turn to these in the analysis of the topological register of loss in chapter 5. Here, war devastation in buildings and the natural environment is used to show the ways in which losses are evaluated in the zones of abandonment and question the processes through which property is separated from junk. I consider these processes as part of the constitution of the abject, as techniques of dejection where speech propels the work of silencing.

The second section, *crevices*, delves into the entanglements of these layers, where these registers provide the scales for calibrating loss on the basis of which further minor losses are excluded. These are the losses of others, those not specifically targeted in the first place, but caught in the entanglements of refugeehood nevertheless: migrants, women, and Turkish-Cypriots in the south. Accordingly, chapter 6 examines the experience of groups who have been alienated from the majority population through the constructions of refugeehood analyzed in the first section: nonnationals, including recognized refugees, asylum seekers, and other irregular migrants. These categories, I argue, call forth a concept of protection and state responsibility that jars with the staple image of the refugee as a national victim-subject. Chapter 7 surveys a range of gender-based exclusions arising from the governance of refugeehood, arguing that the gendered aspects of refugee concepts have positioned women as a particular kind of subject. This form of subjectivity has been central to the reproduction of the nation through family constitution and domestic life, the organization of which vis-à-vis refugeehood is critically examined here. In the last chapter of the section, the construction of Greek-Cypriot refugeehood is reconsidered against its main category of exclusion, Turkish-Cypriot refugees. Revisiting some of the legal and material registers that have, often inadvertently, resulted in the exclusion of various other groups, this chapter elucidates how these registers have been oriented against the figure of the enemy, personified by Turkish-Cypriots. I argue here that the figure of this enemy refugee is an absent presence in the constructions of refugeehood examined throughout the book.

The conclusion projects these arguments into considerations for theorizing displacement and refugeehood. It revisits some of the parameters that refugee protection has often taken for granted and which the ethnographic findings here question: that refugees flee from conflict settings into nonconflict environments, that international legal protection can be decontextualized from local social and legal concepts, that refugee status is a unified socio-legal category, and that refugee identity is marked by a sense of temporariness.

Taken together, the data from this study show that refugeehood is an essential component of the ways in which citizenship is conceptualized and structured. That it can provide the means for establishing, maintaining, and reproducing discrimination, both in law and in everyday life. And that ultimately, it affects a much wider group of people than those recognized under the "refugee" label. Writing these lines against the specter of a Europe crumpling under the weight of anti-immigrant discourse in the summer of 2016, I am suggesting, among other things, that we pay reflexive attention to how structures and rhetorics, which seem today surprising, are actually the outcome of these deeply imbricated structures of discrimination, not only in Cyprus, but apparently across Europe and possibly far beyond.

TWO **FRAMING**

The Governmentality of Major Losses

THE NECROPOLITICAL REGISTER

What is then the matrix of refugeehood that *minor losses* become caught in? This chapter can be thought of as a bridge leading into the two sections that examine, consecutively, layers, over which registers of refugeehood are spread, and crevices, in which refugeehood entraps people. In this bridge, I revisit the baseline of Cypriot refugeehood—the major losses against which other losses are judged and come to be seen as minor.

Effie Voutira has argued some time ago that the conceptualization of refugee identity in Greece, tightly connected to the 1923 forced exchange of populations between Greece and Turkey has determined Greece's refugee policy up to the present. It created shared understandings, a form of common knowledge, about what refugee means. This has guided, she argues, the reception of foreign asylum seekers, which until very recently, was shaped by the

> cultural assumption concerning the genuineness of the "refugee" label, which presumes that the only *true* refugees must be of Greek origin ... [and hence] is biased because of these cultural assumptions, which imply that Sudanese, Palestinian, Ethiopian, Iraqi or Afghani asylum seekers are seen as "foreign" refugees: and thus as essentially "others," whose treatment is to be guided exclusively by a rigid application of the 1951 Refugee Convention, which is not "common knowledge." (2003, 74, emphasis in original)

This has been the Greek-Cypriot view in Cyprus as well, where refugees (*prósfiyes*) are thought to be those Greek-Cypriots who fled from their homes in the north of the island during the war of 1974. Migration here too is historically framed within the legacy of the Greco-Turkish conflict, but in a much more complex sense.

The law and policy that this framing produces are thoroughly imbricated in the most material infrastructures left by the war: ethnic demarcation lines on the ground, abandoned or damaged buildings, mined areas, neglected urban centers, low-skill employment positions, immigration regimes that hinge on legal and illegal entry points. The legal apparatus that determine refugee status are inflected by the same border that makes a South Asian waiter pine for his former home: the Green Line. As the arch-symbol of the conflict, the Green Line provides a measure for counting all those major losses that official rhetoric on each side recounts against the other; it also forecloses, in the process, the stories of minor losses explored in the following chapters. The foreclosure of these minor losses is integral but not tantamount to the discounting of the Other's losses. These losses of the Other (and not multiple lesser others) are the explicit aim of official rhetoric and refer to the singular ethnic Other on the other side of a binary. Their discounting takes the form of omission and uncertainty—two tropes that have become ingrained in accounts of the conflict.

To focus on these minor losses of the conflict we need to ask anew, "What are its major losses?" According to Greek-Cypriot rhetoric, the Cyprus problem is one of "invasion and occupation" (*próvlima isvolís ke katohís*). The invasion happened on July 20, 1974 and resulted in killings, rapes, lootings, and displacement; the occupation continues to violate 36 percent of the island's territory. Even without numbers, there is counting entailed in this definition—that of the Greek-Cypriot losses from the invasion in the form of territory. The same rhetoric also counts two hundred thousand refugees and 1,619 missing presons. And there is also a subtraction, a counting out, of those losses—the people killed, raped, and displaced, and the properties looted prior to the invasion. These are people from across the communities in Cyprus from earlier stages of the conflict, as well as people tortured and killed in the coup that preceded the invasion. This discounting is ethnic (e.g., Turkish-Cypriot losses), political (losses of the Left), gendered (losses of women), and temporal (Greek-Cypriot and Armenian losses, for example, prior to the invasion). Counting also becomes accounting through the constitution of a population defined by major losses, and the shirking of responsibility for those other minor losses.

A necropolitical register is set up, determining which deaths count and which do not, which injured lives should be attended to and which not. The categories of this register are hugely important therefore as tools of governmentality. Writing on drone targeting in Afghanistan, Allison shows that such categorizations end up being more important as categories than representations of what "actual humans are doing," as the key question becomes their membership in the population "that is liable for putting to death" (2015,123). This is not a scandal only of virtual wars (Der Derian 2000), I want to claim, but a continuation of governmentalities that have been working on the living as much as on the dead throughout modernity. It spurs a Foucauldian archaeological tracing of discourse to further interrogate the categories that have been mobilized in the necropolitical register in Cyprus. What exactly are these categories, I therefore ask, and how have they been connected to past governmental logics?

Such archaeology would need to consider colonialism and its legacy. Indeed slavery and plantation colonialism stand out as the arch-images employed by Mbembe in his development of the notion of necropolitics (2003). More benign forms of colonialism, however, such as that of European Cyprus, are no less necropolitical; if anything, that necropolitical conflict order drives their postconflict democratic everyday, putting into question the very temporality of conflict/postconflict. At stake here, as Mbembe suggests, is the imaginary of colonies as places where the law is suspended, the political thrown into disarray, war is constant, and peace cannot be attained:

> colonies are zones in which war and disorder, internal and external figures of the political, stand side by side or alternate with each other … they do not imply the mobilization of sovereign subjects (citizens) who respect each other as enemies … [i]t is thus impossible to conclude peace with them. (ibid., 24)

The impossibility of peace, Mbembe is suggesting, is part and parcel of colonial legacies and their necropolitical governmentalities. But if such governmentality is staked on the discounting of the colonized as citizens and as enemies, a discounting of their involvement also in analyses is often an inadvertent result. Mbembe may recognize, but does not dwell on how the colonized have implicated themselves in the very wars that colonialism refuses to legitimize.

In my accounting here, I want to maintain a postcolonial analytic lens while also recounting the involvement of the colonized in violence and responsibility.

A HISTORY OF CATEGORIES

It is indicative that of the numerous analyses of the conflict, only a handful attempts to inventory losses, in terms of property and casualties; when they do, these inventories tend to be fragmentary. These inventories are instructive of the governmentality of the conflict that has determined the foreclosing of lesser stories that have become caught in the discursive cross fire. In my initial encounters with academic literature on the Cyprus conflict, I was struck by the concern with objectivity and engagement that pervades it, and the frequency with which either or both goals are belied (Demetriou 2008). I now realize that the problem is not necessarily political investment in one or other political end but a more profound one: it is with the emulation of governmental logics in academic research. Inventories of loss are invaluable pointers to that governmentality.

The fragmentary nature of those inventories is striking. The numbers of the dead, wounded, missing, and displaced are broken down in many different ways, each of which speaks to a specific analytic perspective. Unsurprisingly, key among them is the ethnic demographic. This ethnic separation of the Turkish-Cypriot dead from the Greek-Cypriot dead might appear obvious, but it should still prompt the question of how this has come to be so, how we define the conflict as solidly dichotomic, and how Greek-Cypriot and Turkish-Cypriot have emerged and solidified as mutually exclusive categories. It is indeed curious, on the first count, that the hybridities and exclusions of this binary have only recently been looked at (Constantinou 2007; 2008; see also Pattie 1997). And it is equally curious, on the second count, that attempts to unpack Greek-Cypriot and Turkish-Cypriot identities have involved comments about internal fractures but have not questioned their opposition (Mavratsas 1997; Ramm 2006; Vural and Peristianis 2008).[1]

Analytically, the employment of this dichotomic logic has pinpointed 1958 as the start of interethnic violence proper. That is the year of the mob killing of eight Greek-Cypriots from Kontemenos village, as they passed through an agitated Turkish-Cypriot crowd in the village of Gönyeli. The eight had been arrested with twenty-seven others by the British police at the height of the anticolonial struggle, on suspicions of preparing an attack against the nearby Turkish-Cypriot village of Ayios Vasilios and the mixed village of Skylloura. They were not brought to a police station due to Turkish-Cypriot rioting, and they were released to walk home (Crawshaw 1978, 289). In the following weeks, interethnic violence left fifty-six Greek- and fifty-three Turkish-Cypriots dead. It is telling that Nancy Crawshaw, a foreign correspondent for the *Manchester Guardian* between 1955 and 1959, in one of the earliest authoritative accounts of that period, marks out events of June and July, 1958, in a table of casualties as "inter-communal violence" victims, separate from the violence generated in the course of the anticolonial struggle between 1955 and 1959. In the course of that violence, Greek-Cypriots had killed Turkish-Cypriots and vice versa both before and after 1958.

In that period, the military call for decolonization was led by the Greek-Cypriot organization EOKA and was tantamount to union with Greece (*énosis*). Turkish-Cypriot opposition generated opposing fighters' corps (Volkan, then TMT) and a call for division (*taksim*). Until 1958, interethnic fighting was generally viewed as an offshoot of EOKA violence against the British colonists, who employed Turkish-Cypriots in the police force tasked with quelling the rebellion. Crawshaw's casualty tables list eight civilian and twenty-two police casualties on the Turkish-Cypriot side until 1958 compared to 105 servicemen, twelve police, and twenty-six civilians on the British side, and fifteen police and 207 civilians on the Greek side (406–8).[2] It is worth asking why the Gönyeli incident should be singled out in a context where decolonization spurred deep intercommunal insecurities. These did not instantly spring up in 1958. The inauguration of EOKA's activities in 1955 sparked, in the same year, the worst pogroms against the Greek community seen in Istanbul. They also mobilized Turkish-Cypriot riots when British colonists appeared to be considering EOKA demands and as EOKA began to kill Turkish-Cypriot policemen. During the riots in May, 1956, Turkish-Cypriots set fire to a church and killed a parishioner in the Greek-Cypriot neighborhood of Ayios Loucas in Nicosia. By that year, British colonists were installing barbed wire in central Nicosia along what was initially called the "Mason-Dixon line" to separate the Greek from the Turkish neighborhoods (ibid., 175, 231).[3] The categorization of Gönyeli violence—but not the previous instance of Ayios Loucas—as interethnic is telling of a governmentality that takes Turkish-Cypriots as incidental to a Greco-British dispute divesting them of agency and responsibility. That rioting had in fact led to the eviction of about three hundred Greek-Cypriots from the parish. These early forced displacements are also evicted from the demography of major losses, which are at this point focused on life and not livelihood. It is the colonial governmentality under which both citizen and enemy subjectivities are refused "and where 'peace' is more likely to take on the face of a 'war without end'" (Mbembe 2003, 23). The moment of the emergence of the category, "inter-communal violence," is a moment of necropolitical governance that delegitimized colonial war. So to delve into the necropolitics of that moment, we need to recognize it as the fundamental governing apparatus that renders peace impossible.

And if the pinpointing of interethnic violence is problematic, so is the separation of "inter-" from "intra-" communal violence, which is another major feature of the inventory. As a key trope of counting EOKA violence, the vast difference between the eight Turkish-Cypriot and the 207 Greek-Cypriot civilians that fell victim to EOKA (and even the difference between that number and the total number of 143 British casualties) has been important in showing the ideological emphasis placed on ethnic loyalty. The 207 victims are depicted as traitors, understood to have included informers, leftists, and holders of dissenting views. They would have also included former EOKA members, and arrested active members who may have buckled under torture, but these victims are not talked about. That EOKA was more concerned with charging Greek-Cypriot leftists with treason is undeniable—the list of casualties includes eighteen prominent Communist Party members.[4] But this remains a muted part of Cypriot history today, confined largely to publications of the communist party (AKEL),[5] which although it is one of the two largest Greek-Cypriot parties, has maintained a subsidiary role in official history discourse. That history, recounted in school history books from the early grades, celebrates the lives of many of the 240 or so EOKA members killed in that period as "martyred heroes," tellingly missing from Crawshaw's inventory.[6]

To separate out the killing of co-ethnics due to their perceived or actual collusion with ethnic enemies as being outside the interethnic conflict is to subscribe to a view of ethnicity as an objective category and not one of ascription. And it is also to bracket out native responsibilities. It is a move that eases the reading of partition as a way to manage "the transition from colonial sovereignty to postcoloniality" even if partition is not "directly attributable to colonial power" (Morton 2014, 20). To read against the grain of colonial and postcolonial categories, then, complicates the record of loss and responsibility. This is brought home starkly when we consider that in later phases of the conflict, paramilitaries continued to target their co-ethnics for activities as diverse as buying or selling to ethnic others, sheltering them, fraternizing with them, and, of course, marrying them. Consider the case of Metin, who in his seventies in 2003, was eager to tell me of a love affair with a Greek-Cypriot woman, which he had had in his youth. It ended when EOKA killed her brother as intimidation, he said with a pained frown only after I asked him what happened to her. To classify that violence, which left the interethnic couple physically unharmed but scarred for life, would be to write off both its origins and its effects. Yet this is exactly what is done in the analysis of the 1960s period, a major phase of the conflict, following the end of the anticolonial struggle in 1959. The killings of 1963 that mark the start of this postcolonial period point to a periodization that fragments the conflict into phases and brushes over its continuities.

Topographically, 1958 signaled the separation of urban municipalities, and concomitant eviction of Greek-Cypriot businesses from the now Turkish center of Nicosia. This municipal separation (see also Markides 2001) was at the heart of budgetary disputes in the bicommunal parliament that emerged with independence in 1960, leading to budget vetoing by the Turkish-Cypriot delegates who felt their community was being divested by the Greek-Cypriot majority. The vetoes led to a proposal for constitutional reform by the Greek-Cypriot president, which effectively dissolved the power-sharing structure at the heart of the Constitution. Within a tense political climate, Greek-Cypriot police fired on and killed two Turkish-Cypriots just outside the Turkish quarter in Nicosia on December 21, 1963, sparking widespread violence. Two days later, the wife and children of a Turkish officer were found murdered in their bathroom—an incident commemorated by Turkish-Cypriot authorities in the transformation of the house where it occurred into the Museum of Barbarism. British forces stationed in the sovereign bases that the UK kept after decolonization were called upon to form a joint peacekeeping force with the Greek and Turkish military contingents stationed on the island as part of a tripartite agreement written into the 1960 Constitution.

It is this force, the Joint Force, that is credited with establishing the Green Line in January 1964, a reference still formally reserved for the Nicosia section of the UN Buffer Zone.[7] The force was to later morph into the

United Nations Force in Cyprus (UNFICYP), established through Resolution 186 (March 4, 1964) at the request of the Republic of Cyprus and the UK. By the end of 1964, the violence had left 191 Turkish-Cypriots and 133 Greek-Cypriots dead, while another 173 Turkish-Cypriots, and forty-one Greek-Cypriots were classified as missing (Patrick 1976, 46).[8] Among the battles that took place was the one in Mouttalos neighborhood, for the capture of the Turkish-Cypriot quarter of Paphos on March 9 (and upon the conclusion of ceasefire and hostage-exchange agreements). The battle, which killed fourteen Turkish-Cypriots and eleven Greek-Cypriots, had been prompted by the hostage-taking of Greek-Cypriots in the town's market, which had happened in response to the shooting of a Turkish-Cypriot (ibid., 62). Another major event was the attack on the Nicosia suburb of Omorphita/Kaymakli by a Greek-Cypriot paramilitary group that killed uncertain numbers of Turkish-Cypriots and took around five hundred hostage. In the next four years, violence was a daily occurrence, the last flare-up registered in 1967 when the Turkish-Cypriot village of Kofinou was attacked and twenty-two Turkish-Cypriots were killed. The village had been a TMT stronghold, but also the place from which Turkish-Cypriots had attacked a nearby monastery on January 1, 1964. There they shot three monks dead, on suspicion that the monastery's dogs had killed the villagers' sheep.

Over this period Richard Patrick, an UNFICYP officer who later returned to the island to write his thesis on the Cyprus conflict, records sixty-four Turkish-Cypriot deaths due to conflict, fifty-eight by Greek-Cypriots, and an additional thirteen Turkish-Cypriots missing (ibid., 364). His 1972 study is a rare example of detailed and careful inventorying of casualties. It includes charts showing Turkish-Cypriot "violent deaths" (365) in the period 1963–1967, which distinguish between inter- and intra-communal, military and civilian, and conflict-related and personally motivated deaths (exemplified as domestic and business disputes). He also correlates media coverage of violence with geography and offers a categorization of incidents on the basis of intensity along a tripartite scale: most critical, major, and minor incidents. Yet the periodization on which this analysis rests would suggest that incidents are distinct from each other across time, an assumption belied by the evidence. In one of the most traumatic incidents of January 1964, a mass grave was discovered in Ayios Vasilios containing the bodies of twenty-one Turkish-Cypriots, killed a month earlier during a Greek-Cypriot attack on the village and neighboring Skylloura. Patrick notes allegations linking these murders, which had also included torture, to the Gönyeli incident of 1958 (50).

Martin Packard, an officer in the Joint Force during its first six months of operation, describes vividly the patrolling of Nicosia villages in the peacekeeping effort (2008). Reconstructed from his notes four decades after the events, Packard's account is a critique of the British foreign office policy of the time, which he suggests was oriented towards partition (5–6). This goal had not been clearly communicated to the Joint Force staff (enabling Packard to continue pursuing reconciliation in his local dealings). He writes:

> In contrast to better-known later efforts at top-down mediation in Cyprus, the process in which I was involved started from the clientele of village coffee-houses and moved upwards through the various levels of leadership. (7)

His Joint Force had "a mandate to deal at individual or village level with confrontations, disputes, shortages, fears and absences of governmental authority" but had succeeded, by the time of the hand over to UNFICYP to provide "linkage between divided ministries, a back-channel between the political heads of the two communities and help with the groundwork for a series of island-wide bi-communal projects" (7). The employment of allochronic language ("bi-communal" now recognized as a reference to peace initiatives after 1974) is telling of the temporal links that stretch across the knowledge field of the Cyprus conflict and within which its periodization is enmeshed. What ultimately Packard is describing in 2008 are efforts that brought peacemaking into confrontation with peacekeeping, as later literature would have it (Richmond 1994; 2001).

The major locations of violence in this period (Kofinou, Ayios Vasilios, Kokkina/Erenköy, Kaymakli/Omorphita) included strategic points for the control of movement and transport through the territory. An argument has been put forward to read the 1963–1964 period accordingly as marking a Gramscian-like shift from a war of position to an open war of movement.[9] Transport—in buses, especially—had been the main method through which Turkish-Cypriots disappeared in this period. This is an alternative reading—focusing on military logic—different from a focus on selective losses that index only the Other's barbarity. But Patrick's inventories speak of further possibilities: mixed motives, ambivalent causes, uncertain attributions. A military stronghold might also be implicated in spirals of violence that even cross the animal-human divide (the example of dogs and sheep above). Packard's account similarly illuminates the ambivalent motives of governmental practices (partition for the FCO, coexistence for the Joint Force), but also raises questions about the motives of those subjected to such practices. In many analyses, there is an underlying assumption that these motives are decisive in explaining the conflict, as I have shown by the separation between inter- and intra-communal violence. People who chose to stay together in mixed villages during this period are presented as exemplary of the positive aspects of coexistence. In Dali, a village where such coexistence is celebrated to this day, Packard presents a different perspective: in early 1964, Turkish-Cypriots were "actively prevented" from leaving by their Greek-Cypriot neighbors and "it was elicited that the villagers who were being so constrained were those of which the head of the family had significant financial debts to the Greek-Cypriots" (2008, 72). In Ayia Marina, where the Turkish-Cypriot head

> made a number of statements to the [Greek-Cypriot] press describing his satisfaction with Greek Cypriot policy and his earnest desire that the two communities continue to live together in accustomed harmony … [it transpired that] the Turkish Cypriots would already have left if not for the fact that only that day [January 22, 1964] had the government Grain Commission begun to move the village's accumulated harvest into central storage. (ibid., 121)

Elsewhere he notes the opposite: Turkish-Cypriots were reluctant to leave but intimidated and coerced by TMT, a situation highlighted in much of Greek-Cypriot official discourse.

Today these uncertainties are returning, as their results are coming to light. There are the unmarked graves, in wells, riverbeds, caves, and fields, dug up by experts employed by a UN-directed Committee of Missing Persons (henceforth CMP), tasked with another inventory: to unearth and identify the dead from the period of the 1960s and post-invasion 1974. This work seeks to impose order on uncertainty by identifying the bones and returning them to relatives—commingled bones in mass graves, an expert tells me, is one of the Committee's greatest problems. Other uncertainties, the cause of death and attribution of responsibility, are ones that remain muted. The Committee has an amnesty-oriented mandate that limits their research and provision of information on both those counts. Those exhumations today, therefore, allow only partial solution to the uncertainty as they un-mingle and identify the bones. In so doing, they open a space in which further accountability can only be demanded, but without guarantees that the call will be heeded.

A HISTORY OF NUMBERS

According to the first UNFICYP report on June 15, 1964, around fifty-five thousand Turkish-Cypriots were in need of humanitarian relief in that year, of whom 16,900 had been displaced from their homes (§92) and fifteen hundred lived in refugee camps around Nicosia (§93). The area in northern Nicosia today known as Göçmenköy, meaning "refugee village," grew out of those camps, which primarity housed people displaced after the attack on Omorphita. A follow-up report on September 10 speaks of destruction of 527 houses and looting of another two thousand in 109 mostly Turkish-Cypriot or mixed villages (§180), raising the number of Turkish-Cypriot refugees (term used in the original) to twenty-five thousand (§190).

This first official demographic accounting of the violence is telling. It sets the terms on the basis of which the conflict is governmentalized and managed. In this report, displacement is recognized as Turkish-Cypriot displacement. Yet the report notes that Greek-Cypriot houses were also damaged and destroyed in the fighting. Most notably, Greek-Cypriots left villages in Tillyria, after Greek-Cypriot attacks of a Turkish-Cypriot coastal village in the area, which was functioning as an entry point of arms from Turkey. This action by Greek-Cypriots elicited the napalm bombing of the area by Turkish planes in August 1964. UNFICYP reported that "combined action" had killed fifty-five Greek-Cypriots, twenty-eight of them civilians (UNFICYP Report 1964, 24). The report does not detail however the situation of these and other Greek-Cypriot refugees. These refugees were cared for by the government of the Republic of Cyprus and were not officially labeled as refugees but as victims of the Turks (*tourkóplikti*, as chapter 4 explains). The Turkish-Cypriot refugees, as a formal category in the UNFICYP report, were people to whom this care was denied. On those terms then, the refugee category emerges as a category of victimhood, to be defined and managed by the state—who is and is not a refugee is a decision of the sovereign who provides the relief. It is not an objective, experiential reality. This is significant because it spells the terms upon which certain categories of those displaced—including around three thousand Armenians expelled from the Turkish quarter of Nicosia in late 1963—came to be excluded from the refugee record, as this later became scripted into post-1974 history.

That later phase of the conflict began with a Greek-Cypriot coup against the president whom the nationalist Right saw as unable or unwilling to effect *énosis*. The nationalists argued, on July 15, 1974, as they rolled National Guard tanks onto the streets and overtook police stations, that they would instead bring about change themselves and in consort with the dictatorial regime in Greece at the time. By the end of the week, July 20, 1974, Turkey had landed troops on the northern shores of the island seeking to protect Turkish-Cypriots. In accounting for those losses, the government of the Republic of Cyprus has emphasized the figure of two hundred thousand Greek-Cypriots who fled their homes in the north as invading forces approached. The ceasefire arrangements of that war also displaced over fifty thousand Turkish-Cypriots. A Republic of Cyprus Press and Information Office (PIO) report from October 1974 mentions that police recorded 192 civilians killed, two hundred cases of girls and women being raped, and an unstated number of Greek-Cypriot prisoners of war transported to Turkey (PIO 1974, 41). Another three thousand Greek-Cypriots (ibid., 43) were reported to have been missing, a number which later dropped to 1,619 as prisoners were exchanged and then to 1,427 by 1981, when records were formalized and the CMP set up to investigate these cases see also Davis (2017a). The CMP's terms of reference also included by this time 329 cases of missing Turkish-Cypriots from 1974 and the 214 missing people from the 1960s period[10]—numbers which had up to then remained unmentioned. And they excluded victims of the coup.

This early PIO report explicitly lobbied the international community for support and did so through graphic imagery of the suffering population: torn bodies, bombed-out neighborhoods, corpses protruding from the wreckage, elderly refugees sitting on the ground, young women crying. It estimated Greek-Cypriot refugees at 191,259 and inventoried their needs in detail. These refugees, now fully recognized as such, are pitted against the Turkish-Cypriot "so called refugees," whom Turkey is "endeavouring ... to concentrate by force ... in one area [and to] ... create an artificial 'refugee problem' in order to secure support of world opinion [*sic*]" (ibid., 50). The refugee category emerges here as an ethnically exclusive one: one's refugeehood renders the Other's a pretense.

A special report from the United Nations High Commission for Refugees (UNHCR) on September 4, 1974, speaks of 163,800 Greek-Cypriots displaced from the north and 7,800 Turkish-Cypriots who are homeless in the north. The report also foresees that thirty-four thousand Turkish-Cypriots in the south and twenty thousand Greek-Cypriots in the north "are or shortly will be in need of assistance" (§4). The report counts the missing as 2,180 out of which 580 had by then been located (§11). The UN Secretary General's report at the end of the year 1974 notes complaints received about three hundred deaths of Greek-Cypriot civilians and 195 Turkish civilians, committed by the other side respectively (S11568, §37). After an agreement in August 1975 that still remains debatable (Third Vienna Agreement), 8,033 Turkish-Cypriots were transferred from the south to the north (S11900, §10) while Greek-Cypriot refugee numbers stabilized at 183,000 (ibid., §35). Politicians still argue about whether the transfers were an emergency humanitarian measure or an exchange of populations agreement. In the south, only sixty-two Turkish-Cypriots now remained, while in the north one thousand Maronites and nine thousand Greek-Cypriots were registered for UNFICYP assistance (§36)—both of those numbers dwindled in later years. The number of displaced Turkish-Cypriots in the north was then forty thousand (ibid.).

In the periodization of the conflict these numbers represent 1974 as a single event: Turkey's military attack on Cyprus. On the one hand, this conflates two phases of the war (July and August), the first of which appears from accounts to have employed especially brutal tactics to intimidate Greek-Cypriot populations into vacating their areas. On the other hand though, it conflates the coup (July 15), instigated by the Greek-Cypriot National Guard on orders from the junta leadership in Greece, with the invasion of the Turkish army (July 20). Greek-Cypriot rhetoric often refers to these two events as "a twin [or double] crime." In doing so, it places emphasis on the far greater trauma (in terms of casualties) of the second and castigates the first but without fully accounting for casualties and perpetrators. Such numbers are indeed difficult to ascertain, as we now know that at least some of the missing Greek-Cypriots registered as victims of the war were killed during the coup.

It was not until 2014 that the Republic of Cyprus published a list of fatalities during the coup. These were categorized as follows: forty-one fatalities among the resistance fighters (seven of whom had been recorded as missing), sixteen civilians (one recorded as missing), five from the Greek military contingent based on the island since its independence (one recorded as missing) and thirty-six fatalities (seven of whom were civilians, twenty-three recorded as missing).[11] The category of fatalities (*pesóndes*), in general, designates their difference from victim fatalities (*pesóndes thímada*) referring to civilians killed by coupists; from resistance fatalities (*pesóndes andista-siakí*) referring to civilians who took up arms against the coupists including paramilitaries and twenty armed-forces personnel; and from fatalities hailing from Greece (*Elladhídes pesóndes*), all of whom are military. The unspecified fatalities category (*pesóndes*) then is the category that refers to coupists themselves, which evidently does not comprise only the National Guard (the institution leading the coup), but also paramilitaries outside of it. The governmentality of this categorization speaks of the difficulty the state has faced in accounting for its own failures on multiple fronts: in terms of upholding the rule of law in the 1960s (and allowing militias to thrive), in terms of holding co-ethnic perpetrators to account after 1974, and in terms of recognizing that the former two were questions of state failure (or also of state failure) and not (only) the result of Cyprus's victimization on a global scale. This general victimization discourse has guided official rhetoric since 1974, allowing it to claim that the Cypriot state had from the start (1950s) been a pawn in grander schemes hatched out in the context of the Cold War. In doing so, it has upheld a binary perspective, whereby responsibility is an all-or-nothing question.[12] Accordingly, this argument has allowed official rhetoric to divest its proponents of any responsibility for all of the losses described so far.

Thus categorized, the all-important distinction between inter- and intra-ethnic violence that has hitherto determined the inventorying of loss, now morphs into a dichotomy between victims and perpetrators of a double crime, whereby the first are understood as being co-ethnics, the latter as ethnic Others and those who helped them. Ethnic differentiation is not undermined but rather entrenched, as the civil war phase of 1974 is subsumed under the Turkish-invasion narrative. Accordingly, commandos who had been killed in battles during the coup participating in it willingly or under duress and hurriedly buried in graves marked with the designation "unknown" had been subsumed under the "missing" category until the late 1990s. And when attempts to identify and return remains to families were carried out in 2010, an even more complicated story emerged. Correspondence between remains and names (for those whose names had been marked on the graves) was found to be flawed during the exhumations in 2011. The families of some contested the circumstances of their loved one's death—essentially contesting their identification as "coupist, one family maintaining that their relative had been executed by fellow officers for refusing to partake in the coup." When some of the identifications were finally concluded in 2014, twelve of the dead were given, amid much criticism from the Left, a state funeral.[13] In the necropolitical governmentality frame (Mbembe 2003; Dillon and Reid 2009; Stepputat 2014) shaped until that time, the separation of dead coupists and dead resisters had been tacitly acknowledged and maintained. It was now time, the Minister of Interior delivering the eulogy said, "to look in the eye and admit the simple and elementary truth that those on the one side and those on the other side fell in the course of carrying out their duty, which we have not had the nobleness and bravery to do until now" (newsit.com.cy). Tacit as it had been, that acknowledgment was now dissolved. The impossibility of knowing who did what was folded into a common call of duty, allowing that duty to remain unquestioned.

An AKEL publication of late 1974, and widely circulated for a number of years after, provides a counterpoint to the official version presented in the PIO report. It dwells explicitly on the dead heroes of the party killed in the coup, providing accounts of survivors imprisoned and tortured, outlining failures of the coupist government (in power from July 15 to 23, 1974) to manage the country's defense in response to the invasion, and celebrating solidarity with Turkish-Cypriot people, whom they see as also victimized by the conflict and their nationalist leaderships (AKEL 1974). The publication (AKEL 1974), prefaced by President Makarios himself, displays many of the key elements of leftist discourse that has guided counter-histories of the conflict since then. It displays some of the same imagery of victimhood as the PIO report, but also includes graphic imagery of violence from the 1960s (where the victims are presumably Turkish-Cypriots but not explicitly identified as such), alongside images that celebrate coexistence (common demonstrations, party events, and daily interactions). But this counter-history has never become officially sanctioned beyond the double crime rhetoric. On that basis, the memorialization of dead coupists as casualties of the coup in general simply extends the official double crime line into that area of counter-hegemonic necropolitics that had tacitly been recognized as being under AKEL's authority. By speaking of what had been silenced, the counternarrative force is taken away from the left. Claimed now by a liberal discourse of acknowledgement and the right to mourn, the political import of AKEL's counter-history became irrelevant. The past was far away, and everyone in the end deserves a funeral; victims are victims, after all.

At around the same time that casualty categorization was applied to the Greek-Cypriots in the early 2000s, the Republic also publicized an official list of exactly five hundred Turkish-Cypriot names registered as missing (*Government Gazette* 3713, May 12, 2003). The list is telling of the same governmentality of counting loss. The ethnic Other appears here as a round number, which includes, in 2003, 126 victims of a massacre exacted on the populations of three villages in August 1974 (Aloa, Sandallar, and Maratha), whose remains had been unearthed by the end of that year. Note that even then, the Committee for Missing Persons (CMP) was tasked with determining the fate of 543 Turkish-Cypriots at the start of its activities. Even the most progressive initiatives of acknowledgment of the losses of the ethnic Other continue to be guided by the concern to discount those losses—in the form of now a flippant approach to counting that rounds off to the nearest hundred.

These counts were the last mass casualties of the conflict. During the long ceasefire that followed, seven Greek-Cypriot and three Turkish-Cypriot soldiers were killed in sporadic incidents on the Buffer Zone, while UNFICYP counts fifteen fatalities from "malicious acts."[14] The last two Greek-Cypriots to be killed on the Buffer Zone have become, since their death in 1996, the last heroic victims of the conflict. A bikers' demonstration in August 1996 that broke through the Buffer Zone from the south was met with an organized force of extreme nationalists from the north who beat a Greek-Cypriot to death and shot his cousin on the day of the funeral, as he tried to bring down a Turkish flag near the spot of the earlier killing. The images of these last two casualties still adorn the Greek-Cypriot checkpoint in central Nicosia. They are images that epitomize the ethnic losses against a brutal Other.

SILENCING MINOR LOSSES

The demographics of Cypriot losses reveal a necropolitical register of postcolonial transition. The discounting of the deaths of the Other exhibit in Mbembe's words a colonial "economy of biopower [where], the function of racism is to regulate the distribution of death and to make possible the murderous functions of the state" (2003, 17). Yet in the uncertain accounting of one's own deaths as deaths of martyrs, victims, or traitors—an uncertainty exhibited most clearly in the blurred terminology regarding militants that the last section reviewed—an uncertain positioning of the state is also exhibited that shares characteristics of what Mbembe categorizes under contemporary forms of necropower (ibid., 25–35). For Mbembe, necropower is "the working of [a] specific terror formation" traced through from slavery to colonialism and late modernity, which combines disciplinary, biopolitical and necropolitical power. It ultimately hinges on the sovereign "capacity to define who is *disposable* and who is not" and does so on the level not of individuals but of populations, via the claim of a state's "divine right to exist" (ibid., 27). Under this lens, we can understand the insistence of Cypriot necropolitics of major losses on assigning blame and revoking responsibility (Papadakis 2005; 1998) not only as a collective sharing of trauma but also as a political mechanism working to uphold the state. Counting the dead in specific ways, and discounting some deaths from the register, is less about mourning and enabling us to get on with things and more about telling us who we are, who others are, and who among us are not quite us.

Accordingly, in the counting and in the failing to account for losses, the ultimate victims are neither the heroes, nor the martyrs, neither the innocent, nor the survivors; the ultimate victim is the state itself, dissolved, usurped, betrayed, attacked, mutilated, and barely surviving. This state, the Republic of Cyprus, is the victim in Greek-Cypriot discourse, and arguably Turkish-Cypriot discourse too. The divergence is on the question of how this state has survived and the merits of its survival into a future peace. It is a state that is connected to a homeland through divergent interpretations about this homeland (Greece for the staple nationalist discourse, Cyprus in the leftist one, in parallel Turkey and Cyprus for Turkish-Cypriot discourse). And it is a state that in emerging from an anticolonial conflict is staked on being counted within a modern international system of sovereign states and in having decisively broken with its colonial past.

In the necropolitics of postcoloniality, the dead and the missing, counted together or separately, are categorically different kinds of losses to refugees. The remains that surface in recent years through exhumations undertaken by the CMP speak of the terrors of "unspeakable death[s] ... [l]ying beneath the terror of the sacred ... [in] the permanent remembrance of a torn body hewn in a thousand pieces" (Mbembe 2003, 27). This fracturing of bodies indexes a past governmentality, one in which sovereignty was more integral but also more horrifying. The images that appear in propaganda publications of the 1960s and 1970s are exceptionally graphic, concentrating on the burned, shot, or mutilated body. National struggle museums still largely showcase this necropolitical gaze.[15] The survivors of the horrors of conflict, those wounded, raped, and mostly those who survived the loss of their families (the relatives of the missing), turned into the prime symbols of security at the sight of the Other's death (ibid., 36). The mothers of the missing are a familiar and haunting image to Greek-Cypriots growing up after the war—clad in black, holding photos of their loved ones, and demonstrating their pain and anger at the Ledra Palace checkpoint in Nicosia. They are images that the passage of time, increasingly after the 1990s, has turned from news items to stills: metaimages of photos of women holding other photos. They have become governmental apparatus for remembering what the pain of Cyprus is. Highly feminized, these symbols stood for the victimization of the homeland (see also Roussou 1986; Anthias 1989).

Reading critically the inventories of loss allows us to see more clearly how and why the conflict has been memorialized under these particular tropes. The analytic task ahead is not to see beyond the numbers but through them. Commenting on the images of death-squad murders in Brazil, Smith argues that they create an "excess spectacle of death [which] . . . indicates that police violence is following a social script of white supremacy that is infused into the mundane" (2013, 186). The mourning emphasized and the mourning foreclosed by the imagery of death and its incorporation into the mundane are registers of necropower and indicative, in Cyprus as in Brazil, of "the necropolitics of the state and genealogy of policing" (ibid.). I therefore turn, in the chapters that follow, to the views on the ground not in order to recount a story as alternative to the numbers but as a story that has been reappropriated alongside that of the numbers. I read an ethnographic record of memoirs and oral histories through a lens calibrated on the critical perspective of necropolitical demographics.

Considering Packard's account as such a memoir, we see that in the affective register, what looks like solidarity might also have involved economic gain, and what looks like co-ethnic murder might also involve the policing of inter-ethnic reproduction. The way in which numbers become tools of knowledge, whether by inventorying or obliteration (writing them out of qualitative studies), defines how the conflict is governed—by the state, academically, and in the everyday. Speaking of another case of "computing" loss, that of counting the dead of the Armenian genocide of 1915, Altınay (2014) poses the question of Islamized survivors whose stories had remained untold until 2004. Elsewhere, in presenting the surfacing of such stories as counters to state discourse on multiple levels (2006), she also foregrounds the considerable labor that goes into this silencing, which perpetuates it for decades. This silencing here forecloses mourning and robs it of its critical potential (Morton 2014). What silence people keep and what they mourn are political undertakings that conduct and counter-conduct subjects.

The question I am prompted to ask here is about the different modalities that mobilize such labor: keeping silent and feigning ignorance at the moment of the event, fearful silences in repressive aftermaths, hushed mutterings of resentment in leftist environments, familial avoidances of war talk. All this labor has supported a governmentality of the conflict in Cyprus that for the last half century has solidified around a knowledge of loss with a hollow center. Packard speaks of locals in coffee shops in 1964 who claimed to have seen and heard nothing as co-villagers and neighbors were abducted, shot, or taken off buses never to be seen again, and neighboring villages and ethnic quarters evacuated in fear in the aftermath of such incidents. He also describes widespread looting of these evacuated quarters and people scurrying away from his patrol as it surveyed the damage. People who have lived through events and witnessed them have kept most of that knowledge to themselves; people born after those events have known of killings, troubles, or atrocities, but have also known that their knowledge was incomplete.

Among many Cypriots, the story of the Green Line is no longer a tired story of deaths and recrimination that the state has promoted selectively over the last half century. An alternative knowledge is offered in the legendary explanation of its color. This holds that it comes from a green pen, chanced upon on that December evening (December 28, 1963) by the British commander of the Joint Force, Peter Young, who drew up the Nicosia separation map two days before its signature (also corroborated in Packard 2008, 25). The same legend exists for the drawing of the Palestine-Israel border agreed upon in 1949 but tabled at the UN under Resolution 181 (November 29, 1947), a time that interestingly coincides with Peter Young's earlier posting in Palestine. The ethnographic quality of the legend relates something of the cultural concepts that have come to define the Cyprus conflict. That the substance of the conflict, here in the form of actual division lines that have profound effects on the daily life and deaths of people, is decided by higher powers, and often on flimsy logics, such as the chance presence of a pen. In this otherwise archetypical form of postcolonial subjectivity the balance is tipped towards a victimized construction of the native as a subject who is powerless but also innocent. In a Bhabha-esque (1994) twist, the postcolonial predicament becomes a technique for absolving Cypriots' responsibility for the conflict. The central character in the story of the Green Line is the green pen and its whimsical presence.

Contrast this to the regretful comments elicited after the death of a great aunt in 2014. The memory to which her closest affines returned was the moment in 1964 when the neighboring Turkish-Cypriot village was being abandoned and her own co-villagers were seen on the streets with loot. She had been held back from reproaching them, venting instead her anger at home. The fear of intra-ethnic repercussions was great and she was from a village on the other side of Cyprus, a foreigner. The labor, I want to argue, that went into keeping her silent then was not momentary. It continued to work on the silencing of that shared memory within the family's elder generation, and perhaps on the reflexive worries about the thin line separating silence and complicity for years after. That is the governmentality that frames Cypriot conflict subjectivities.

It is the same governmentality that foreclosed the question of who those sixty-two Turkish-Cypriots cited in UNFICYP's report were that stayed behind in 1974, and why they did so. It also foreclosed questions about the Armenians who were evicted from their Nicosia quarter in 1964 after it was enclosed within the Turkish-Cypriot enclave because they had colluded with Greek-Cypriots. And about the Maronites of Ayia Marina village, who had sheltered Turkish-Cypriots from Skylloura in the same year and warned by Greek-Cypriot militias to refrain from providing such help. And indeed, of people who survived on the Other side after 1974. In the period after 2003, a number of stories emerged of people who were discovering inter-ethnic relatives: a half-sibling from a Turkish-Cypriot's failed marriage to a Greek-Cypriot before he fathered co-ethnic children; a mother who had to explain to her adult Turkish-Cypriot son that she had been born a Greek-Cypriot before marrying and converting so that he could claim in 2003 a passport from the authorities in the south using her official Christian name; the female basket weaver in northern Nicosia's market to whom other stall owners referred for decades as *Rum* (the name Turkish-Cypriots use for Greek-Cypriots), indicating affection but also marking out her difference, the difference of a person who stayed on the wrong side. The gendered aspects of these examples also raise the urgent question of the counting of women's losses and the failure to see women as anything other than patriarchal subjects. These stories have been foreclosed through labor on the part of political subjects who have upheld, even in transgressing, the national script. Acknowledging them would have allowed acknowledgment of those other losses that undermine the myth of ethnic distinction. It would have poked holes on that imbricated roof structure of loss that holds us together collectively as victim subjects of the Cyprus conflict.

FIGURE SI.1. Paintings by Costas Economou: Storm clouds, watercolor, 1974, 27 cm. x 36 cm. (top); The loneliness of refugeehood, oil on canvas, 1981, 47 cm. x 52 cm. (center); Theano's loneliness, oil on canvas, 1995, 22.5 cm. x 29.5 cm. (bottom).

1 LAYERS

Notes toward a Global Everyday

The back wall of the archbishopric in the old part of Nicosia is a prime spot for graffiti slogans. Scrawled in blue spray paint, one of them reads, in the summer of 2017, "Kyrenia – Varosi = Return." These are two towns in the north, key sites of Greek-Cypriot displacement and the main reference points in political demands for the settlement. The palimpsestic answer of another graffiti author, below it and in black paint, instructs the original authors to "learn maths, you fascist s**." As unauthorized performances of marginal discourse, these exchanges are not necessarily astonishing. They instead bring into the realm of the unauthorized, the radical, a well-rehearsed rhetoric of nationalism and its main counternarrative that rejects it as partial, inane, and ultimately destructive. In this unauthorized field, as opposed to other more public fields, nationalism can be completely written off as legitimate utterance, the language of numerics being employed to dismiss the grammatical script.

Even though outright dismissal of this sort does not feature in public discourse, the conflict between scripted narration and a counternarration, in as far as it questions which losses count and how, is abundant not only in slogans but also art in Cyprus: photography, poetry, literature, and cinema are rife with depictions of the major losses surveyed in the last chapter.[1] There, the tropes of victimhood and protest are heavily employed to portray both major and minor losses. Exemplary of the first, painter Yiorgos Skotinos's series "Cycle of Protest" illustrates atrocities during the invasion via violated bodies that resemble ancient figurines, thus connecting pain to history;[2] and in terms of minor losses, Vasos Argyrides's opera *Manoli . . . !* exposes the impunity over coup killings through a mother's protest and its silencing by a chorus representing the state and the law, bringing into view and questioning the presuppositions of unities in authorized histories.[3] Pushing counternarration further, is an artwork by Nurtane Karagil depicting Turkish-Cypriot displacement through the sketched figures of Makarios and bare-breasted Aphrodite in double. She stands for the two population transfers coded under her name post-war. This child-like drawing caused a controversy after local authorities asked the Greek-Cypriot curator (who refused), in February 2017, to withdraw it from a collective exhibition celebrating Paphos as European Cultural Capital.[4]

All these performances communicate the loss, trauma, victimhood, silencing, and protest, which the last chapter prefigured as constituents of Cypriot subjectivity. As acts of citizenship that distinguish activist citizens who "engage in writing scripts and creating the scene" from active citizens who "act out already written scripts" (Isin 2008, 38), they transform certain citizens, whether from majority or marginal populations, into actors (ibid., 39). Such acts hover between deeds and performance, process and outcomes, conduct and enactment (ibid., 23). And they are political in negotiating the relationship with the Other (ibid., 35). But the conflict between narration and counternarration is also predicated on the conflict between protest and its circumscription. Acts of citizenship are particular kinds of counter-conduct in the Foucauldian sense, I argue below, and as such, their emancipatory component remains indeterminate. The continuum between assisting the conduct of others and affirming the possibility of being conducted otherwise is not always marked out.

This is what concerns me in the theorization of loss as the subjectivizing mode in the governmentality of refugeehood. Costas Economou (1925–2016), the artist in my grandmother's family, once explained that despite what I would have expected from his continuous interest in political developments, his political works of art were few. Engravings of a wounded horse and rider was the exemplar he chose; and an oil painting of a lone, old woman refugee in a deserted landscape had been especially successful in international exhibitions: "depictions like this went a long way with critics." But the topic of 1974 was too scripted to work on, he felt. And so, the few works that he did produce on it were personal: his depressed mother-in-law in the refugee painting, a subtly critical depiction of defeat in the horse etching. Acts of citizenship in Cyprus are performed in reference to the script of refugeehood because this is what delimits both conduct and counter-conduct. The chapters in this section explore this limit on the registers of affect, law, and space. At this limit, I want to argue, the space of citizenship is opened up and destabilized through the caesura of acts, but these nevertheless arise on the continuum of counter-conduct.

The layers of paint on graffiti walls that mark the law and the illegal, authorized and unauthorized, infraction and whitewashing are good metaphors for the space of subjectivity I am talking about. It is a space that holds potential for acts to emerge. It is a space where what Rancière calls "dissensus" can be exposed (2011). The dialogue scrawled on the wall, the discussion over the artistic depiction of a political leader, the musical intervention to vocalize what has been silenced, are acts that point to a recognition that the "common is divided," to a conflict about who speaks, to a conflict about "what has to be heard as the voice of pain and what has to be heard as an argument on injustice" (Rancière 2011, 1–2). This is a circumscribed space, an outside of which is illusory.

And this is not only the predicament of the Cyprus conflict. Tazzioli, commenting on the theorization of acts of citizenship, contends that such circumscription defines the analysis and not the act, an analysis that remains implanted in a Western-centered interpretation of activism (2015, 58). I want to agree with the impossibility of an outside that she poses, but want to also suggest that this has less to do with orientalism and more to do with the difficulty of theorizing away from emancipation. The Tunisian migrants she studied are indeed putting into question norms on which the migration regime is founded and often at the cost of their individual and collective freedom (2015, 59; 76–78). But their claim to a right to arrive in a Europe of their own making (of liberty and human rights) is also based on (Eurocentric, perhaps also oriental?) constructions of what Europe should signify for the rest of the world. What I am proposing as a point of focus is the negotiation between imposing caesuras on the existing order to open up new spaces for thought and action and constantly co-emerging with the field in which these acts take place (in reconstructing, for example, Europe between security and solidarity, humanitarianism and incarceration, autonomous migrants, activists, and state authorities). In Cyprus, loss gets similarly reconstructed between nationalism and its rejection, pain and accusation, exposition and refusal.

Performance and performativity *pace* Butler (1993; 1997a) are important in this negotiation for understanding the production of regulation and its simultaneous destabilization. What is important to remember is that subjection can also proceed through performance. The state also performs; indeed, power is enacted through performance. The display of death, as for example through vigilante executions in Brazil, or its hiding through disappearance (Smith 2013) are performances of necropower. And therefore, the question is to be able to hold both the promise and the circumscription of the act in focus at once.

I have elsewhere explored the employment of a specific, anthropological, everyday as a way to do this (Demetriou 2016a). I read this "everyday" as an alternative to Heidegger's—a shift that also requires a reorientation of understandings of the political. In this, I agree with Isin that "the question of the stranger as the essence of the political eludes Heidegger" (2008, 35). This question, I argue, comes to the fore in the encounter with death and mourning, making loss a particularly salient site for exploring this politics. At the same time, I take seriously the stark warning that Chandler and Reid (2018) offer against anthropology-inspired reifications of "indigeneity." The valorisation of practices that might look like resistance to colonialism modern-style, they show, can easily become blind to the ways in which in a neoliberal world, these practices end up being folded into new orchestrations of power (such as for example, when indigenous communities are called in to provide knowledge for environmental projects). Drawing attention to the bleak everyday of suicide in Canadian indigenous communities instead, Chandler and Reid appear to suggest a shift of focus from indigeneity as an emancipatory platform to focussing on preventing the "indigenization of contemporary neoliberal governmentalities" (ibid., 2). Such a shift is part of how I reread Heidegger's everyday. The contemplation that Being-towards-Death has to confront in its everydayness, is not its own death only, which is never experienced post-factum, but the actual experience of the death of others. This grappling with everydayness then becomes an ethnographic exercise, such as emerges in the work of Veena Das, when she analyzes the recuperation of an ordinary everyday following devastating events such as the Bhopal disaster or the violence of India's Partition (1995; 2007). It is an engagement that "descends," as she puts it, into the ordinary, rather than sublimate normality into philosophical contemplation as Heidegger offers, or, to heed Chandler and Reid, extol indigenous existence within neoliberal adversity as the answer to neoliberalism.

Following from all this, I want to propose that not (only) eman-cipation but (also) loss and mourning constitute the ground for rethinking acts of citizenship. And that these acts are not only the performative acts of art or unauthorized script, but can also arise in the everyday. This is what I examine under the terms of a Foucauldian counter-conduct (Foucault 2006). For Foucault, "counter-conduct" is a term used to describe particular forms of protest, and, I suggest, indeed acts that might not be readily rec-ognized as protest, dissent, insubordination, etc. What I find useful in the concept of counter-conduct is the emphasis on the negotiation between the potential to destabilize governmental structures and the fields within which it is circumscribed.

Mourning, it has been argued, has a critical political potential (Morton 2014) that could indeed be counter-conductive. The graffiti dialogue is but a small example of the contestations in which this potential is mired: some mourning tropes overtake the margins and implode delinquency into state discourse (e.g., equating villages of displacement to the nationalist dis-course of return), foreclosing the potential of the act. Mourning is not an act but the affective disposition from which the act arises. And it is configured within relations of power. The necropower involved here defines who remains in a state of injury, how that mourning is performed, how it is authored as performance, and to what extent this is authorized. Loss, as a field of conduct and counter-conduct, is the space where the act and its circumscription are negotiated. These acts engender potential as well as violence. And it is to this violence, perpetrated in postconflict subjectivity, that I turn. And to how exactly, through this perpetuation, postcolonial peace is foreclosed (Mbembe 2003). How are the politics of mourning and imagery utilized, what are their complicity, their critical potential, and where are these limits? How is violence silenced and/or rendered immaterial without necessarily being confronted? And what are the structures by which past violence and its silencing reemerge and are reconfigured in Cyprus's late modernity? These are questions of how minor losses become such through counter-conduct.

The layered way in which I ask these questions in the next three chapters is not to imply a separation between the affective, the legal, and the topological registers. Rather, it is an analytic gesture of partitioning that eluci-dates the specific forms that the imbrication of these layers takes. In my exam-ination of the affective layer, therefore, I do not suggest that legal or spatial dimensions are not relevant. I rather argue that the construction of a collective notion of refugeehood (what I call a "generalized refugeehood") prompts specific performative repertoires, examined in chapter 3, which interact with the development of legal norms and legal conduct and counter-conduct examined in chapter 4. And that, in turn, this conduct and counter-conduct are tightly connected to the ordering of territory and the contestations that surround this ordering. It is to better illuminate these imbrications that I first explore the workings of performativity in mourning (chapter 3), then the development of the legal apparatus of exception (chapter 4), and finally the limits of sovereignty in the governmentality of space and objects (chapter 5). In parallel, chapter 3 charts the contours of dissensus arising from the work of reflection on performativity as this enters the mundane, which the following two chapters take up and explore in terms of imbrication in the legal and topological registers. As all three chapters make clear, these three layers are anything but separable: affect arises from the materialities of space (see also Navaro-Yashin 2012), is oriented by law, and it informs both the management of the landscape and the development of the law. Each of these three chapters examines different angles of all these entangled processes.

The implications of what I propose in this section for current thinking on refugeehood are twofold. First, I propose that citizenship in postconflict societies operates in a particular modality. It is circumscribed by an orientation towards a very particular Other, often racialized, and arguably also sexed. It is on this specific figure that other others are calibrated, minoritized, excluded, or integrated (I examine this more closely in the next section, "crevices"). Postconflict citizenship is a spectrum not only based on the ideal subject, but also ordered on the ultimate Other. This is another way to read Arendt's remarks on the stateless as the figure standing opposite the citizen and amid other statuses of non-belonging (1994, 344–84), a figure whose emergence she locates in World War I (1914). This orientation towards the Other has a highly performative aspect. And knowledge of this performative aspect, which implies knowledge of the limits of that orientation, also circumscribes this subjectivity.

My second point is that this has implications everywhere today, when post-9/11 and (post-?) War on Terror without a declared end but with renewed and shifting theaters, conflict is no longer "over there." We are all postconflict subjects. And I insist on "postconflict" not as a heuristic device

to connect my Cyprus data to the global condition. We are postconflict subjects in a situation that like in Cyprus, holds conflict in abeyance, just far and
close enough, on news screens of flare-ups, in a zone of waiting between comfortable and tense ceasefire. The "post" of postconflict points to the ordering
capacity of conflict on this subjectivity but also to its constant receding from
view. The subject is always in a beyond of conflict, but ordered by the conflict nevertheless.

And if citizenship is globalizing through methods such as the stan-
dardization of biometrics for travel, techniques of surveillance, and policies
that circumvent human and political rights (Rygiel 2010), postconflict citizenship is globalizing also. Consider the export of methods that govern conflict from states such as Israel, which are exemplars of conflict societies, to
states such as the United States, which lead the global War on Terror. Practices
are shared not only on this level. In June 2017, Israeli military exercises were
carried out in Troodos Mountains in Cyprus, under a bilateral cooperation
agreement, because the area offered similarities to war zones in southern
Lebanon and southern Syria. Emulation and simulation play a role in the
migration of conflict across the global order. Performance is also a device for
enacting global forms of power.

In a different way, postconflict refugeehood is also globalizing. One
of the legal cases I discuss in chapter 4, concerning displacement in Cyprus
(*Loizidou vs. Turkey*) is now a textbook example in refugee law concerning
the responsibility to protect. And this is increasingly significant in a world
where the externalization of borders and other techniques of creating exceptions in territorial jurisdiction are encompassing more and more of the spaces
where refugees and migrants are able to move. And in the other direction,
the globalization of postconflict citizenship also means that "policy laundering" (Rygiel 2010, 61) can return practices of othering back to the conflict societies that struggle to overcome them. The EU-Turkey statement of
2016, which allows migrants to be returned to Turkey from Europe and EU
member states to accept resettling Syrian refugees according to a quota system,
has prompted Cypriot authorities to qualify a preference for three hundred
Orthodox Christians, following similar qualifications of other member states,
as I explain in chapter 6. The othering that defines postconflict subjectivity
has a long afterlife; and it morphs as it travels through space and time. And it
is morphing globally.

THREE **DISSENTING LOSSES**
The Affective Register

GOVERNING A SUBJECTIVITY OF LOSS

The contours of Cypriot post-conflict subjectivity arise in the major losses surveyed in chapter 2. In the aftermath of the war and territorial division in 1974,
all citizens can claim to have suffered loss of their state, but the state can claim
to have heroically survived. A state-centered victimology has formed the basis
for constructing a hegemonic victimhood, under the sign of a generalized refugeehood: we have all lost our lands. And if in its Greek-Cypriot version the
state marks the point where loss is lamented but survival also triumphs, in its
Turkish-Cypriot version the triumph of setting up a new state justifies losses
of the 1960s; and in both cases, the toll of these triumphs is questionable, the
political victories post-1974 incomplete. The state of the Republic of Cyprus
survived but with political and territorial division; a new state exists in the
northern part of the island but without sovereignty and lacking international
recognition and economic self-sufficiency.

In turn, this incompleteness, muted in the official rhetoric, has
formed a chasm between this rhetoric and the everyday experience of the state.
To Cypriot political subjects, there is an accepted and obvious distinction
between formal politics and everyday knowledge, and this often surfaces in
the dialogue between governmental and opposition politics. The disagreement
about what the state of the state is, and what it should be, has become embedded
in political experience, discourse, and practice. Navaro-Yashin has called this
a political subjectivity constituted around the "make-believe state" (2012),
upholding the "as if" of the state, functioning as if one's state is recognized
and sovereign while knowing it is not, in the case of Turkish-Cypriots. I claim
that the "as if" operates for Greek-Cypriots too who have contended with a

state founded constitutionally on power sharing but which has been largely in suspension for the better part of the last half-century.[1] A higher-ranking civil servant once informally remarked in a Greek-Cypriot group discussing the legal parameters of a prospective federal settlement that "we have taken half of the Constitution and placed it in the deep freeze for the last 50 years." In our jovial environment, the comment was meant to recognize the "as if" of the state that everyone knows but does not publicly discuss.

So the consensus on the victimology of the state has developed within this same field of dissensual dynamics: knowing and recognizing privately but not saying publicly. In the fracture of consensus, Rancière recognizes a paradox of democratic governance, which while being predicated on the participation of citizens in political life ("government by the people for the people") also tries to circumscribe this participation. This prompts a "reduction of political action [which] leads to the empowerment of 'private life' or 'pursuit of happiness,' which, in turn, leads to an increase in the aspirations and demands that work to undermine political authority and civic behavior" (2010, 47). The issue at stake is the potential of dissensus to question the democratic-neoliberal edifice, when new collectivities emerge from it that question the private/public understandings at the heart of this paradox. Another way to read the democratic paradox is in the function of performance and performativity—incessantly drawing and erasing a line between what is known and what is done, political rhetoric and critical praxis. The collectivities emerging here are forming around minor losses. And they are questioning whose losses are major as well as what loss is and how it is counted. Refugeehood is the starting point of this questioning.

Refugeehood, in the post-war state, was largely used to furnish the images of loss presented in chapter 2 with an expansive quality, linking the body to the land, and the land to the masses. The tragedy of loss did not concern only the specific individuals who were maimed, raped, or related to those who died, as depicted in the graphic publications mentioned in that chapter. It concerned the multitude, and this multitude was made into a spectacle in another set of images—the images of the rows of tents in the refugee camps set up in the aftermath of the war and in existence until the end of 1975. Tents were first replaced by prefab housing units in the settlements in 1975–1976. Soon after, more permanent housing in large-scale complexes became available. Maria Hajipavlou, placed at the Press and Information Office at the time, speaks of governmental pressure on policy-makers concerned to dismantle the tent settlements as soon as possible: "Makarios insisted that refugees should get everything that they want, otherwise they would rebel." But short-lived as the tented camps were, their images persisted in public discourse for years after. These images were interspersed with those of individual victims, on whose faces (chiefly of young women crying, hands on their cheeks, and children holding up photos of missing fathers) the abysmal depths of loss invited communal empathy.[2]

But as the suspension of the conflict has persisted, a different governmental politics has emerged. As peace negotiations stalled and the political establishment in the north sought international recognition (a goal that remains, for Greek-Cypriot politicians, the most reprehensible of all Turkish-Cypriot claims), different forms of territorial sovereignty began to reshape the postcolonial geography. Sovereign British bases and sites retained for British military use had been key clauses in the decolonization agreement since independence (Treaty of Establishment, August 16, 1960). They provided the first response units following the clashes of 1963, and marked the south-easternmost limit for advancing Turkish military forces in the second phase of the invasion in August 1974. Enclaves administered by Turkish-Cypriots had circumscribed ethnically pure, safe areas during the conflict years of the 1960s. Their administration evolved into the state that unilaterally declared independence in 1983. The UN-administered Buffer Zone evolved in parallel with these developments from the Green Line in inner city Nicosia to a zone across the length of the island. In all of these spaces sovereignty is claimed, questioned, contested, undermined; and re-emerges through the violence of the law and the violence of its absence. Cyprus appears as an exemplar of what Mbembe described as the postcolonial space ordered by necropower: "a patchwork of overlapping and incomplete rights to rule ..., inextricably superimposed and tangled, in which different de facto juridical instances are geographically interwoven and plural allegiances, asymmetrical suzerainties, and enclaves abound" (31).

Over the decades, the state's ambivalent and patchwork-like existence began to weigh in on the gap between rhetoric and experience. A sovereign Greek-Cypriot political space became increasingly untenable conceptually, as much as territorially. The territorial fracture and ambivalence also had an affective aspect. The particular aspect of that enmity-driven survival logic that rested on refugeehood began to fracture, as the general condition of displacement became narrower. The recognition of people as refugees and the granting of rights and benefits by the state was increasingly at odds with a rhetoric that presented the loss of homelands as a communal one. In this postcolonial politics of loss, refugeehood began functioning as the affective field that exposes the hiatus between the rhetorically projected consensus of slogans such as "we are all refugees" and the dissensus of those who feel they have lost more, or at least differently, than others. This is what I begin to explore in this chapter.

The chapter examines the affective register on which refugeehood is evaluated. It surveys differing descriptions of loss among Greek-Cypriot refugees and analyzes the ways in which differently situated discourses conform to and confront the hegemonic narrative. As people deconstruct this narrative as a political device, they rearticulate their losses within a frame that attaches political affect to both home and property. This political affect is the condition of dissensus, expressed forcefully in relation to restorative-justice mechanisms and the ethical positions they invoke. Through the Cyprus example, I propose that a more nuanced understanding of how loss is affectively registered can be instructive for the way refugee return and compensation are managed. Similar questions can be asked in Bosnia, for example, where much has been said of material reparations within a binary frame based on ethnic logic (Jansen 2006; Dahlman and Tuathail 2005; Phuong 2000). Affect, Jansen suggests, is today redrawing Sarajevan mental maps that have material effects on people's residence choices and property values (in Demetriou and Dimova, 2018). My Cyprus material tells me, at least in the long term, that affect may take different forms and shape discourses and choices at variance with each other. It is this variability that I seek to understand anthropologically.

In my early work on Cyprus (2006), I argued that the island's division, especially as it is marked by the Green Line in Nicosia, is a symptom of Greek-Cypriot political subjectivity in the Lacanian sense. It is a symptom that produces the kinds of *jouissance* that Žižek dwells on (2000) to claim that what is in fact deplored (the symptom) is fundamental to the subject and that it is its loss and not its presence that produces catastrophic anxiety. The debilitating effects of such dwelling in loss have been raised by a number of critics of traditional approaches to refugee relief. Nyers (2006), for example, argues that the construction of refugees in terms of bare life (as those who have lost everything) renders the recovery of political life impossible. One can either be refugee or political subject, but not both. The currency of such critique is evident recently where, for example, humanitarian intervention is expanding beyond the mere preservation of life into the support of the emotional and the social, if not quite the political. Clowns Without Borders is present in refugee camps from Lesvos to Iraqi Kurdistan offering emotional relief from war trauma and creating connections "so that celebrations of laughter can continue."[3] This is a far cry from the situation in 1970s Cyprus, where loss was managed on the basis of national unity and set the terms for this management through the decades. But despite this difference, I want to propose that theoretically the Cyprus data speaks to that space where political life is recuperated and reinhabited by people despite the insistence on loss, and even through it.

Division indeed animates the whole constitution of being Greek-Cypriot, and it is omnipresent in social and political life, and on the landscape. Looking at the exploitation of its branding value, "celebration" might well describe the forms that this affect takes. Nicosia's municipality describes the city as the "the last divided capital city of Europe" in all its insignia,[4] and the Green Line is a major point of focus, even after the opening of three major crossing points in the capital. Lines painted in the middle of downtown streets guide tourists through the key landmarks of central Nicosia and through the checkpoint, but also along sections of the Green Line, inviting them to experience the division. Even after a significant reduction of troops in the city centre in the last decade, such a walk along the Green Line still includes, in front of steel gates or walls of concrete and sandbags, the sight of soldiers at their posts, rifles on their shoulders, behind signs banning both access and photography (while in fact inviting the latter).

A postage stamp featuring the etching of a refugee girl sitting in front of a line of barbed wire was issued in 1974, and it is a compulsory addition to all letters mailed out of the Republic, two cents per stamp going to the Greek-Cypriot refugee fund (see figure 3.1). Refugeehood and division, private loss and communal loss of "our lands" become one. The stamp was produced as an international campaign tool. Initially, a special seal was pressed into whatever postage stamp was being used. The separate refugee stamp was developed later in 1974 and initially featured a mother and child, an etching made by the Greek artist Tassos, who had been collaborating with the postal service since 1962. The lone child figure, by the same artist, replaced the mother-and-child dyad

FIGURE 3.1. Development of the refugee stamp: Stamp print on random postage stamp reading "refugee fund" in three languages from 1974 (left); stamp featuring mother and child engraving used between 1974 and 1977 (top right); refugee girl with barbed wire engraving used on stamps since 1977 (bottom right).

in 1977. The stamps are today bought, licked, and pressed on a daily basis; but also they go unnoticed, bypassed on that same basis. The original stamp series is not archived at the central post office where I sought it, but it is available for sale in antique and souvenir shops in downtown Nicosia. Refugeehood, as referent for division, is increasingly communally circumscribed, its "culturally intimate" (Herzfeld 1997) aspects overtaking the outward-looking international campaign focus. The public exhibition of pain gave way slowly to an invocation of banal nationalism (Billig 1995) working mostly on the private level. The stamps and their erratic presence as commodities but not archives indicate the simultaneous connection and disconnection between "Man *and* citizen" posited by Rancière as part of subjectivation in liberal democracy (2010, 56). Citizenship recedes from view and becomes suspended over collection and transaction.

This receding from view of the citizen subject is evidenced elsewhere too. Wall graffiti of the kind mentioned in this section's introductory notes—against the division, the Turkish army, the invasion—which were scrawled near many central Nicosia military posts, are now confined to more remote areas and pop up only selectively in the manner described earlier. A recurring slogan in such graffiti (oftentimes produced by the military personnel at such outposts) continues to be the injunction in Greek that "our borders are not here; our borders are in Kyrenia" (*ta sínorá mas íne stin Kerýnia*), interpellating through indexing the island's northernmost town, a generalized refugeehood, under which the whole nation (an appellation that is itself uncertain) is displaced. The graffiti are read in a hurry, seen from cars driving by, and the images don't register.

As cultural feature, tourist brand, and interpellatory device, division is the sinthome that holds together the Borromean knot of Greek-Cypriot subjectivity. If the ultimate object of desire is a resolution of the conflict, we might posit the imaginary as all those interpretations of such a resolution that each of us might fantasize or fear; and anxiety would emanate from it if only in the recognition of that subjective incongruity between self and community. That community, articulated in all those pronouncements that present the "we" in unity would make up the symbolic. And the impossible real would in turn be the specter of actual conflict resolution. That specter was one that Greek-Cypriots rejected in voting down the Annan Plan in 2004. It is also the specter of coexistence as it takes place on an everyday level and in ways that are largely uncelebrated, marginalized, and unarticulated. This is the working of the sinthome in the banal modes of habitus. And it runs through the top levels of conflict governance too.

Post-2004, the high-level negotiation process between the leaders of the Greek- and Turkish-Cypriot communities, has moved substantially beyond baseline agreements of the terms of a settlement, envisioned as a "bizonal bicommunal federation" ever since 1977. But in the move, they have also become much more bureaucratized and technical, involving less the leaders' opinions and more the consensus among experts on topics such as constitutional provisions, demographic and area correlations, and monetary compatibilities. Committees of experts have been meeting since 2004 to pose and (perhaps less) to answer questions about the categories of property ownership registered in each side; to figure out ways to codify loss (lack of development, loss of income, loss of use, loss of access, etc.); to consider scenarios of claims and return under differing electoral systems; to correlate territorial jurisdiction with coastline proportions—in short, to establish the parameters of govern-mentality in the time of the "as if." An as if (as if the settlement was agreed, as if it had been accepted by the public, as if political interests were monolithic and unchangeable and aligned with ethnic identification) chiefly based on the assumption that Greek-Cypriots and Turkish-Cypriots behave and will con-tinue to behave as *proper* Greek-Cypriot and Turkish-Cypriot subjects.

GENERALIZED REFUGEEHOOD

Elsewhere (Demetriou 2007) I argued that the opening of the border in April 2003 was an event that spurred a dramatic reconfiguration of this subjectivity, momentarily putting into question the way in which the field of the political had been ordered around loss. In the aftermath of the opening of the border, I claimed, the state reasserted its role as a guarantor of the limits of political discourse and of that field of the political. Crossers, many of whom were ref-ugees, were admonished by government and refugee-association representa-tives that this crossing was not a return; one should not be a guest in one's own home, return would be when the land was liberated. This reconfiguration of subjectivity enacted by the crossers had drawn on discourses that were previ-ously available but did not figure prominently in official rhetoric, unlike the discourse on "return upon liberation" that the state employed. Those other discourses spoke of reunification, rapprochement with Turkish-Cypriots, rec-onciliation over historic violence, and return to a past of peaceful coexistence. The minute ways in which Cypriots experienced the political post-2003 are inextricably tied to the processes of reunification taking shape on the ground but which nevertheless are unarticulated. This other specter of the real, a real that is seeping through the closely knotted structure of division has a different potential from the 2004 referendum. It has the potential to unhinge subjec-tivity not by exposing the real as an imminent possibility, but by undoing the expectation of grand redemption.

As a principal manifestation of this order, refugeehood has provided the victimology, as we have seen, articulated in the symbolic; and it has fur-nished the imaginary of return. It has also driven the incision into the real by prompting hitherto foreclosed evaluations about such returns. But how does such an injured state operate as the basis of subjectivity in the first place? In a chapter on "Wounded Attachments," Wendy Brown posits the middle class as the address of injured identities. The success of capitalism, she says, has been to hold up this middle class as an ideal in "a phantasmic past, an imagined idyllic, unfettered, and uncorrupted historical moment [when] ... housing was affordable, men supported families on single incomes, drugs were confined to urban ghettos" and not as a failure to deliver prosperity to nonclassed subjects such as homosexuals, single women, and people of color

> who lack the protections of marriage ... who are strained and impoverished ... disproportionately affected by unemployment, punishing urban housing costs, and inadequate health care programs, [and] ... subjected to unwarranted harassment, figured as criminals, ignored by cab drivers. (1995, 60–61)

And she concludes that this predicament is what stifles dissent, what allows the work of subjection to proceed unresisted, what founds the "language of recognition" as a "language of unfreedom" (ibid., 66). When the terms of the debate have been set in the frame of some categories and not others (the middle class), recognition is folded into and circumscribed by the only discourse available: liberal capitalism. At stake here is the relationship between interpellation, habitus, injury, and dissensus. The claims of the injured subjects are rendered irrelevant to the discourse of the ideal, their critical potential evacuated. But what happens when it is an injured subject that is held up as ideal, when the site of injury, a specific site of injury, is highlighted and privileged? My data suggests that these links must be readdressed through a consideration of performance.

    If the middle class is an injurious identity featured as ideal, refugeehood in Cyprus works in the opposite terms but towards the same end: it is an injured identity held up as the ideal of injury and occlusive of the exclusions around it. Injuries, I suggest, can rhetorically become a site of privilege, and they do so at the cost of proliferating exclusions. And again, Cyprus is not exceptional. Injured subjects have been held up across radicalized nationalist political space, reclaiming a political *bios* purported to have been lost through too much liberalism. Trump's electoral campaign of 2016 comes readily to mind, premised as it was, on the injuries suffered by white populations across the rustbelt and beyond; as does that of the Brexit front in the UK, spotlighting the injuries of the white working class (see also Evans 2017). The backlash we are seeing there and elsewhere today on whatever progress had been made to

those planes of injury Brown identified in 1995, is partly the result of a duplicitous rhetorical connection between injury and privilege. We need to dwell
upon this connection and its long-term effects. And as Stevens proposes, we
need to recognize that such duplicity is not an accident in the system (2017b).
In the case of the deportations of US citizens, who are wrongly classified as
"aliens" that she examines, she finds that "the rates of agent and guard abuse,
false confessions, and erratic judicial opinions in the United States are higher
and often have more serious consequences in deportation proceedings than in
the sphere of criminal arrests and trials" (ibid., 228). An ideal liberal democracy
that apportions reparations to injury "just right" is untenable. It is untenable
because exclusion is part and parcel of liberal state governmentality and determines from the start the way injuries are addressed, even if the precise calibrations turn out to be accidental.

In Cyprus, the call of those excluded is not that they are injured
because they are not middle class, but that they fall outside the ideal of injury.
Their call is that they too are injured, they too are refugees, and their falling
short from that ideal does not diminish the injury, it worsens it. Brown's answer
to the problem of injured subjectivity is the mustering of collectivity against
a nihilistic slip into individualizing therapeutic discourse (ibid., 74–75). The
countering of subjection prompted by refugeehood in Cyprus is the fracturing
of that collectivity. It is when refugeehood, in its function as interpellatory
device, is experienced as failing to properly address specific injuries that its
promise of generalizability can begin to be countered. On this basis, exclusion
comes into plain sight upon the realization that these specific injuries do not
precisely require new mechanisms of address but the expansion of current
ones. It's not that different governmental instruments need to be hatched out to
address the losses of different groups of refugees. It is simply that these different
groups should be counted as refugees too. Exclusion per se is the problem.

But how does its appearance come about? What I have been calling
"generalized refugeehood" describes the condition whereby loss works to bind
collectivity. It is integral to subjectivity in a way that invites us to explain it in
the Freudian terms of melancholia. "Melancholia is, like mourning, a reaction
to the real loss of the love-object, but it also has a condition which either is
absent from normal mourning, or, where it is present, transforms it into patho-
logical mourning," writes Freud (2005, 210). And it is not solely an individual
matter but can be political too: "[m]ourning is commonly the reaction to the

loss of a beloved person *or an abstraction taking the place of the person, such as fatherland, freedom, an ideal* and so on" (ibid., 203, emphasis added). Far from driving a wedge between the personal and the political, mourning, even from its Freudian origins, is deeply political. Mourning is the invocation of the empty space left by the subject without rights, the subject effaced (Rancière 2010, 66–69) that prompts others to act on those rights and thus starts the process of subjectivation. Melancholia is characterized by a "disorder of self-esteem, the loss of object [having] been transformed into a loss of ego" (ibid., 204). Moreover, ambivalence is a precondition to melancholia (ibid., 211). Melancholia proceeds through "battles of ambivalence," which are repressed until the point of conclusion, when they represent themselves "to consciousness as a conflict between one part of the ego and the critical agency" (ibid., 216).

Seen as a melancholic condition then, refugeehood dwells on those losses that are not death (the major losses explored at the end of the previous chapter) and progresses on a plane of ambivalence that invites critical political reflection. This is not because some refugee psyche is collectivized among Greek-Cypriots but because specific structures have been set up to institutionalize such melancholic aspects of mourning (images, text and songs, emphatic presentations of the Green Line, public education, media discourse, patterns of political negotiation). Loss is articulated as a hegemonic discourse that speaks of the northern part of the island as being lost to the Turkish occupier (*Túrko kataktití*) that is the main object of mourning. The loss is a collective loss of the Greek-Cypriot community; the lands lost are "our ancestral homes" (*patroghonikés mas estíes*), the homes that bore our forefathers. This rhetoric imbues representations of northern Cyprus in elementary schoolbooks and extends to large parts of the formal and informal curriculum, so that the generations being educated post-1974 are viscerally familiar with this concept of loss. It is a primary site of their interpellation as Greek-Cypriot subjects. Up until 2014, the exercise books used by elementary-school pupils depicted Kyrenia Harbour or the shores of Famagusta on the cover (figure 3.2). The caption "*Dhen Xehnó*," meaning "I don't forget," a phrase that became the key slogan of Greek-Cypriot nationalism in the years following 1974 (see also Yakinthou 2008; Constantinou 1995) is still used to title exhibition spaces of pupils' work in schools. Children in preschool classes are introduced to nationalism surrounding national celebrations with visions of lands in chains, awaiting their liberation, crying for the return of their owners and inhabitants (see also

Zembylas 2012; Spyrou 2006; Christou 2007). This imagery is abundant in publications of refugee associations such as *Adhúloti Kerínya* (literally meaning "Kyrenia refusing enslavement") and municipalities in exile, which represent refugees from specific areas in the north and tasked with creating community among dispersed individuals.

FIGURE 3.2. *Dhen Xehnó* (I don't forget) educational campaign: Ministry-issued exercise books featuring the "I don't forget" logo and pre-1974 photographs of Varosha from 1984 and 1986 respectively (top); wall display in school entrance hall in winter 2016, featuring pre-1974 pictures of Kyrenia and other locations in the north under the title caption "I learn, I don't forget, and I struggle" (bottom).

Refugeehood emerges in such constructions as the locus of grievability. It is what makes our injury grievable by "cultural reflex," as Butler would say, and the injury of others not (2011, 36). But this location of grievability is also what opens up the space of the political. This grievability involves substantial political work, work on behalf of structures of sovereignty, known since Antigone buried her brother against the law of state and family.[5] What happens in the current moment is that grievability comes to determine the "resurgence of sovereignty within governmentality" (Butler 2004, 56). This allows the return of the absolutism of decisions over life and death, which for Foucault would have died with the emergence of a governmentality that seeks to manage life and not to kill (Foucault 2006). Its return is "animated by an aggressive nostalgia that seeks to do away with the separation of powers" (Butler 2004, 61) only that now this sovereign power is not fully and centrally located in the state, but dispersed along the "patchwork of incomplete rights to rule" (Mbembe 2003) and unaccountable.

Grievability is political because it develops as a "cultural reflex," but it is also political because that reflex can be countered. Butler uses the example of Guantanamo detainees who produced poetry on polystyrene cups and scraps of paper, to locate an affect proceeding from loss, which involves injury and rage, and can lead to further injury, but can also lead to the determination to "limit the injury ... through an active struggle with and against aggression" (ibid., 172). This is to say that alongside the revengeful violence that we saw reproducing the conflict in the last chapter, another form of political action, which is not pacifism in the passive sense but a struggle informed by the same negative affects of injury, can counter the governmentality of loss. The struggle is not a struggle within some individual ethical compass; it is a struggle against nothing less than foundational state structures and their interpellatory effects. "Who needs Althusser or the police" Butler rhetorically asks, "when the raging speech of the melancholic himself wields the power of self-annihilation?" (ibid., 174). The political affective struggle of loss is against interpellation—it is critical and reflective work that takes account of the performative.

In the generalized condition of refugeehood, where mourning has acquired a high rhetorical value, the performative is integrated into the understandings of loss. Children grow to know that their literature-essay scores are immediately boosted when they tackle the island's division in those terms of grieving. And they often produce these essays within ambivalent frames of expedience and sentiment. I suspect that the students are also often graded in the same ambivalent terms. When a mother I know complained to the teacher that images of "enslaved Pendadhaktylos" Mountain kept her five-year-old daughter awake at nights, the teacher laughed it off. It would pass; it was nothing to worry about. Despite the omnipresence of the rhetoric of enslavement of the lands, there is a level at which it is accepted as exaggeration—almost like a fairytale that eventually the political subject grows up to accept for the fiction that it is. And yet, it is not quite fiction but rather a performative, in Austin's sense—it does not merely describe enslavement but effects it (1962, 6). It is speech that acts. It interpellates subjects to look out for those specific views of Kyrenia they saw in their schoolbooks when they are actually there visiting for the first time, as many youngsters told me after 2003; it elicits nightmares and creates worried parents. How far the political subject grows up to accept the fairy tale for the fiction that it is, is actually uncertain. The rhetoric acts in an illocutionary manner (i.e., by bringing about consequences), but the explicit intention of that act to do so (its perlocutionary force) cannot be written off; it sits at the limits between illocution and perlocution (ibid., 94–121). At this limit a governmentality of neuropolitics (Isin 2004) arises, working through the cultivation of "anxieties and uncertainties" (ibid., 223). For Isin, such governmentality has unfolded since the 1990s in the domains of economy, the body, the environment, the digital network, the home, and the border (226–32). But it may also be possible to propose that this governmentality is globalizing since 9/11, and is, in fact, part of the postconflict governmentality I sketched in this section's introduction.

The destabilization between fiction and performative forces is a level that has eluded many academic critics of victimhood rhetoric in Cyprus, who have been at pains to redress the exaggeration, provide facts (such as inventories of loss), and unmask the rhetoric for the propaganda that it is. But it is the anthropological question instead that I want to pose in this book: why is it that for many Greek-Cypriots, irrespective of political persuasion, the rhetorical quality of this discourse of enslaved lands is taken for granted? What are the performative politics of mourning here? What struggles of ambivalence is at work? Perhaps ultimately, the role of education is not solely or primarily to educate into a national mythology, but to educate (if inadvertently, or perhaps in spite of itself) into the performativity of that national mythology. This is what allows it to be laughed off and to persist. It is also what allows it to exist alongside discourses that in political terms would be seen as irreconcilable (e.g., the peaceful coexistence of Greek- and Turkish-Cypriots) and yet are espoused by the same state institutions that sustain the rhetoric of collective loss. These ambivalences, which came to the fore most forcefully in the 2003–2004 period, when the border opened and a peace plan tabled, are the points we must turn to in tracing the affective register of loss.

PROPER AND DISSENSUAL REFUGEES

The demand that "all refugees [should reutn] to their houses" (*óli i prósfiyes sta spítia tous*) after a settlement has been a diachronic slogan since 1974. With the opening of the checkpoints in 2003, Greek-Cypriots were faced with a dilemma of crossing or refusing to cross. Their authorities advised that their safety in the north could not be guaranteed (see also Demetriou 2007). Yet people flocked to the crossing points in their thousands. These were initial confrontations with the specter of the real. In the first governmental statement issued after the opening of the checkpoints, there are no less than ten references to "law," "legality," and "illegality," one to the UN Security Council Resolutions, and one to international judicial decisions, but no mention of citizens' right to make decisions about their movements (PIO April 23, 2003). The Greek-Cypriot subject was asserted as a subject of law, not a subject of freedom. On the same day, a former attorney general stated that individuals cannot recognize states, and that therefore the showing of passports required of Greek-Cypriots would not amount to treason, and it would not be illegal as the government implicitly argued. It was this last statement, and not the government's assertion of sovereignty that was credited by many Greek-Cypriots as having persuaded them to cross. It was at once a subversive and a depoliticizing statement (I cross not because I want to make a political statement but because I have been assured I cannot). The subject's freedom was reasserted through their dissociation from law and not within it. To fully understand the import of these propositions in destabilizing affective structures, we need to look to the discourse on statehood developed until then and its relation to the citizen subject.

Up to that point, when the Green Line was impenetrable and crossing required special permits, the Greek-Cypriot governmental rhetoric had held that the showing of passports in order to cross was morally reprehensible because it implied recognition of the "illegal pseudo-state" in the north. In the post-1974 social contract, the preservation of the state, its very substance and existence, was cast as the duty of every Greek-Cypriot citizen. This "substance and existence of our state" (*i kratikí mas ipóstasi / ontótita*) was invoked routinely to support (or criticize, accordingly) any policy on the national issue, pressing the point that particular acts, especially those not condoned by the state (primarily crossing and engaging in citizens' reconciliation) were not simply frivolous or naïve, but jeopardized the very existence of the state. Such "bicommunalists," as civil society activists who crossed were known, threatened the "substance and existence of the state" because they submitted an internationally valid Republic of Cyprus passport for inspection by the authorities of the "illegal" state in the north; and thus contributed to the "indirect recognition of the pseudo-state" (*émmesi anaghnórisi tou psevdhokrátous*). Consequently, in as far as entry into the north was prohibited by the Turkish-Cypriot authorities (prior to the opening of the border), the question of individual responsibility for crossing was a marginal issue. The imparting of the state in the passport-holding citizens' care was an implicit form of interpellation. And it worked on the affective basis of generalized refugeehood.

But the possibility of crossing in 2003 brought these conditions of subjectivity into conflict, rendering the question of crossing or not crossing of fundamental importance to the being of the Greek-Cypriot subject: should she see her land or withhold showing her passport? Socialize with Turkish-Cypriot compatriots or risk the substance and existence of the state? Crossing meant realizing one's duty as a proper refugee (actual refugees, as well as second- and third-generation ones and people for whom the north was imagined as "our lost land") and as a supporter of a settlement that would provide for harmonious and peaceful coexistence between Greek- and Turkish-Cypriots. Not crossing, on the other hand, meant resisting the longing for the land or coexistence for the sake of upholding the state.

Greek-Cypriot refugees I have spoken to since then appeared ambivalent vis-à-vis both these constructions. People who had refused to cross post-2003 did not point to recognition as the key obstacle. Others, who had rejected the UN plan, did not rationalize their choice on the basis of collective return. Crucially, individuals who had refused to cross had subsequently voted in favor of the UN plan. Individual rationales differed from official discourse. Roula is one of those individuals. She was sixty-one in 2011 when she shared her account with me. She had been displaced from a social-housing settlement in northern Nicosia to a refugee settlement in the southern part of the city. She might be classified as a conservative, and parts of her account adhere to nationalist rhetoric. Yet, other parts emphatically contradict it. This is how she rationalized her decision not to cross:

> If I knew I would be safe I would return, but to go and then have them [Turks] come again to take us, no. If I am safer here, I don't mind not going. . . . I still cannot bring myself to go and see [the house]. . . . Because I saw the war, because my husband was wounded, I have a phobia inside me. Not because I hate them [Turkish-Cypriots] that I don't go. But I have a phobia—even when it thunders I still think of the war.

Collective return as a point of principle is not an issue for Roula as refugee associations often posit (claiming that return means the return of all refugees). It is security on a personal level that is. On this same level, crossing becomes an issue of personal negotiation, not ethical or political injunction. The loss that legitimizes her otherwise nationalist refusal to cross is not the rhetoric of enslaved lands. Neither is it the material loss of the house, which she described as not much better than the one she now lives in. It is the psychological trauma of flight and its aftermath, amplified by her husband's involvement in the war and the longterm damage he has suffered to his leg.

Nadia, who was a teenager at the time of the war when she fled her home in the Varosha area of Famagusta, spoke of trauma and insecurity in very different terms. She recalled the time spent in tented settlements waiting to reach some place of safety:

> At some point an acquaintance who had joined the army came and reported horrible things that were happening on both sides. This somehow comforted me in the sense that it was about the war doing horrible things to everyone. He was not out to blame the Turks, as the others were doing. He said "war is a terrible thing because I saw Greek-Cypriots do things that I did not believe humans could do" . . . he said he'd seen a Turkish-Cypriot old man being tied to a jeep and dragged until he died.

These atrocities, described alongside her mother's fear that the advancing Turkish army would rape her daughters, a fear that ultimately informed their flight, became a point of commonality in the dehumanization that war effects on people, regardless of their ethnic belonging. This reconciliational aspect of trauma, which has since led Nadia to a number of rapprochement initiatives, does not ameliorate the experience of the loss she feels as total and irredeemable. She acknowledged she still mourns for the experiences that no political settlement can now return to her:

> You tend to idealize things, so for me even if I were given ten times the value of the house it would not be the same. I want my house back, I want my city back, I want my neighborhood back, I want my smells back, I want to be able to run again on the beach, where I used to run as a child. Can you understand this, without having lived it?

Loss emerges in these two narratives as formative of the two women's political subjectivation. It provides the ground for their positioning as political subjects, their views about the ethnic conflict and its resolution, their decisions in the material conjunctures of the present and the projected expectations of a future that seems increasingly counterintuitive. Yet, it is clear that the nationalism-reconciliation spectrum on which their positionings might be attempted cannot account for the critical reflection that underlies them. They both speak as political subjects who have outgrown the anthropomorphized image of enslaved lands. In Roula's case, refusal to cross is not a principled position beyond question, but a pained stance that makes individual sense. In the case of Nadia, the sharing of pain across communities does not detract from the sense of injustice at having lost her teenage sense of social self. By appropriating their losses in different ways, the two women show the limits of collective appropriations and the attendant readings of loss as a mechanism for typifying political attitudes in the correlation between the level of the state and that of the individual. One cannot speak of "Greek-Cypriot attitudes to loss," I would therefore suggest, without discounting the processes of critical reflection that constitute them.

Such critical reflection would also push the analysis to ask, "Who are Greek-Cypriots in the first place?" This is a question that seems to me foreclosed only if one already adopts a position of ethnic determinism. One clear example of this, but not the only one, is the minority groups that are counted in law as religious groups within the Greek-Cypriot community (the Armenians, the Maronites, and the Latins). The narratives of loss that they recount diverge even more significantly from the schemas of conductive discourse, as the next chapter shows. Alongside them, we should also consider Roma people, included in the Turkish-Cypriot community, who have never been officially recognized as a separate group under any legal regime. I return to this issue in chapter 8. I would like to prefigure these discussions from the point of view of affective attachments.

Thus, for example, Armenians experienced refugeehood in very different ways from most Greek-Cypriots, even though the categories that determined this experience have not been explicitly oriented towards marking this distinction. Whereas Greek-Cypriots displaced in 1974 are officially recognized by the state as "refugees" (*prósfiyes*), those displaced prior to this point are categorized as *tourkóplikti* literally meaning "those struck by the Turks." This is a poignant differentiating factor that elevates temporal difference to the ethnic level, given that the majority of displaced Armenians hail from Nicosia and were displaced in 1964, as chapter 2 showed. Armenians are thus *tourkóplikti*, while most displaced Greek-Cypriots are classified as *ektopisthéndes* (displaced) in formal legal language and *prósfiyes* (refugees) in more general parlance, including some policy discourse, as the next chapter explains.

Arpik, a teenager at the time of the family's displacement from the Armenian quarter of Nicosia in 1964, related, in 2010, this experience as distinct to that of majority Greek-Cypriots from which she was made to feel alienated:

> Unfortunately we are not considered *prósfiyes* (refugees). We are *tourkóplikti* (struck by the Turks). Those from 1963 are *tourkóplikti* (struck by the Turks), 1974 *prósfiyes* (refugees). And we did not receive any of the advantages, whereas for you [Greek Cypriots] there are various options. Sometimes I hear Greek-Cypriot refugees talk about 1974, especially younger people, and I tell them "hey, I've lived like this since 1963!" and they get surprised, they don't know.... Mrs. Anna, from Kyrenia, when we said to her that we lost too, she used to say "this is different!" (*állon toúton!*). We did not understand at first, then we realized she didn't count our loss as much as hers. What does this mean? Property is property!

If Roula's and Nadia's approaches to loss individualize their experiences, Arpik's communalizes it, but does so within a frame that puts the idea of

Greek-Cypriot community in question. By foregrounding her experience as an Armenian first and foremost, she calls attention to the silencing of losses other than Greek-Cypriot (and/or Turkish-Cypriot ones). This presents an anxiety to communicate what state and other discourses of classification have been failing to account for—that is, the particularities of individuals' losses. This failure is more totalizing in the case of Armenians because the silence has been propped up by legal technologies (the categorizations of "refugees" and "those struck by the Turks") but nevertheless present in other minority accounts. Ethnic exclusion might be inadvertent or capricious (Stevens 2017a), but it is founded in law nevertheless.

In the case of the displaced Maronites, most fled in 1974, but a significant number have also been enclaved within the northern part of the island in areas where the control of the Turkish army has been particularly strong. Of those, some were displaced to the southern part of the island controlled by the government of the Republic subsequent to 1974. Maronites have also had easier access to their properties since 1974, and many have repossessed them following the opening of the checkpoints in 2003. In late 2017, plans were being proposed for the withdrawal of Turkish army troops from Maronite villages and their repopulation by returning Maronites and their descendants. This experience contrasts with that of Greek-Cypriots, enclaved in the region of Karpasia, who have endured much harsher terms of enclavement and are seen as one of the prime heroic victims in Greek-Cypriot discourse. No repopulation plans were considered for them in 2017. And it also contrasts with the situation of the Roma, who live in the south as the opposite enclaved Turkish-Cypriot population in the terms of humanitarian assistance of UNFICYP, but who have never enjoyed the legal status of a separate group, and who have been shunned by both the Greek- and Turkish-Cypriot authorities. These differing experiences have punctured the experience of loss among members of these minority groups. Law here props up ethnicity as an issue not of loss but of recovery.

Thus, in the Maronite case, the loss experienced might be put to question. As individuals who relocated to the south were allowed to visit enclaved relatives in the north post-1974, they have been seen as different to other Greek-Cypriot refugees. Michel, who was three when his parents left the house in the village of Kormakitis in 1974 to resettle in Limassol, thus articulates a different sense of loss, which, like in Arpik's case, is strongly correlated to the sense of community and to feelings of alienation from the Greek-Cypriot majority:

> Greek-Cypriots would consider us some kind of traitors for going back [to visit relatives on weekends] ... I remember the sense of hatred for the Turks that was inculcated in us at school. I remember going back to the village and hearing people speak in Turkish, including my father, and I used to get angry.... My views of course changed afterwards, in London, and after the Annan Plan, when I met Turkish-Cypriots.... The first time I crossed after 2003 was the first time I actually felt able to travel elsewhere other than the village and meet Turkish-Cypriots[6] ... I felt the same surprise as everyone else after the Annan Plan when I saw restaurants and shops.

Paradoxically, the reconstitution of the Maronite community after the flight of 1974 took place, in Michel's analysis, at the community's own expense. As he explains of the level of state policy,

> [E]ven though the Maronite representative kept asking for one refugee settlement to be reserved only for Maronites this was not done. It was not done for other communities either ... but as a result, the Maronites dispersed and today there is an 80% of mixed marriages, so the community is disappearing. In the past mixed marriages were the exception. Also, there was no attention paid to other ways of keeping the community together, through its own cultural spaces. [But] as individuals, they were helped as much as everyone.

The efforts of the state to reconstitute refugees as a community had the effect of nullifying other ethno-cultural differences that existed prior to the critical point of 1974. This was not antithetical to the representation of Maronite access to lost villages and properties as a form of treason. It actually went hand in hand with the state rhetoric of collectivizing a sense of refugeehood as the proper condition of the Greek-Cypriot subject. And here lies precisely the force of all the articulations examined so far. In their different ways, they all put this purported collectivity of Greek-Cypriot refugees into question. They speak of sentiments and attitudes that are framed by this concept of the proper Greek-Cypriot refugee subject, but they describe processes of political subjectivation that undermine the collectivity at its core. All four individuals are communicating their distance from this proper refugee subject, and all do so with regret. It is precisely from this perspective that the analysis of loss can become instructive as explanation of the quagmire of positionalities that are proverbially said to plague the refugee/property issue in Cyprus today. Refugees may pine differently for homes, or be affected by different policies and structures, but what they all feel keenly is the disconnect, inadvertent, accidental, or intentional, from legal projections of proper refugeehood.

PERFORMATIVE LOSS

At the funeral of the great aunt I mentioned in chapter 2, the middle-aged mayor of the village she had come from, which was then occupied, asked to deliver a eulogy. The speech included references to her family and early years in the village, skipped over her adult life in her husband's village, and ended with a lament of an uneasy rest, until her bones would finally be able to be carried and buried in their rightful place, the ancestral village. He was sure, he said, that this would be the first priority of her children on that blessed day of return. Her children, along with the rest of the audience, were sure of his certainty of the opposite. At the very least, the admonition for reburial when the time came was contrary to the traditional injunction of married couples being buried together. Had she been from a different village in the south, there would be no question that the rightful resting place would have been her matrimonial grave, not her parental. What the mayor's injunction sought to underscore was the performativity of refugeehood, not the possibility of a realizable act. This was well understood by the congregation, who were not in the least surprised. We all recognized it was his duty as mayor of an occupied village, presiding over a dispersed population with no longer a fixed territorial centre, to attend such funerals and offer such injunctions.

As eulogy, the speech asserted my aunt's inclusion into that sphere of major losses that constitute refugeehood as an ideal version of Greek-Cypriot subjectivity. Only that my aunt was not strictly speaking a refugee. She had not fled in 1974, but had moved out of the village long before then. And she had never received refugee benefits. It was not until the point of that performance that her minor losses were admitted into the realm of major losses—and only for that performative moment where speech acted to make her a refugee. But in that very same moment that minor loss became major loss, the abyss separating the two was exposed. This exposition is the performative work that refugeehood does on an everyday level. Every time a claim about the Cyprus problem is made, those hegemonic images of loss I have been describing are brought forth and are recognized as performative losses. Refugeehood is held up as an injured but privileged status, while simultaneously it is clear that this privilege is only for some refugees, a group from which in fact, in myriad ways, all of us putative refugees are excluded. The privilege is there to interpellate, and it interpellates through performative excess. And every time that recognition happens, the exclusions on which that ideal of loss is predicated peer out from the crevices of that imbricated structure.

It is in those crevices between the legal, the material, and the affective that dissensus begins to be formed. Dissensus arises because of the perceptions of injustice within the legal (and this is true for major losses too), but it is propped up by the hiatus between rhetoric and performativity. In analyzing this process further, I turn in the next chapter to the legal register of refugeehood. I explore the juridical underpinnings of the subjective constitution described here as another layer from within which insurgencies develop.

FOUR

GOVERNING LOSS

The Legal Register

THE PROPER SUBJECTS OF LOSS

If, on the affective register of Cypriot refugeehood, performativity enables the emergence of dissensus, what are those moments at which dissensus materializes into acts of citizenship? This chapter traces the emergence of dissensus more closely, considers it alongside counter-conduct, and analyzes the specific fields within which acts arise and that circumscribe those acts. I turn to the legal register here, to better understand the development of the refugee category as a domain of subjectivity, a domain circumscribing power and contestation. Law works here to index democracy, sovereignty, and their absence, and it is at these interstices that refugeehood comes to mark a specific kind of citizenship.

Rancière (2010), locates a paradox in the enunciation of democracy, which puts in motion the process of subjectivation: "Democracy . . . entails that there is never merely *one* subject, since political subjects exist in the interval *between* different identities, between *Man* and *citizen*" (56). Subjectivation circumscribes the field of citizenship as a field of contestation between exclusion and inclusion, between the universal (man as subject of rights by birth) and the particular (citizen as a specific bearer of rights): "in this process, Man and citizen are used as political names whose legal inscription is itself the product of a political process" (ibid.). We might contrast, or complement this, with Kristeva's (1982) reading of the political via the figure of Oedipus, whereby she sees the transition from tyranny to democracy in ancient Athens as being involved in the transformation of the sovereign into a citizen subject (read in the move from *Oedipus Rex* to *Oedipus at Colonus*). The question I am asking is: what is entailed in the process of democracy that renders the sovereign a citizen subject? What exactly is the difference between sovereign and democratic subjects? And what lies in the transition from one to the other? Can we ever say that this transition is complete? The abject, which is Kristeva's main concern, is inserted in this process of subjectivation and in the making and unmaking of citizenship and of refugeehood.

Studies such as Rygiel's (2010) have shown how biopolitical processes like biometrics and other forms of identification post-9/11 are increasingly focusing on the creation of abject subjects whose citizenship needs to be "unmade" (Nyers 2006). She argues that by eliminating compliant subjects (i.e., those who do not only submit information about themselves but also "fit" into particular categories of living and behavior) a population of "abjects" is created (Rygiel 2010, 156–59). The democratic paradox here consists in the centrality of a war mentality (Reid 2014), where the security of all lies in the rooting out of terrorists, a category which is omnipresent and spectacularized in the War on Terror. At the other pole of spectacle imagery is the figure of the migrant denizen, whose disposability "evokes the always-already established (if obscene) fact of an at-least potential relegation of the world's 'citizens' to their properly abject condition as 'bare life' . . . [concealing and announcing] the universal disposability of all labor" (De Genova 2013, 1194). In thinking of these two cases together (abject subjects and migrant denizens), and against my Cyprus data, I want to reconsider the relations between abjection, subjectivation, and the democratic process.

In Cyprus, the performativity that spreads over the political, as I have shown, operates in a postconflict (and postcolonial) temporality. Peace may be pending, but no war here produces casualties, making the UNFICYP mission a follow-up tour to those in Afghanistan, for example, in the case of the British contingent. In this gray terrain of ceasefire that has eluded both the devastation of recent conflicts in the neighborhood (e.g., Libya, Syria, Egypt) and the War on Terror in the West proper (United States, United Kingdom, France, Belgium, Germany, etc.), the spectacle around which the political continues to re-emerge is the refugee as victim and as us. The restoration of democratic process after 1974, to whatever extent it has progressed, did so on the subjectivation of this figure into the emblematic citizen. But it has done so by also producing a myriad of abjections and by silencing the one abjection that makes the refugee a denizen—the refugee Other. This is what I trace here, through a genealogical inquiry into the legal and social constitution of the Cypriot categories of refugeehood.

To the extent that loss founds the political in Cyprus, as explained in chapter 3, its legal mobilization in the processes of subjectivation speaks to nothing less than the constitution of community, demos, and the powers that attach to it in the democratic process. And that includes the subjects of exclusion, of lesser losses, those injured otherwise. Terms such as "refugees," "displaced," and "struck by the Turks" (*prósfiyes, ektopisthéndes, tourkóplikti*), which we have seen figure on the affective register of loss, sit alongside other categories of victimhood in Greek-Cypriot legal discourse that calibrate the losses of 1974 (the dead, the missing, those injured), even if they emanate from violence of other times. As such, they are techniques of population in a Foucauldian sense: they mark the boundaries within which people and bodies are to be governed, and they mark out other populations, minor populations, and those not part of the population. But chiefly, they mark out those who have lost their homes in 1974 (refugees/*prósfiyes*) as the population of victimhood at the center of governmental concern. And in marking this population out, they also draw out the gradations of this loss: refugees proper ("displaced" [in law]/*ektopisthéndes*), the displaced from other periods (*tourkóplikti*), owners of property but not primary residences, families of the displaced, caregivers to the displaced (categories which the law has treated in variable ways over the years).

Post-1974 refugees have been the subjects of a number of legal instruments employed by the Republic of Cyprus to regulate access to rights, which would enable those displaced in 1974 to rebuild their lives in the southern part of the island by alleviating some of the burden of the material losses they had suffered. These instruments often refer to the "displaced, those who have suffered and other persons" (*ektopisthéndes, pathóndes ke álla prósopa*) as the main formal categories of victimhood who come under the special protection of the law. These categories constitute articulations of who is a proper victim and who is not, even where the categories appear inclusive. The "displaced, those who have suffered and other persons" is thus a category predicated on specific understandings of refugeehood used here to generate the proper subjects of loss. Law is the instrument by which these major and minor losses are differentiated. It is that tool of surgical precision that tells Arpik that even though she can count herself as refugee experientially, in technical terms there can be no material compensation to ameliorate her loss. It also rendered my aunt a carer of her displaced mother after 1974, probably keeping her on the village community's register and allowing the mayor on her funeral to declare her a refugee.

Gradations of citizenship that calibrate the inside/outside spectrum (Soguk 1999; Isin 2004) refer in the Cypriot context back to loss. The Civil Registry and Migration Department of the Ministry of the Interior summarizes its activities under six categories: issuing of nationality and citizenship documents, issuing of passports and other travel documents, issuing identity cards, issuing refugee cards, issuing displacement certifications, and certifying civil marriages.[1] As the key categories across which citizenship is calibrated, these six areas speak of the special operation of loss in determining the kind of citizen subject one is—not one, but two forms of apparatus, refugee cards and displacement certificates, qualify the citizenship of refugeehood (their difference, gendered to a large extent, is explored further in chapter 7). Loss, so thoroughly implicated in determining citizenship in Cyprus, founds the whole edifice of political existence in all its imbricated forms. An archaeology in the Foucauldian sense of working back to that foundation would look at the transition points in the discursive construction of the law—the coming into being of "displacement" and "refugee" identity in legal discourse. This archaeological analysis is undertaken here. The aim of this chapter is to reconstruct that process of founding the subject of rights as the subject of loss from that point in 1974 when loss was chaotic, everywhere, and hardly governable. And to deconstruct how, in rendering it governable, it was scrutinized, calibrated, evaluated, and judged in court. And in turn to reconstruct again, how that governance elicited counter-conducts as well as conducts of the self on the very same legal plane from which it began.

TROGLODYTES CYPRIOTES

On August 30, 1974, the *Official Gazette* announced the approval of Law 39/1974, forbidding the shooting, killing, catching, or chasing of game or wild birds, unless under a special hunting license (§4.1). The Law lists seventeen types of wild birds thus protected (§10.1), among them the Eurasian wren, *Troglodytes Cypriotes*. For a parliament that was functioning amid the chaos of governmental takeover and war since July 15, the protection of wildlife from poachers seems a strange point of priority. At least stranger than the new regulation of import taxes (Law 36/1974, announced on August 26) and transport vehicles (37/1974, August 26, 1974). Read alongside Law 38/1974, which restricts gun possession and regulates hunting gun licenses in that context, 39/1974 could have been an attempt to reinvest the state with powers over the means of violence: the Minister of the Interior with the power to issue licenses, and the police with powers to prosecute. In the previous period, both had been key sites in the breakdown of order, where forces that eventually turned against the government were given space to grow. The return of a democratic sovereign was perhaps being announced through the regulation of what can be killed and what not—beginning with wildlife. Or perhaps they were laws already passed, but which the publication of the *Official Gazette*, suspended between July 12 and August 26, had simply failed to report. Even in that case, from a performative perspective at least, these laws depict a state which still in shock, is attempting to relegitimize itself by continuing from where it left off. It was not until October 1, 1974 that legal announcements in the *Official Gazette* would unequivocally reflect the war situation.

But on another level, the protection of the Eurasian wren is symbolic of a governmentality that is yet to speak its name: the protection of the displaced. In Greek, "troglodyte" is a word that describes burrowers—those animals or humans who live in makeshift dwellings or use the dwellings built by others. It is also used for the uncivilized, cave people. Irrespective of lawmakers' initial intentions, it is tempting to read the inclusion of this species as metaphorical of a category of subjects, human troglodytes, that the law had up to then been unwilling to acknowledge and take responsibility for, because they were largely Other. During the 1960s, as we saw in chapter 2, tent-dwellers were mainly confined to Turkish-Cypriot enclaves, unseen and barred from access to the Greek-Cypriot majority. And when they were otherwise, they were classified as *tourkóplikti*, as we have seen with Arpik, and then, not in official law, but rather in media discourse and common parlance. It was Greek-Cypriot newspapers and not the law that first reported on *tourkóplikti*. *Tourkóplikti* were neither persons of concern to UNHCR, like Turkish-Cypriots, since they enjoyed the protection of their state, nor the subjects of specific and concerted policy to effectively alleviate their losses. Now, post-war, when the tent-dwelling population largely consisted of Greek-Cypriots, makeshift-dwellers, would gradually become the law's main target.

And when they did, it was largely because these tent-dwellers were subjected to a degree of discrimination by the rest of the population that was considered immoral for co-ethnics to exhibit. The first laws on the displaced protected them from inflated rents, payment pressures, and eviction. One of the recurring themes in accounts of refugees that I collected in 2000s was their hostile reception by non-displaced locals. "They used to tell their kids 'eat your food otherwise the refugees will come and take it,' as if we were scavengers," they would say with resentment. Scavengers, troglodytes, beggars: these were the undersides of the formal discourse on loss—a discourse that set up refugees as its heroic subjects but which, on account of its performative formality also produced the failures of empathy, humanitarianism, and solidarity that these subjects experienced.

The law came to mediate these two approaches to refugees—exaltation and scorn—in the first years after the war. This was a hesitant mediation at first, especially as regards the proper naming of refugees. *Ektopisthís* (plural *ektopisthéndes*), meaning "displaced," did not come into legal use until February 1976, when Law 4/1976 defined "displaced tenant" as "a person who, in the period immediately preceding the Turkish invasion had their permanent residence in an area which, due to the invasion has become inaccessible" (preamble). The point of this law was to alleviate the problem of inflated rent prices in areas where those rendered "displaced and homeless" (*ektopisthéndes ke ásteyi*) sought refuge, and in so doing, it also announced the equation between forcible movement and lack of a dwelling, activity and material circumstances. A previous law in 1975 had included a provision to freeze and lower rent prices, to halt rent payment for properties in "inaccessible areas" (*aprospélastes periohés*) and to regulate by Ministerial Council orders rent rates in "distressed areas" (*dhispraghoúses periohés*) i.e., areas where "due to proximity to dangerous points on account of the recent events normal activity has been negatively affected so as to necessitate relief measures" (36/1975, §3.2).

Even before then, Law 51/1974 ordered a 20 percent decrease in all residential rent prices. Other laws had also forbidden redundancy layoffs (50/1974), yet at the same time suspended social compensation for such dismissal (1/1975), regulated payment obligations for sales in "affected areas" [another term used to designate "inaccessible" and "distressed" areas] (9/1975), regulated social welfare (10/1975) and social security (11/1975). They also instituted benefits for National Guard personnel missing or killed in action (24/1975) and for the families of civilians killed or impaired in the war (25/1975). Recall that this would have been the time when rebellion in tented settlements loomed as a fear in the highest level of government. The legal formulation of the displaced as a population category therefore, in Foucauldian terms, arose at the point of the shift from a sovereign governmentality that ruled on the "let live" of species (birds and humans) to a governmentality of welfare biopolitics that determined economic relations and ensured that people had a roof over their heads. This was also the shift from the "right of death" of interethnic violence, coup and war, to the "power over life" in the face of humanitarian disaster (Foucault 1990, 133–60). And that biopolitical governance was inscribed onto the contours of ethnic, social, and political categorization already drawn.

In this shift, the subject of loss co-emerges with the subject of refugeehood and in a way that in a global context departs significantly from the strict parameters of the 1951 Convention. The loss of home, and not the fear of persecution, is here foregrounded. The calibration of the refugee body with the body of the population (Foucault 2004) is done through the connection of loss of home to loss of homeland. But this calibration implied a new set of regulatory apparatus with their own divesting effects.

In that famous passage from the *History of Sexuality*, Foucault sees the sovereign law of deciding between life and death as an extension of a "historical type of society in which power was exercized mainly as a means of deduction [of wealth, goods, products, labour, blood]" (1990, 136). Its morphing into biopower, he says, required a transformation of the law accordingly:

> the action of the norm, at the expense of the juridical system of the law ... Such a power [biopower] has to qualify, measure, appraise, and hierarchize, rather than display itself in its murderous splendor; it does not have to draw the line that separates the enemies of the sovereign from his obedient subjects; it effects distributions around the norm ... the law operates more and more as a norm, and ... the judicial institution is increasingly incorporated into a continuum of apparatuses (medical, administrative, and so on) whose functions are for the most part regulatory. (ibid., 144)

Recent readings of these lines and his governmentality lecture (2007) have transposed the concept of biopower onto contemporary governmentalities that seek to "ungovern" (Constantinou and Opondo 2016) or make the state's lethality appear ordinary (Povinelli 2011, 153), or to spell an affront on the separation of powers in democracy (Butler 2006, 61). In earlier work, I had looked at the laws about land use in a minority region in Greece as a biopolitical mechanism of divestment that employed the idiom of "care of the state" to achieve the opposite of prosperity (Demetriou 2013). In Cyprus, Erdal Ilican has discussed the emergence of Cypriot subjects as a corollary to property redistributions on both sides since 1974 (2011). Drawing on these insights, I am suggesting here that the legal governance of refugeehood post-1974 allows us to see biopower as devastating at precisely those moments when it appears most benevolent. The social justice that legislation in the latter half of the 1970s foregrounded brings into relief the lack of social solidarity that existed on the communal level and also the lack of state social consciousness in earlier years. In looking at the development of the law after this point, I am concerned with that transition of the law into norm and the precise ways in which it is "incorporated into a continuum of apparatuses." For the Cyprus data tells me that it is an all but smooth process: the law quavers and is put in question as this incorporation progresses and hits upon contradictions and hesitations.

LEGISLATING REFUGEEHOOD AND EMERGENCY

The legal language of the 1970s reveals an uncertain and malleable situation, a governmental structure still in formation that is unsure of how to name. The law's operation as norm was crucial at this point of abnormality but for the same reason also hesitant. The first legal definition to be formulated after the war did not refer to the population or the state but to the situation itself: *ékrythmos katástasis* (unstable situation) is defined in Law 49/1974, the first that announces the legal regulation of exception, setting temporary exit restrictions on citizens of the Republic. That law defines an unstable situation as "meaning the situation brought about as a result of the Turkish invasion, which continues to exist until the Ministerial Council, by notification in the Official Gazette sets a date for the ending of this situation" (§2). That notification is yet to appear more than fifty years on; instead, the definition of unstable situation has been used in all legislation enacted to the present day that concerns refugee or other welfare benefits and property arrangements affected by that Event of 1974. It is this instability, and not displacement, which signifies the original *legal* event.

Before the term "displaced" was formulated as *ektopisthís*, the victim subject was referred to as *"enikiastís apodhedhighménos epireasthís ousiodhós ek tis ékrythmou katastáseos* [a tenant proven to have been substantially affected by the unstable situation]" (Law 51/1975 §5.1b). It is a wordiness that suggests inability to regulate effectively and hope that this status would be short-lived. But also a wordiness that ties the loss of habitual home to refugeehood. This construction departs from analyses on refugees and emergency in the international context. Nyers argues that the link between the two hinges on the loss of political identity, whereby the refugee is produced as the "accident" of "ontogenetic practices of modern statism . . . to secure the 'normality' of citizenship" (2006, 9). In Cyprus, the link is established on the basis of home and not political community. In this sense, the inquiry into refugeehood beyond the 1951 Convention allows us to view it as a governmental apparatus that produces exclusion, not against citizenship, but within the confluence of both citizenship and refugeehood. The unstable situation, which characterized the situation of displaced Greek-Cypriots before they were legally defined, was the given against which people had to prove their relation and prove it substantially. *Ékrythmos* is a temporal definition of abnormality, literally meaning "out of rhythm" (i.e., out of sync, or a time "out of joint" as Hamlet would say). In thus naming the abnormal, the law normalized the exclusion of others whose abnormality was located outside that key moment in 1974.

These others were not immediately named. Such abnormality was not used in law prior to 1974 and does not appear in the legal regulation of the 1960s unstable situation. That instability was only retrospectively recognized, and this is shown by the introduction of the term *tourkópliktos* as a category defining previous displacements—it was used after the definitions of "proper" displacement (the displacement of 1974) had solidified. The law did not in fact define the term *tourkópliktos* until 2005. The concept first appeared as a category before the law in 1984 when an amendment to the Law on Rent Prices (39/1984 amending 23/1983) included under the term "displaced," also anybody "who, on 21 December 1963, was residing in a house owned by themselves in inaccessible territory and is not an owner of a residence in territory controlled by the state" (39/1984 §3.a). A later amendment broadened the temporal definition to ownership "immediately preceding the invasion" (138/1991 §2) while another one distinguished the three temporal categories of displaced on the basis of 1974, 1963, and "preceding the invasion" (2[1]/1993 § 2). In 2005, Law 46[1]/2005 consolidated and revised the terms under which housing assistance was provided to "the displaced, those who have suffered and other persons."

This spelled the introduction of the term *tourkópliktos* as a formal legal category. Under that law, *tourkópliktos* came to define "any Greek-Cypriot whose normal residence had become inaccessible prior to 1974 as a result of intercommunal disturbances" (§2). In the same year, another amendment reintroduced the previous proviso that to be considered *tourkópliktos* a person should own no other residence in the Republic-controlled areas (141/2005, §2). An explanatory note accompanying this amendment purports to clarify that the original intention of Law 46[1]/2005 was to extend the term to *any* Greek-Cypriot (*káthe Ellinokýprios*) who lost his or her residence in the intercommunal violence but that the point of the amendment was to specify the *quality* (*idhiótita*) of the *tourkópliktos* category as "a category of entitlement to housing assistance" (141/2005). In broadening refugeehood, two concerns thus remain: loss of property (here shifting from loss of "home") and ethnic belonging.

Under these terms, Arpik would not, strictly speaking, qualify as a displaced subject, even as one who is not a proper displaced person (*ektopisthísa*) but merely struck by the Turks (*tourkóplikti*). She would not qualify because at the moment that the law brought this category of victimhood into its purview, it already rendered an affective status (that of having suffered displacement), a status of material claim (through providing or refusing access to benefits). This is the case for most *tourkóplikti* nowadays, who, nearly two generations on from 1964, had, by the coming into force of Law 141/2005, already rebuilt their lives and those of their children outside the state's rehousing and rehabilitation schemes. When Arpik laments that she is not recognized as a refugee but merely a person struck by the Turks, she is not lamenting only this exclusion. She is also lamenting the suspicion that her being denied access to displacement status also has to do with her ethnicity. And indeed, she might theoretically be right. For in that brief moment when the law recognized *tourkoplikti* in the broad context of victimhood under the phrase "any Greek-Cypriot," it was unclear whether Armenians, officially members of the Greek-Cypriot *community* but yet not Greek-Cypriots *proper*, could be counted as victim subjects.

Arpik did not know the legal history of the term she applied to herself. She was also unsure of entitlements that went with it which she remembers her parents receiving, possibly post-1974: "My mother received some support for the rent at some point, but I cannot remember when it began. It was 50 Cypriot pounds. It was not immediately after, it was later," she reminisced probably referring to the 1984 law. As she raised the issue of the difference of her loss, she was also adamant that her claim took account of forgone material benefits, but that it was mostly about recognition. It was the social exclusion from proper refugeehood that she felt bitter about. The centrality of the category *tourkóplikti* in Arpik's narrative of loss and social integration goes beyond the strictly legal. In 2011, her articulation of the term suggests that it already had a substantial effect on her relationships with Greek-Cypriots before its legal codification in 2005. In this sense, it is indicative of the law's work in normalizing a social reality already in place. In contrast to the postwar laws that attempted to mold this reality through social intervention, the 2005 law merely reproduced an awkward, highly politicized term conceived originally on the plane of media propaganda, which had passed over the years into public discourse.

The legal terms of refugeehood index, by exclusion, the demarcation of a particular part of the population—indeed a section quite apart from the population: Turkish-Cypriots. In contrast to the hesitation over the term *prós-fiyes* (seen in the wordiness of early post-1974 laws), the category *tourkóplikti* is a rather crass formulation that aims quite obviously to exclude Turkish-Cypriots and their flight from the experience of displacement. In these terms, it follows formal political rhetoric, of the kind I described in earlier chapters—rhetoric which depicts Turkish-Cypriots solely as aggressors and never as victims. It is the rhetoric of school history books that describe the violence that began on December 21, 1963 as *tourkoandarsía* (Turkish mutiny). The pertinent point here is that this period of violence is being projected in nationalist/state discourse as a period of Greek-Cypriot victimization, when the vast majority of displaced, killed, and wounded, were in fact Turkish-Cypriots. Naming victims as *tourkóplikti* (struck by the Turks) makes the victimization of Turkish-Cypriots a historical blind spot as it categorically excludes from the conceptualization of victim those who have most claim to the status. In this sense, it parallels denialist strategies of the Armenian genocide or the Holocaust, which draw on the loss of life on the other side or acts of resistance on the part of persecuted communities, to present organized killing as provoked or as a war between equals. By the same token, the discourse of *tourko-antarsía* silences aggression and discrimination against Turkish-Cypriots and implies that the suspension of their political rights that preceded 1974 was a justifiable defense of order on the part of Greek-Cypriots who were faced with a mutiny. It is a step beyond the belittling of the violence that the more widespread formulation *fasaríes* (fracas, commotion, noise) communicates in the discourse of people who have lived through them. *Fasaríes* would thus be akin to the formulation "troubles" as used for the case of Northern Ireland (Aretxaga 1997); *tourkoandarsía* is its more propagandist, but also more technical, and thus more normative version. That normative work is what the legal appearance of the term *tourkópliktos* completes.

And it does this political work in a specific context. The 2005 law was passed a year after the referendum on the Annan Plan, in which 76 percent of the Greek-Cypriots rejected a proposal to reunite the island in a federal state. Much of the public debate on that plan had concerned its property provisions and had prompted widespread discussion over what refugeehood and return might mean. The government, which advocated a NO vote, had claimed in the prereferendum campaign that with a rejection of the peace plan rights to property would not be lost and that measures would be taken to alleviate financial adversities that refugees and their families and descendants continued to experience (e.g., lack of access to title deeds for the temporary purpose-built housing they had been offered by the government after the war). That alleviation is what the 2005 law, with its official formulation of *tourkóplikti*, enacts. The refugee subject, now multiply categorized and properly labelled, has become a postconflict subject. The conflict, by implication, has entered its "post" era. And yet, this transition remains silenced, unwilling to speak its name.

Contrast this genealogy to that for refugees (*prósfiyes*). As a legal category, *tourkóplikti* stands in stark contrast to the careful, if hesitant, legal formulation of displacement status in the 1970s. That formulation did not transpose the publically used *prósfiyes* (refugees) into law, but instead came to settle on "displaced" (*ektopisthéndes*) after considerable experimentation with wordy descriptions of statuses of loss. *Prósfiyes* would in fact be a legal misnomer, as the people it has been applied to are in current legal convention "internally displaced persons" (IDPs), having been displaced from homes in the northern part of the island, to the southern part.

Yet, as the war in Cyprus pre-existed the formulation of IDPs as a category of international law, reference to those displaced in 1974 as refugees is surprisingly frequent in documents other than strict national law, including the oft-cited United Nations Council Resolution 361 of August 30, 1974, which reads:

> [The Security Council] [e]xpresses its grave concern at the plight of the *refugees* and other persons displaced as a result of the situation in Cyprus and urges the parties concerned, in conjunction with the Secretary-General, to search for peaceful solutions to the problems of *refugees* and take appropriate measures to provide for their relief and welfare and to permit persons who wish to do so to return to their homes in safety. (§4, emphasis added)

The Resolution appears less concerned to comply with a strict application to the UN Convention in naming "refugees" but more hesitant in naming "the situation" that produced them. Public discourse has drawn on this faulty application of the refugee category to present 1974 refugees as exceptionally victimized because they are "refugees in their own homeland" (*prósfiyes stin ídhiá tous tin patrídha*)—an otherwise contradictory designation meant to underscore the unfathomable logic of the Cyprus conflict. However, law itself has not presented "refugee" as a formal category, even though the legal instruments that regulate this status, and access to rights and benefits relating to it, are produced by a parliamentary committee under the appellation "Committee on Refugees-Enclaved-Missing-Adversely Affected Persons" (*Epitropí Prosfíghon-Englovizménon-Aghnooouménon-Pathónton*).

It is in this context that refugee subjectivity, thus far a largely affective status, gained material and financial substance and became—much more than was previously the case—a rights-bearing status. But it is also this context that elicited dissensus; the context that revealed much more forcefully than was previously the case the minor losses, the acknowledgment of which had been denied, and with it the access to material benefits.

IMPROPER REFUGEES

In this context, one of the faultlines along which dissensus appeared to be emerging for the refugees I spoke to in 2011 was ethnicity. Via temporality, as we saw in chapter 3, Armenians were rendered *tourkóplikti*. Maronites were rendered as not quite displaced since they could visit their enclaved families on weekends

once a month on special permits. But similarly those enclaved Maronite relatives were not quite enclaved themselves, at least not in experiencing the level
of oppression that Greek-Cypriot enclaved experienced in Karpasia region (see
also Conclusion). The parliamentary Committee on Refugees-Enclaved-Missing-
Adversely Affected Persons focuses its work on those enclaved subjects and the
decimation of their population through the years and less so on the Maronites.
Michel's memories of the Maronite village from where he had been displaced
at age four were shaped mostly through visits to such enclaved relatives. He
remembers month-long approvals processes, difficulties in crossing, customs
checks on both sides, time checks at various points en route, obligatory bribes
to the Turkish-Cypriot police (of washing detergent and instant coffee), and
queues of Greek-Cypriot enclaved at the checkpoint crossing the opposite way,
where they would be made to wait for five to six hours in order to see their close
family. This, as we saw him verbalize in chapter 3, made Maronite students like
him suspect to their Greek-Cypriot classmates.

But this suspicion also jarred with his feelings of belonging in a community of loss that bore no distinction to Greek-Cypriots. His family left the
village during the second Turkish offensive in August 1974 and headed first for
the Troodos Mountains, then for Limassol where they settled for the first few
years before ending up in Nicosia. The hardship he remembers parallels the
hostile reception of the general refugee population in the south: "We were about
fifteen of us in one house, and I remember we had problems with the landlord. He
did not like having so many people." This similarity, like in Arpik's case, jarred
with the experience of being made acutely aware of his difference as a Maronite
refugee as the idea of treason hovered over the perceptions of Greek-Cypriot
classmates who heard of his visits back and forth. It also jarred with the differential reconstitution of ethnic community. As Greek-Cypriot refugee communities became organized through associations and municipalities of occupied
towns, they were able to partly overcome the difficulties of having been settled in
different geographical regions. However, as Michel explained, Maronite losses,
in being mitigated by the dispersal of alternative housing across the island, ultimately led to the loss of community through marrying out (and into the Greek-
Cypriot community).Ethnic dissolution foreclosed to a large extent the work
of cultural reconstitution that maintained Greek-Cypriot communities of loss.

For the Maronites of the Kormakitis area, their minor loss is different
from the loss Arpik articulates. But it is equally tinged by the sting of ethnic

difference, even as this difference allowed them to return to the village post-2003, to claim properties, fix houses, and recreate a semblance of village life on weekend excursions, now easier and more jovial. The enclaved of Kormakitis could be seen as an example of how life would be governed following a settlement. They have access and rights to property, the right to decide on village governance, a nonvoting representative in the Republic's government, and identity cards but no political rights in the north. Yet the denigration, with which their status is treated by majorities on both sides (a treasonous hint for Greek-Cypriots and exclusion from Turkish-Cypriot public life), is also a cautionary tale for how that future coexistence carries its own new losses.

Even Latins, who otherwise appear to have been almost completely integrated into the Greek-Cypriot population, have in some instances experienced refugeehood differently. In 1974, Jeannette was married and in her thirties when she abandoned her home in Famagusta. She was privileged because she had opportunities to visit her house on several occasions following the war and recover items from it as other houses in the neighborhood were being looted, in more or less organized fashion. She was reminded, on these occasions, by the Turkish-Cypriot policemen who escorted her to the house, that she was being granted this opportunity, only because she was different from Greek-Cypriots—because she was a Catholic. Insisting that there is nothing that distinguishes her from Greek-Cypriots, apart from some of the foods learnt from her mother and the occasional newsletter she receives from the Latin representative, Jeanette felt that her loss was the same as that of her Greek-Cypriot former neighbors. Famagusta for Jeanette was the location of the best years of her life, the place where her daughter took her first steps. Her family was one of the last to leave the neighborhood. On the day of the Turkish advance, she was in the town distributing supplies with other women.

> An acquaintance saw me and asked "what are you still doing here?" . . . We got in the car and drove off, my daughter held a small bag where she had packed all her dolls, she was almost ten. . . . For many years she did not go anywhere without her bag. She also could not look at soldiers. She still cries when she sees Turkish soldiers. It has affected these children a lot.

The family eventually ended up in the British base of Dhekelia among other Greek-Cypriots. Jeanette also found herself helping with the humanitarian effort at the Achna camp, set up within the base. The camp was just outside the village of Achna, which had been overrun by the Turkish military in one of the bloodiest operations of the war, which left eighty-four people missing (Uludağ 2005, 75). The camp housed an estimated sixty thousand refugees and has become emblematic of life in tented camps in that period. A church constructed to memorialize camped existence in Achna forest, erected on the site years later, is designed as a canvas tent. "It was a dreadful situation," Jeanette remembers. "I saw people going like this [putting her hands together in the shape of a cup] to receive food because there were no plates to put it in." The family ended up in Limassol, where Jeanette had to come to terms with the perceptions developing around refugee identity.

> There I saw the difference. The Limassolians were lamenting the cargo they had lost in the ships in the port, they complained about the refugees, saw us as intruders who threw out the British tenants and they had to rent to us instead, and so on. Nicosia was not like this because Nicosia, well half of it suffered too.

All these experiences are confirmations that Jeanette's loss was indistinguishable from that of her Greek-Cypriot neighbors. Indeed, from her humanitarian determination down to the anthropomorphizing the town, her discourse exudes her near-total integration into the Greek-Cypriot community of loss. The point at which Jeanette's loss was differentiated was recovery of the valuables left behind. Her Latin background, which allowed her access to the house according to her Turkish-Cypriot police escorts, was pondered in disappointment. It was "a difference I never felt," she said, "but they saw it," and they made sure she was aware they saw it. Looking back, Jeanette points to the gap between things that she has salvaged—a television, books, a chest of drawers, photographs—and the feel of a home, which was lost forever.

> OK, so I got all these things back. What did I understand? Most of them withered in the meantime and were thrown away anyway. Sometimes I search for pictures, or other small things, your sense of place, where things were, is lost. Some people don't even have that of course. I know people who buried their jewelry in the ground, under their trees, and lost it forever.

Jeanette's minor losses are significant precisely in their minor capacity. The valuables she recovered might have provided some sort of consolation, but the emphasis on her difference, which she has had to accept in return, seems to bear its own scars. Her ethnicity simply allowed her to witness the process of property turning into junk, that in the case of proper losses, as the next chapter explains, has been arrested and frozen. Her involvement in refugee relief postwar is in these terms a claim to proper refugeehood, against the fear of impropriety that resurfaces time and again in these narratives.

Consider another story, that of Dimitris. He was born two years after the 1974 war, to Greek-Cypriot parents who were displaced twice: once in the 1960s from the north Nicosia suburb of Trahonas, going from one side of the settlement to the other "just across the river," and then from their new dwelling in the next neighborhood in 1974. They are both *tourkóplikti* and *prósfiyes*. They are also left wing, and his father had been targeted during the coup by the nationalist paramilitaries, luckily escaping capture and possible torture and imprisonment because he was not in the house when coupists came. Through his childhood and adulthood, Dimitris has striven to square the official rhetoric of displacement and loss being propagated through the postwar educational system he grew up in and the personal experiences that his parents and relatives recounted.

> To hear my relatives talk about this loss is—so much pain and sense of being wronged . . . My father tells me for example, that the Paphiotes, from where he originally hails, are now rich, their land has acquired value, and he received nothing despite all he lost[2] . . . Three camp-beds is what they got, I still remember them clearly, wooden folding frames with a canvas because my father's one ended up in my grandmother's house and I slept on it on holiday visits. And I used to be told "this is one of the few things that you father got from this whole story [*pou doun' tin istorían oúllin*]."

His words exemplify the uneven distribution of the negative effects of war on the population—uneven effects which were also found in the Turkish-Cypriot community (Erdal Ilican 2011). This uneven distribution was propagated as future generations grew up and is the main concern of the Central Agency for the Equal Distribution of Burden, set up in 1989 to provide housing assistance to the children of refugees. But this redress is unlikely to be used by Dimitris, who feels wronged twice as a refugee and again for being alienated from the performatives of proper refugeehood.

> We would learn all these songs and poems by heart and sing them. OK, they are nice, but it's something that does not relate to you directly ... it becomes staged at some point.... Someone who was born two years later, or fifteen years later and figures as the passionate nostalgist of return [*énthermos nostalgós tis epistrofís*]—it does not make sense. You hear "soundbites" from people who were born after, for example.... I won't call it staged [*siké*], I will say trite [*tetrimméno*].... I talk to people who verbalize this sense of injustice saying "I will never get to enjoy my house." What does this mean? It means you will not enjoy it under your terms because of your own issues.... I hear all this empty rhetoric, which is actually not empty at all, it has a very specific content: division.

What Dimitris verbalizes is the impossible ideal of a refugee identity that national discourse has set up—an ideal from which actual refugees often feel excluded. For if Dimitris, whose father was displaced twice and is therefore entitled to claim a double sense of loss, feels alienated by the norms of proper refugeehood, then it is the improprieties of loss that we should seek to understand. What makes Dimitris an improper refugee is not the qualification of his losses, as in the other cases we have seen (people telling him he is a different sort of refugee), but in the failure between the calibration of body and population (himself being unable to feel like a refugee as he should). A counter-conductive affect of refugeehood operates here in the mode of Foucauldian *parrhēsia*, a conduct of self premised on differentiating truth from the staged and trite. He refuses to equate home with homeland and in this becomes a dissensual subject. The gap between "Man and citizen" that subjectivates him is the gap between his actual refugeehood and the refugeehood that posits the ideal refugee-citizen. And if these improprieties appear as aspects of dissensus in social and informal discourse, over the last decade or so, this dissensus has also figured on the legal plane.

JURIDICAL COUNTER-CONDUCT

Legal analysts refer to the *Loizidou vs. Turkey* case at the European Court of Human Rights as a cornerstone in litigation concerning refugees, property, and the obligation to protect (Koskenniemi and Leino 2002; Moloney 2004; Mowbray 2005). Titina Loizidou is an owner of property in Kyrenia. She filed a lawsuit against Turkey in 1989 for denial of access to her property and sought compensation for loss of use. In 1996, her right to access and use her property was recognized and compensation of 1.5 million euro was awarded, paid seven years later (ECtHR, Case 40/1993/435/514). Following this, other cases were tried, some having been hailed as "national victories," others as losses in the increasingly politicized litigation field of the 2000s (Erdal Ilican 2011).

Since the late 1990s, Titina Loizidou's name has come to signify an ideal form of refugeehood for Greek-Cypriots. Displaced from Kyrenia, claiming her right to return, and taking on the Turkish army who barred her access not just through the invasion but by arresting and imprisoning her in 1996 when she tried to cross the Green Line during a women's protest, and most importantly winning that battle, she bares all the hallmarks of the proper refugee subject. And yet, for the purposes of the Republic's law, she is not technically displaced, since she had moved to Nicosia before the invasion. In the text of the case, the ECtHR makes no mention of "refugee" or "displacement," and the field of concern bears no relation to the 1951 Convention. Her exclusion from displaced subjectivity, in the eyes of international litigation, is irrelevant to the violation of rights she has suffered, which are rights to property and not refugee rights. The lack of correspondence between 1951 Convention and ECHR parameters expose the tensions and contestations involved in the governmentality of refugeehood at the level of the international. And they point to the spaces between national policy and international law where counter-conduct may arise.

It could be said that the Loizidou case does not tell a story only of resistance against the Turkish occupation. It also counter-conducts the governmentality of refugeehood of the Cypriot state, through engendering an iconic refugee subject away from the legal parameters of displacement and destabilizing differentiations and connections between home and property and the putatively clear definitions that surround each. This is indicative of the intricate ways in which legal discourse has worked in Cyprus through the political as a *dispositif* of subjection: holding up the refugee persona as a generalized refugee (in claiming that everyone is a refugee) yet setting up legal criteria that made it difficult to actually claim that status—if one was displaced prior to 1974, or propertied, or a minority member, a leftist, middle-class, and so on.

This concurrent generalizability and exclusion lies at the heart of the feelings of resentment that I presented in the previous section. The plane of litigation that the *Loizidou* case opened up, in shifting the legal persona of concern from refugee/displaced to property owner, seems to have offered a platform for the expression of those sentiments in differing ways. The litigants I spoke to, who have filed cases after *Loizidou* and who often hold that case up as an inspiration, articulate these variable ways of conducting refugeehood otherwise on that legal plane. In this sense, their cases can be seen as acts of citizenship. But it is also interesting to note that as such acts, they often do not exhaust themselves on the legal plane. In many cases they exude an affect that engulfs the law and extends beyond it. Loizidou's incarceration by Turkish authorities during the "Women Walk Home" march, the case would suggest, was the moment that provided the affective basis (fear, anger, humiliation, perhaps—all rolled into a sense of injustice) for turning the woman activist into an active litigant.

Meletis Apostolides is the first Greek-Cypriot to have sued individuals instead of the Turkish state and to have pursued the action in local courts instead of the ECtHR. The case began in 2004, when shortly after the opening of the Green Line Apostolides, a middle-aged Greek-Cypriot architect and a refugee from the village of Lapithos in the Kyrenia region, visited his family home. Although he developed friendly relations with the Turkish-Cypriot family now living in the house, he also discovered that the plot next to the house, also owned by him, had been sold to a foreign couple. David and Linda Orams, pensioners from England, had constructed a villa on the plot as a retirement residence. Meletis Apostolides filed a local case with the Nicosia district court, which decided in his favor in the same year, a decision upheld by the Supreme Court. As the execution of the decision (the Orams vacating the property) could not be pursued in the inaccessible areas, the case was transferred to the UK, on the basis of an EU-wide execution of judgment agreement. From there, the case was referred to the European Court of Justice on the question of applicability and a final decision in 2010 confirmed the decision of the Cypriot courts.

The *Apostolides v. Orams* case was the first property case in Cyprus related to the conflict that pitted individuals against each other. Its landmark status was argued to have opened the way for possible intercommunal suits that might displace the adversarial nature of the conflict from the person-to-state level to the interpersonal. Aware of these arguments, Meletis Apostolides explained how his quest for reunification of the island, and not the attempt to foster enmity, informed his actions throughout.

> The first congratulations I received were from Turkish-Cypriots. They understood that it was not an act directed against them.... Property, for me, and Cypriot refugees in general, is not only a material question—it is about connections to homes that stretch back for generations; my mother's home was built by my grandmother in the 1860s. Therefore for me it is a crucial point, this connection between reunification, return, and the property issue.

A key point in deciding on litigation was the identity of the Orams as non-Cypriots: "I could understand Turkish-Cypriots living in my home, because they need a place to live too. But I cannot understand a foreigner who comes to invest on this land cheaply and who, by acting so, contributes to the worsening of an already complicated problem." Apostolides is aware that he treads a fine line between an iconic Greek-Cypriot refugee who sued people in the north, and the ethnic enmity fostered by nationalist presentations of his case. As an act of citizenship, the case could be seen as ambivalent. But if so, it is an ambivalence answered by Apostolides's acts in fields beyond the legal: his peace activism and his poetry.

In a collection of poems written in 2011, he speaks of his experiences as a leftist soldier ordered about during the coup, of witnessing the deaths of friends and enemies with regret during the war, of Turkish-Cypriot friends encountered through his reconciliation activities, of his mother's visit to the house and his encounter with his legal opponents. The poems are in general mournful, exuding feelings of disappointment and regret. Anger is only expressed in two poems, one addressed to the Orams and another to a land developer he met in Lapithos. "'This house is mine,' / you said / without looking at me," the first poem starts. "You ignored me. / You continued to water the flowers. / Later you accepted / that you took a risk. / Justice / had already taken / its course." The litigation case is described, in a matter-of-fact way, as a question of countering disregard. Justice is called in to recover the affect rejected in the encounter with the future legal opponent.

It is a performative gesture, in this sense, recognized as such through another performative, the poem. "I do not believe that political matters will be solved through the courts," Apostolides had pondered with me in 2011. What is at stake is reconciliation between people, "like Europe did after WWII, for future generations as well," he had said. In these terms, we could see his poetry as a strategy alongside litigation, and alongside his reconciliation activism through which he counter-conducts his refugee subjectivity. And if the litigation he has pursued repositioned him within the proper frame of refugee conduct, his insistence in making his claims heard clearly rubs against the limit between conduct and counter-conduct. The last poem in the collection derides the mournful performatives of refugeehood promoted by the state through commemorative events held every July and contrasts them with his own feelings of loss:

> Black [clothing]
> is in fashion
> this July.
> It has always suited me.
> In the end, all of us settled.

I would like to suggest that despite announcing the performatives of the self as more genuine that those of the state ("black has always suited me"), the last line works to destabilize the loss of purity, to question whether in the end there can be untainted, pure, mourning: "all of us settled" (teliká, voleftíkame óli). Apostolides's case in this sense speaks to the difficult question of how one can mobilize affect to "speak truth to power" (Foucault 2011) when that affect is already claimed by the state. The space of parrhēsia claimed by Dimitris may already be taken.

If mourning is already packed with state power, then what affect can possibly counter-conduct the affective politics of loss? The next case I examine answers this by displacing affect altogether from the domain of refugeehood and resituating loss squarely within the economic domain. Mike Tymvios has become a political outcast since his own case against Turkey turned into a legal battle with the Republic of Cyprus. Tymvios had in earlier times been praised for having represented Cyprus in the Olympics in shooting. Mike Tymvios's land in the north was passed on through family. He has never felt any particular connection to it, had never been a displaced person in the eyes of the law. Tymvios is not a refugee in a legal or affective sense; he is a property owner. His case was lodged at the ECtHR in 1990 (*Eugenia Michaelidou Developments Ltd and Michael Tymvios v.*

Turkey, Application no. 16163/90). In lodging the case, Tymvios claimed the right to enjoy a property he owned in the area of Tymbou village (and then registered under a company he owned with his wife). The Court ruled in October 2003 in his favor and awarded costs and expenses but reserved its decision regarding the claimed amount of 270,000 CYP (about 540,000 USD) for pecuniary and non-pecuniary damage, inviting the parties to settle between them.

While up to then the case followed the precedent of *Loizidou v. Turkey*, the negotiations phase catapulted Mike Tymvios to notoriety after he accepted an offer from the Immovable Property Commission (IPC) for exchange of his property instead of returning the original land to him. This is a body set up by Turkey in northern Cyprus, on the request of the ECtHR, following the *Loizidou* case. It is a local-remedy structure (i.e., a local body to settle property disputes before they reach the ECtHR). The government of the Republic has since claimed that the IPC is not a body that it recognizes and has urged Greek-Cypriot refugees to refrain from filing cases with this com-mission, lest it result in eventual recognition of governmental structures in the north, or more crucially, provide a settlement of the property issue de facto. In an April 2008 judgment, the ECtHR confirmed the conclusion of the *Tymvios* case in a friendly settlement in which the land in question was exchanged for land under the authority of the IPC and an additional sum of one million USD (to cover remaining valuation estimates and claimed damages).

The IPC claims control over properties abandoned by Turkish-Cypriots in the south. The titles to these properties were handed to Turkish-Cypriot authorities post-1974 in exchange for housing and ownership rights in Greek-Cypriot "abandoned properties" in the north (Erdal Ilican 2011). However, under Republic of Cyprus law, Turkish-Cypriot properties in the south fall under the administration of a special department within the Ministry of the Interior known as "the Custodian for Turkish-Cypriot properties" (explored further in chapter 8). This includes property owned by the Turkish-Cypriot Communal Chamber (effectively disbanded in 1963), which the land in question formerly was, before passing under Tymvios's ownership. This meant that whereas the IPC claimed the property in exchange was theirs to give, the Custodian department refused to recognize the agreement and execute its terms. Turkey was effectively using the case, it seemed, to render the property issue a dispute between the Republic and its citizens.

Aware of this, Tymvios addressed a letter to the Republic's government explaining the offer and proposing to transfer his legal rights to the government "so that I would not need to agree to a friendly settlement and pursue the case in the Court." In other words, he asked his own government to buy the land in the north from him. The government ignored his letter, prompting him to accept the settlement.

> When I was declared bankrupt for a sum of €700,000 and I presented the court with a collateral of property in the occupied areas, which, had I owned it in the free areas would be worth 100 million instead of 40 [the total sum calculated in the IPC compensation offer], I was deemed "not worthy of credit" (*mi axióhreos*) because this property was in the occupied areas and [in the eyes of the state] had a value of 0.... Because the Turks happened to have entered from Kyrenia, are we to accept that we were simply the unlucky ones who have to lose our properties? This is the question.

Tymvios sued the Republic for blocking the settlement at the ECtHR, and in 2012, the Republic approved the exchange deal. This resolution is indicative of Mike Tymvios's success in navigating the increasingly complex entanglement of law and politics on the property issue—but it is a less certain success on the level of social relations and public discourse. Mike Tymvios engaged in the legal performance in all its excesses, becoming the ideal property litigant for fighting the case to the end and on the basis of the letter of the law. No affect of loss of home or homeland, no interpellation into refugee citizenship. Instead, there is awareness that one is playing the game—opponents and allies are judged on the basis of their performance. Man and citizen are recognized here for the political names that they are. There is no quavering in the gap, no ambivalence about the intentions and reception of the performance. We all know it is staged, and we are all on the stage. This is the realm where citizenship is unconditional, the question of rights as corollary to obligations does not arise. But this is also the citizenship of property owners, not refugees.

And it does not always work. In the case of Eleni Meleagrou, the state challenged was the state in the north. Eleni Meleagrou is a UK-based human rights lawyer. The case resulted from her dissatisfaction with the ability of the IPC to resolve her property claims. She applied to the IPC in November 2006 to test it as a domestic remedy following eight other ECtHR cases (*Demopoulos v. Turkey and 7 other cases, Admissibility*). She requested full reinstatement of eighteen pieces of property, including a family home on the Kyrenia coast, and engaged in negotiations for three years before many of her claims were rejected and compensation offered for the rest. The decision was upheld in June 2011 after appeal. During the course of the proceedings, she filed a case with the ECtHR in May 2009 (ECtHR, 14434/09) claiming ineffectiveness on grounds of independence, language barriers, and lengthy proceedings. It was rejected in 2013.

> I went to try and see if the IPC was effective. And I was perfectly prepared to consider reasonable responses to my demands. . . . It's difficult to say what I was expecting as a just decision. I am not a fool. I understand that people [who may be living in some of the claimed properties] cannot be forced from their houses. . . . If they had negotiated seriously I would have been prepared to consider all sorts of things. But they never did.

Eleni Meleagrou has thought long and hard about the reality of the IPC as a remedy for properties and homes lost, and about how this "sorry situation" came to be (personal communication, 2018). And she has written on this intellectual effort (Paraskeva and Meleagrou 2013; 2018). As a lawyer, Meleagrou took the law at its letter, and she was left feeling fooled. Eleni Meleagrou may feel loss in terms of home, having memories of the house at the center of the claims, but it was curiosity over the legal process that mostly spurred her legal suit. As a litigant subject, she faced the scorn of a state, albeit a make-believe one, which refuses to be interpellated by individuals—in the same way that the Republic of Cyprus had done for Tymvios in the earlier stages of the case.

And as happened again in the case of *Thomas and Eleni Kaoullas v. Republic of Cyprus* (743/2007), a refugee from Famagusta, who sued the government for failing to take into account the financial strain his loss of property had put on himself and his family. Thomas Kaoullas and his wife claimed 109 million CYP (260 million USD) from the government as compensation for loss of income from the various properties and businesses they had lost. They argued that they had received no financial support from the state after their displacement and that the state should have calculated their losses against the taxes they were asked to pay all these years. The case was dismissed as baseless in January 2012 and the appeal rejected by the Supreme Court. In early 2017, Thomas Kaoullas was considering further action at the European level, but had already begun despairing.

Of the litigants mentioned thus far, Thomas Kaoullas is the only one recognized under the law as a displaced person. Speaking as such a proper refugee, he was pushed, he claimed in 2011, to file the suit after finding himself in an extremely difficult financial situation and realizing that the benefits he had received from the state were meager in relation to his losses.

> I was given 6000 CYP, with which I bought a flat, which was too
> small, so I now rent both the house in which I live and the premises I
> use for my business. I already paid 200,000 CYP in rent for these . . .
> I am now 65, and I am still struggling . . . The Limassolian can go to
> the bank, put down his small plot and get a loan, while my property
> is not accepted as collateral.

Throughout our discussion, Thomas Kaoullas returned to the sense of injustice many times, an injustice he sees as running in parallel with the social rejection they had experienced after their flight, when they settled in Limassol and faced inhospitable landlords. Limassol has since seen successive property booms, from which the landless like Kaoullas were excluded. It was spurred largely by foreign investment, which made Limassol the island's offshore finance centre before the banking collapse of 2013. At the height of such a boom in 2007, when Kaoullas lodged the application, the vast difference between the property he had lost and the valuation of properties around him, would have stung. Before applying to the Republic of Cyprus courts, Thomas Kaoullas had applied to the IPC and refused to settle on compensation for part of his property in the north, because the amount offered was too small and the financial strain he was under great.

Of the refugees that I have spoken to over the years, Thomas Kaoullas is perhaps the most sure that given the opportunity he would return to repossess his property and live in Famagusta. He had, by 2011, made a habit of crossing to the north and seeing the property on a weekly basis, counting 350 times, he had said: "Because I have an open wound, I go to my house, I cut my flowers, and I leave, I come to Limassol and I do this with pain in my soul"—affectively too, he is a proper refugee. But as a proper refugee, what

Thomas Kaoullas feels he has faced is scorn of his losses, from both sides: the IPC through the ridiculously small sum they offered, and the Republic through the outright dismissal of the case. A double loss akin to Dimitris's, we could say. And there is a lack of correspondence here between the sense of loss, which complies thoroughly with the home/homeland calibration, and the calibration of that loss in a monetary scale by the powers that be. The seemingly exaggerated amount he claims is perhaps a performance of putting into numbers the sense of immeasurable bitterness he feels. And there is also perhaps the implied suggestion, on the part of the state, that the claims leveled were actually illegitimate, that for all the performatives on refugee losses, refugees like Kaoullas should in fact be thankful for what they got. Far from the ideal citizens they were purported to be, Kaoullas's case showed how refugees like him will always straddle the line between the ideal and the abject. I will return to the issue of abjection in the next chapter.

Looking at these cases together, the calibration of the physical to the species body effected through the correlation of home to homeland is counter-conducted through claims to individual physical properties leveled in individual terms in each case. And in as far as they are claims effected through law, they call forth and recover the congruence between law and justice as relevant to each person; they halt the process of law's slippage into norm (Foucault 1990) by taking the bare facts of law at face value stripping them of the performative habit and reconsidering them as performative acts. We could perhaps speak here of a counter-conduct that poses bare law against the biopower that produces bare life. The most vociferous accounts of counter-conduct presented here have sought (successfully or not) to beat the state at its own game, that game being the performance of legal and exclusionary sovereignty, which drew its legitimacy from the discourse of loss and refugeehood. In the shift from refugee to property owner, the material is negotiated against the political, loss against gain, sovereignty against rights, Man against citizen. Democracy is announced on a terrain of liberalism, where refugeehood is now to be calculated, measured against the politics of peace negotiations (where these cases have been debated) and meted out under the sign of property. In this sense, the cases studied communicate the binds of inclusion and exclusion that the imbricated structures of loss have created. The territorial plane on which these binds emerge and the abjection they generate is what I take up next.

FIVE

ROOTING LOSS

The Topological Register

TOURING ABANDONMENT

Space exudes loss in Cyprus; which is to say that it not only frames but produces its performance. The Green Line, a location of such intense production,
as suggested in previous chapters, is by no means the only one. But it is arguably
the epicenter from which loss ripples outwards on either side. Speaking of a
similar effect, Rozita Dimova (in Demetriou and Dimova, 2018) shows how
mega statues in the center of Skopje are ripple effects of conflict discourse
centered on the Greek-Macedonian border. Memorial statues to fallen heroes
from the conflict's different phases perform similar functions in the villages
and town squares all over Cyprus. But their epicenter is the heart of the capital,
Nicosia's Buffer Zone. This topology inflects the affect of loss differently.
Sandbags, barrels, brick walls, barbed and razor wire, and gates prohibit access
to spaces that can be seen and smelled, traces of which can be transferred in
the paws of wandering cats and dogs.

A 1999 short feature film entitled *Espresso* (Florides and Nicolaides)
plays on the oxymoron of proximity and prohibition through the narrative
of a stray dog, shuttling between the two sides of the Green Line, carrying
messages between the opposing border guards, often in the form of insults
written on paper and hung around its neck. A more recent film, entitled *The
Story of the Green Line,* straddling comedy and drama (Chrysanthou 2016)
uses the same story line as the comic thread of an otherwise somber tale
of people divided by war. *Espresso* was produced as an attempt to counter-
conduct the hegemonic affect of melancholia that artistic renderings of the
Green Line, as seen in chapter 3, had produced up to then: the laments in
children's literature over kites that can fly above the Line while the children

holding them cannot, or the song that urges Pendadhaktylos, the five-finger mountain peak, to "throw [the invaders] off its back." The film counters the prohibition of contact as a game rather than lament. Importantly, in doing so, it also counters the understanding of such contact, which in the hegemonic discourse of loss concerns people and land—specifically Greek-Cypriot people (as generalized refugees) and the lands in the north that they have lost. In reinstalling Turkish-Cypriots as people across the divide, the film reconfigures contact as a relationship between people, even if these are "enemies" who can nevertheless play with each other on more or less equal terms and through the dog, rehumanize each other.

The Green Line is, or was until 2003 at least, one of the few places in which the hegemony of loss can be countered—indeed the materialities of the Green Line prompt such countering if only for the fact that inside the Green Line space persists in different ways, its loss not quite complete. In this epicenter things are not neatly packaged as memorial busts of heroes elsewhere suggest. For one, within the Green Line one does not confront a line but an area—the Buffer Zone. And in that area things are not lost but (also) found. In areas of the Buffer Zone, fields can be cultivated and herds can graze. As a register of loss, the Buffer Zone presents a field where the making and unmaking of presence, absence, materiality, and immateriality coexist. This is what I examine here. As processes that construct the topology of loss, they also show the fields within which resistances arise, the possible locations of crevices within which alternative subjectivities of loss are encountered.

The border-making processes unfolding on the Green Line are fiercely guarded and maintained by a triple military apparatus: Greek-Cypriot National Guard, Turkish military forces, and UNFICYP. Each of these forces may control access and boundaries differently but the combined effect of these governmentalities structures the spatial layer of loss. On a hot August afternoon in 2011, UNFICYP's officer walks us through the kilometer or so length of the section of the Line that is designated for dignitaries' Line Tours. Locals are not normally permitted on these tours, and my inclusion in the group of scholars I am hosting is an exception, occasioned by the institution of new policies about transparency and communication of UNFICYP's role. I repeated the tour in 2016. It is a tour that aims to highlight the work of the

UN mission on the ground, in a place that is considered a restful assignment by troops engaged in active conflict zones.

The tour starts with Annie's house, testament to the whimsical nature of borders and people's insistence in navigating them. Its owner, a Greek-Cypriot woman, lived there until her death in 1991, aged ninety-one. The house has a back wall resting on the Greek-Cypriot side of the border and a front door opening into the UN-controlled area. This meant that for her to meet her shopping and other daily needs, the UN had to escort her out through the iron gate a few paces from her house, out into the Greek-Cypriot side where the market was, and later back in. We are told that UNFICYP adopted her, as her family wanted nothing to do with her after she decided to stay in the house post-1974.[1] Annie's house points to and undermines the governmentality of the Green Line: a Buffer Zone that separates opposing militaries, an area vacated by civilians, a Dead Zone, but also a place from which the restoration of life can begin.

Farther on, Roger's Pass is the gaping shell of a shop, the back wall of which faced a street cut by the Green Line. In order to allow UN military vehicles access to the street running parallel to it in front of the shop, the Canadian contingent rammed the wall with an armored vehicle—and named the spot after a mountain location in British Columbia (Grichting 2009, 211). For a peace corps on strict orders to maintain the status quo, this sledgehammer approach is unorthodox—yet obviously not denounced. On another occasion, the same contingent rammed a metal sheet designating the limits of the Turkish military position. It was their response to the realization that the sheet had been moving forward centimeters at a time until it left no room for the UN vehicles to pass. UNFICYP's work consists largely of patrolling such whimsicalities and devising ways to remedy them. The "10 plus wall" is another such instance: a wall marking the Turkish position began to grow vertically as rows of bricks were added, one at a time. What Weizman has called the "politics of verticality" (2007, 13–16) was performed here in a farcical manner. But UNFICYP played the game. They painted the top layer of bricks white to mark out any unlawful additions; but soon they discovered that a layer of bricks had been added below and the white layer replaced on top. So UNFICYP painted the tenth row down from the top.

There is a wall of tea chests tinkered with in similar manner by the Turkish guards; here it matters whether the boxes face inwards or outwards. And while most of the infractions have been on the Turkish side, Greek-Cypriots have also on occasion played along—painting over and over the outline of a Cyprus map on the road outside one of their positions, the

FIGURE 5.1. Greek-Cypriot military guard post in downtown Nicosia, after successive modifications (concrete lower part, windows with grills and glass on top, and tin roof) to protect soldiers from passersby, autumn 2017.

ever-thicker line extending the limit of their jurisdiction just a few millimeters of paint at a time. One of the tour's highlights is Spear Alley, a narrow street separating the two sides that becomes even narrower between opposing over-hanging balconies from which soldiers would joust their bayonets. It goes to show just how fragile things could have been if these infringements were not performances. Occasionally, changes to the status quo are authorized on grounds of security. Another National Guard post facing a street in a popular entertainment quarter required fencing to protect the soldiers from intoxicated passers-by who, on their way home, threw bottles to taunt them (figure 5.1).

As an introduction to UNFICYP's work in Cyprus, the tour has an overall casual tone. The infringements it highlights are almost laughable, as if the three military forces are in an intermittent game of spot the difference, which the UN arbitrates through daily foot, vehicle, and helicopter patrols. In this arbitration, facts on the ground are always under negotiation. This involves transparency of information about who did what to whom but also about who knows what was really done (Lindley 2007). It involves negoti-ating rules and procedures in an environment where a basic premise is the acceptance that all three sides disagree about where exactly the Green Line is and what precisely the rules of engagement are. And most importantly, it also involves negotiation over the material constitution of the Green Line. UNFICYP's basic reference tool is a 1989 aide-mémoire decoding these three different perceptions about where exactly Buffer Zone limits are. Reports of the UN Secretary General have repeatedly made reference to the refusal of both sides to recognize this document and thus agree "on the exact delin-eation of ceasefire lines" (July 2016 report, S/2016/598). Many UN signposts within the Buffer Zone announce the caveat "UN wire, not CFL [cease fire line]." The topological register is anything but self-evident; it hovers between contestation, physicality, and appearance.

The agreement not to agree (where the boundaries are) is perfor-mative in a Butlerian sense of "performing ... the impossible within the possible" (1997b, 147), acting as if facts on the ground exist while trying to undermine them, but also while recognizing an unspoken limit between what is play and what is serious—a limit performed rather than said, every time playful infringements are treated as serious. To take the performance of drag that Butler uses to elaborate the concept of performativity as instructive

FIGURE 5.2. Sites from the Green Line tour: Annie's house, labelled and protected with barbed wire and wooden pillars (top left); bottles and other equipment in abandoned coffee shop (top right); collected items in the entrance of magic mansion (center left); arrangements in the make-shift museum (bottom right and left).

of the spatial registering of loss on the Green Line, necessitates that we also address the normativities that it destabilizes. "Drag exposes or allegorizes the mundane psychic and performative practices by which heterosexualized genders form themselves through renouncing the *possibility* of homosexuality," Butler writes (ibid., 146), adding that this renouncing constitutes heterosexual melancholy. In political terms, drag counter-conducts by exposing and destabilizing, without necessarily being emplaced in homosexuality, she underscores. Games over Buffer Zone space could be said to similarly "act out" and destabilize the "over here" and "over there"; the Greek, the Turkish, the beyond and the within. And they, in the end, expose the melancholia of loss that supplants the normativity of spatial division. The anthropomorphic figures of the lost land in Greek-Cypriot rhetoric express the disavowal of that normativity: the land that awaits was never lost, and it was never anything but Greek. Yet on the Green Line and its games, that disavowal is upturned: as contests over land become games, what is disavowed is grief itself.

And yet, the drag parallel is not quite complete. Performances cannot quite draw on the exaggeration of drag to expose the normative. In the political work of state sovereignty that these games contest, a sense of gravity can never be abandoned. Our guide points to things left in the Green Line: toys in the street, materials in abandoned shops; we are also told about cars in a dealership that were never sold; and we see books, magazines, and small items neatly placed in a stairway as temporary exhibits in what has been named "magic mansion"; and crockery in a canteen gathering dust but still left sitting there. Other items have been moved and protected in another makeshift museum, visited in 2016: they include books, a sewing machine, a cap, a suitcase, shirts (figure 5.2). Operating procedures treat these items as property; they are someone's belongings, we are told, and it is part of UNFICYP's duty to keep them until they are claimed. It is a logic that miniaturizes loss down to that fine line across which belongings are separated from trash. Will a ball that has gone astray ever be claimed? Or rotting newspapers? Empty beer bottles? I would like to suggest that in taking such losses seriously, all loss is trivialized. The point of the tour, it would thus seem, is exactly to instill in foreign dignitaries this sense of local priorities, in the centimeter-long or centimeter-high territorial claims, that this intervening order (UNFICYP) must take seriously. And yet, in order to be able to continue to take itself seriously, it also needs to recognize, and trivialize, the scale of violence it has to contend with. The superimposition of a mountainous feature onto a rammed wall achieves this performative feat. And it is this very performativity of scale that I suspect allowed the violation of the otherwise clear principle of nonintervention to become a matter of lore, in the case of Roger's Pass, and not a crisis.

Not that this performativity is always serene. Rather embarrassingly, another location toponymically appropriated by peacekeepers is the Mountain of the Moon. It is a hill on which a Greek-Cypriot soldier was shot in 1984 by Turkish soldiers on the opposite side when he taunted them by pulling down his trousers.[2] This story is mentioned but not emphasized in the tour. Nor is another Greek-Cypriot death in June 1996 in a nearby spot, prompted, it is widely held, by sheer bad luck. A Turkish officer became aware of an agreement among soldiers on opposite posts to exchange caps and other items. The officer had his subordinate shoot the enemy.[3] These incidents have prompted not only *Espresso* and *The Story of the Green Line* but also the more somber theatrical play *Kardash, My Brother* (Agisilaou 2004), which focusses on the specific incident and uses it to lament both the soldier's death and the death of coexistence. The line between comedy and drama is the line between life and death. Beyond whatever claim these events may be making on the effectiveness of peacekeeping, they also speak to the performative aspect of blurring the trivial and the fatal. Whether as abusive prank or friendly gesture, or combination of the two (as *Espresso* would suggest), the undermining of authority on the Green Line entails an encounter with the reality of the Cyprus conflict. Its governmentality is of a sovereign order: subject to countering, but also guided by the right to take life. In the Occupy campaign of 2011, the Cypriot flank of the movement took over the Green Line space between two checkpoints in downtown Nicosia. The movement survived for a remarkable six months but was crushed by one of the most violent raids undertaken in recent years by the Republic's special anti-riot police unit.[4] That this violence received no condemnation by either of the other authorities concerned (UNFICYP and Turkish military) is highly suggestive of the extent to which the governmentality of this space is structured first and foremost on the basis of the military-civilian hierarchy and only secondarily on questions about the "letting live" of populations.

This governmental structure in turn shows the parameters on which loss is calibrated in Cyprus. What is distilled in the sovereign government of the Green Line is the militarization of life on the island, a militarization that thrives on the augmentation of some losses and the miniaturization of others. These processes, so clearly seen on the Green Line, become more difficult to discern as they seep into the social fabric away from the Line and are civil(ian) ized. The everyday, the banal, and the mundane are important in the Buffer Zone exactly because of their location. This is the reason they are valuable props to be displayed. In the performance of peacekeeping they signify their absent owners and that absence is made sinthome-atic. The tragedy would be for owners to appear and claim them, for that would spell the end of the performance to foreign dignitaries that need to be convinced of the usefulness of UNFICYP's continued presence in an area of diminishing humanitarian urgency and without frequent casualties. But that would also be laughable. These objects of the everyday speak of a tragedy of loss largely missing from the actual everyday on either side of the space where they are entrapped. But in this very drag-like exaggeration of postconflict realities, they powerfully convey the stakes of performativity.

This may not necessarily be unique to Cyprus. War-torn environments have been shown to have a lasting impact on the populations living in them. Aspects of war devastation in buildings and the natural environment are intertwined with conceptualizations of history and conflict (Stig-Sørensen and Viejo Rose 2015). But they also often expose the underbelly of such conflict societies. They act out the disavowals that allow life to continue to be lived as if those spaces did not exist, as if death did not come about in violent ways, as if the land and people's minds were not divided. If the mourning over major losses in the corporeal sense of body counts and refugees stabilizes Greek-Cypriot subjectivity, this spatial register of loss calls attention to the minor losses that undo this stability.

ECONOMIES OF LOSS

As the stage where the fusion of property and junk is performed, the Green Line prompts questions about the economies that attend such categories of major and minor loss. These economies, I argue in this section, sustain the conflict as an inextricable part of the relation between people and things, political subjects and the materialities around them. In her study of such relations in northern Cyprus, Navaro-Yashin (2012) explains how homes and objects retain an uncanny quality in the Freudian sense that is part of Turkish-Cypriot subjectivity and which is often externalized as political critique of a "culture of loot" (*ganimet*). "Loot" here refers to the widespread looting of the properties abandoned by Greek-Cypriots in 1974 as they fled the Turkish army, but also the political morality of plunder, opportunism, and lack of meritocracy that Turkish-Cypriots see as plaguing their economic and political life (also Erdal Ilican 2011). The overarching discourse of loss that I explore here can be seen in these terms as a refraction of this structure into Greek-Cypriot subjectivity. Remnants of Turkish-Cypriot presence in the south (houses, street names, mosques, cemeteries) are signs of loot that has never been acknowledged collectively, not even by counter-hegemonic discourse as was the case in the north. It surfaces only reluctantly, if at all, at points of ultimate loss—as the example of my aunt's death shows (chapter 2), when reminiscences among her relatives turned to her critique of looting in 1964. But the economy of loss is not only a matter of refraction of cultures of loot. It is also the foundation of an economic logic that ties the psychic to the political and the financial. What is lost to Greek-Cypriots, as we saw in chapter 4, is properties with value, which are also homes they lived in and objects over which they retain political rights of ownership. This may appear as the hegemonic discourse standing on the opposite side of the Turkish-Cypriot counter-hegemonic discourse on loot (as illegitimate gain), but I suggest that the linkages between economy, politics, and affect similarly ground both the hegemonic and the counter-hegemonic, in the north as much as in the south. The topological register on both sides is what furnishes such economic discourses in the governmentality of conflict.

In *Economies of Abandonment*, Povinelli (2011) makes the claim that capitalism in the age of "late liberalism" as she calls it, rests as much on the production of suffering by those whom it divests as on the obfuscation of that suffering. Povinelli is concerned with the dialectic of destruction and production that propels this economic order, and more so with the psychic investments that this process requires, chiefly, she shows, in the form of endurance. The structures of disadvantage appear to arise on a level playing field, and liberal principles make them appear surmountable. But as matter fails to deliver profit, as it turns from property to junk, endurance (of things and of lives) is exhausted. For example, an engine bought by an African American secondhand, which breaks falling from a truck, or a washing machine belonging to an Australian Aboriginal family that during transport loses its lid and no longer runs (ibid., 103, 139)—these are quasi-events in ordinary life that expose the late liberal state's abandonment of minority populations.

I take up the problem of endurance in later chapters. Prefiguring that discussion, I want to concentrate on the potential of detritus to sustain emotional structures and to produce affective events that problematize the political. On the Green Line, the junk that is treated as property produces a disposition towards loss that leaves no room for evaluation of what is kept and what is discarded. It would seem that for the UNFICYP Line Tour guides, it goes without saying that forty-year-old Coca-Cola bottles should continue to be kept as war ruins, along with the cars in the dealership shop. And it goes without saying that the figurative someone whose properties these are, is no longer an individual, but indeed a figure. It is the figurative victim of the conflict whose acknowledgment it is the duty of the viewer to commemorate—during the tour at least.

But this very shift from the individual to the figure is exactly what obfuscates individual suffering in the process of making the conflict so much more than its individual losses. The cars are a symbol of futures envisioned but shattered, a symbol much more powerful than the monetary losses to the individual dealer. I am therefore prompted to ask what is invested in the merging of property and junk that makes the maintenance of conflict a process of production of such affects and what losses that production serves to obfuscate. The minor losses under question here are those that arise in the space of abandonment—they are the quasi-events in Povinelli's argument that make the big Event (the conflict) loom so large that it engulfs individual losses. If late liberalism brackets out recognition by mobilizing concepts of camouflage and espionage in the United States and Australia (ibid., 97–100), one of the key modalities of this process in Cyprus is the conflict. The conflict as communal imaginary sublimates individual losses, turning them from the meaningless (junk) to the ultimate source of meaning (war trauma). That is the way that someone's football can be invoked in the same breath as someone's car without the someone really being conjured up as a person. The belongings of the figurative someone become the cultural treasure that Benjamin describes as horrific because they embody the relations of subjugation that allow rulers to present these items triumphally. They are those "documents of civilization" that also document "barbarism" (Benjamin 1968, 248).

What happens on the Green Line is an enactment of what could be called an "aesthetics of barbarism." Here, things that might never have been revered elicit a mourning for that loot and that violence. And things that could be revered are also sites that condense that mourning. A form of reflection is involved here that Benjamin does not account for—that reflection leads to an acknowledgment of such aesthetics as uncanny, and this is what makes the display performative. The uncanny arises from the separation of people from things, as the former become refugees, here in the sense of being property owners—without their property. The previous chapter discussed the intricate processes involved in shifting from the one to the other in the place of law and the role of affect in qualifying this shift. The question that remains is about the imbrication of both law and affect in the materialities that refugeehood indexes, as this transition is never complete. When and how is property qualified as lost? What kind of property makes one a refugee? These questions were partly answered in the cases of individual refugees: Nadia who laments "her smells," litigants who evaluate their properties in court, Jeanette who saw her prized possessions turn to junk after recovery. But there are also collective property losses that qualify, in parallel terms, the "generalized refugeehood." It is to these that I now turn.

Ledra Palace Hotel, once grand and now serving as UNFICYP barracks, stands definitively on the opposite extreme of "junk," epitomizing the best of the properties lost in the conflict. From its opening as a luxury hotel, Ledra Palace functioned as a space of political negotiation normalizing the aberration of the conflict: it is the place where the leaders of the two ethnic communities met in the 1960s to discuss possible political arrangements to end the violence and allow the displaced to return to their homes. In this process, grandeur and opulence have been stacked in opposition to conflict and violence, rendering the nationalist and militarist links between them invisible. The hotel was also the place where the Greek-Cypriot political establishment celebrated their weddings, socialized, played cards, and attended grand receptions. And it is also where the National Guard allegedly stored ammunition, where war correspondents lodged, and UNFICYP high-ranking officers lived.[5]

Ledra Palace Hotel was a two-story luxury hotel of seventy-eight rooms when it opened in 1949. Its grandeur reached palatial proportions, after the end of colonial rule in the 1960s, with the addition of two wings, then a swimming pool in 1964, another two floors in 1968–1969, and a final addition of rooms raising the count to 240 before its closure in 1974. Being initially a marker of opulence the building became, throughout the latter half of the twentieth century, the chief site of political negotiation in the search for peace until 2002, when the negotiations shifted to Nicosia Airport. Its listing by the Greek-Cypriot authorities in the 1990s as a monumental building is indicative of the imbrications in which the site is enmeshed. It is listed not only because of its architectural value, but also for its political significance; and it is politically invested not only in peace but also in conflict.

The hotel marked the first checkpoint in Nicosia, set up by the UN on arrival in 1964, when a wall of sandbags was erected just before the hotel's entrance. It was at that point that UNFICYP officers took up residence in the hotel's top floor. And while, in Greek-Cypriot accounts, the hotel was shut overnight in 1974—when it was shelled by Turkish fire and taken over by the United Nations—Turkish-Cypriot accounts present it as a battleground since 1963 (Tahsin 1999, 238). Whatever the case, Ledra Palace marked quasi-events of ethnic and social separation; it exemplifies the ethnicization of space that drew Greek-Cypriot Nicosia youth to the hotel in the 1970s and excluded Turkish-Cypriots who were barred from crossing the checkpoint. Turkish-Cypriot men, who were teenagers at the time and living in the neighborhood, remember peeping through the canvas sheets separating the hotel's yard from the Turkish sector, to glimpse at the girls at the swimming pool or the tennis court. Ledra Palace as a space has always been a central location for the conflict, if in a surreptitious way.

Elsewhere I call this process the "militarization of opulence" (Demetriou 2012), a kind of militarization that may be thought of as a particular aspect of the wide-ranging militarization of social life, which Enloe describes (1989; 2000). It is an aspect of militarization that grips the mundane through the display of ostentation that may seem unrelated to violence, in fact contrary to it, but which is actually already militarized. The militarization of opulence is thus a reference to the unfolding of a process whereby domains most seemingly distant to violence (e.g., opulence) become infused in it, having in fact already

FIGURE 5.3. Ledra Palace Hotel in its heyday and in ruin: Featured in a John Hinde postcard from the 1960s, © cardcow.com (top); the hotel's entrance in 2008, with agave plant growing in disused water feature (bottom).

been formed on its basis. This opulent militarization of Ledra Palace took shape in the coexistence of machine guns and Venetian chandeliers; in the changing character of top-floor windows from urban view vistas to surveillance posts; in the shoulder-rubbing of camouflaged men with fashionable and anxious tourists; and in the intense beer-drinking of journalists on assignment, easing the tension of a day's war-zone reporting. The climax of this militarization can be seen now, that the hotel has become a barracks for British UN soldiers. Now, opulence is only there as lack and a different kind of power than ostentation is being negotiated.

As a place that has dramatically changed in forms of occupancy but without ever falling into disuse, Ledra Palace Hotel constitutes a special *topos* where the "production of destruction" (Gonzalez-Ruibal 2008, 254) is ongoing. Gonzalez-Ruibal (2006; 2008) proposes that an "archaeology of destruction" (ibid., 271) pays attention to the political modalities in which this production happens. In the case of Ledra Palace Hotel, these are multiple and imbricated modalities, and they mobilize affect and economic logics to render destruction evental, instantaneous, or gradual. The momentary event of abandonment in 1974 reflects only one political modality in which the Cyprus-conflict imaginary works. The slow process of the hotel's militarization is indicative of others. Both are politically mediated through narratives of loss.

Take the example of the hotel's flora. During the hotel's heyday in the 1960s, the Irish postcard-maker John Hinde produced a card of the hotel that has now become emblematic of the glory lost (figure 5.3). The card features clear blue skies, a front garden with young palm trees and oleander blooms in the foreground. It was probably touched up, as photographic practice then was, for its clear blue skies as much as the brightly coloured oleanders. In the 2000s, when I attended reconciliation meetings in the hotel, the entrance was dominated by an overgrown agave plant in a white plaster structure that I only later realized used to be a water fountain. A former deputy director told me that the fountain was added on the initiative of a manager from Monaco. The same director had also arranged that the mature palm trees be brought over from a coastal village, an innovative transplant in those days, which followed Cote d'Azure practice. It was not the palm trees, the water fountain, nor the oleanders that the deputy director mostly lamented from the hotel's flora. It was the patio at the back known as the "Jasmine Garden," where celebrity musicians used to perform—"nothing left now, they've all dried up." The patio, along with the back garden of the hotel, is actually one of the least degraded areas. It is maintained as an open-air bar and cafeteria, the tennis courts and swimming pool are still used, and the palm trees lining the walkway that separates the patio from the tennis courts are well maintained. The former deputy director reasoned his failure to lament through the fact that "palm trees are easy, they'd survive anyway." The hotel's current occupants, he seemed to suggest, were maintaining the flora in the least care-intensive way, allowing what would survive anyway to do so, the rest condemned to ruination. Roses and oleanders are ephemeral plants, he also reasoned, regarding postcard features; they came and went without marking the hotel's character in any lasting sense.

These comments point to the workings of an economy of loss, where flora indicates the tension between permanence and transience. The affective effort that goes into making jasmine permanent, but not oleanders, marks the difference between loss that is lamented and loss that is discounted. It is this affective effort that made the Jasmine Garden the hotel's jewel, and which underpins the evaluation of its loss as significant. In contradistinction to the oleanders that help frame one of the hotel's most recognized depictions, the jasmine signifies a sense of community taking form in the backyard rather than the public front of the building. The names of singers who sang in the Jasmine Garden, most of them rising to the top of the musical scene in Greece, were remembered with affection, as members of a community of stardom that signified Ledra Palace's grandeur. Signed photographs and press clippings now kept in an album by the deputy director testify both to the construction of that community and the lamentation of its loss.

Much has been written about arboreal metaphors and their links to racism and ethnic cleansing (Comaroff and Comaroff 2001; Lynch 2014). Such transpositions between the floral, the anthropological, and the communal could well be at work here. But I am also arguing that aspects of conflict violence can be articulated not only via deracination but via the language of care too. As Taussig puts it, "[l]ike life, only more so, flowers are beautiful and fragile, and this may be why many people consider them appropriate for death and even more so for disaster" (2003, 111). Lament for lost flowers must be related to the failure to lament or celebrate what survived. And this differential grievability produces the contours of critique while also circumscribing its limits.

There is an exteriority to the subjective experience being communicated here that Navaro-Yashin argues needs to be anthropologically
analyzed beyond the subjectivity paradigm (2007). I propose that *topoi* and
objects do not only anchor memories but are an integral part of the evaluation that gives subjective experience its social meaning. That the register
of this evaluation is essentially that of sentiment (loss in this case), underscores the centrality of the dialectical relationship between grandeur and
ruination in the structure of subjectivity I explore. In that well-known critique of enlightenment dialectics, Adorno and Horkheimer (1979) argue
that contemporary class relations do not drive civilization into progress but
produce culture to numb the masses to ideologies as objectionable as fascism.
Against this conceptual landscape, we could see the polarities between Ledra
Palace's former grandeur—its being a location for producing such numbing
culture—and the trash and ruination that violence left in the very same site
on the Green Line, as marking out the class topologies of loss. The hotel's
business structure as a collaborative enterprise of Greek-Cypriot and foreign
Greek investors was a major step in the consolidation of a local entrepre-
neurial class (also Demetriou 2012). And the ethnic identification of that
class was intimately tied to the recognition of the grandeur symbolized by
the hotel as a point of ethnic and social domination. This is what prompted
none other than the archbishopric, headed at the time by President Makarios,
in his double role, to buy the hotel at a point when the major shareholder was
pulling out—arguing that it should be kept from potentially falling under
Turkish ownership. This antagonistic relationship so forcefully presented at
the social apex, brought about the conversion of this prime property into
trash. And it is its internalization that drives the evaluative mourning that
distinguishes today some losses from others. In recent years, reports have
surfaced at different points regarding the archbishopric's plans to reclaim
Ledra Palace and operate it again, perhaps as a casino hotel. Antagonism is
hard to miss in such plans, which build on presentations of the north—where
casino operations are legal—as a tourism rival to the south.

Another aspect of the cultivation of loss in tandem with politics
and economics is to be seen in the re-collection of particular artifacts from
the hotel's interior. The deputy director nurtured loss through recalling the
high-culture artifacts from inside the building: ballroom panels designed by

an Alexandrian Greek artist; the carved wood paneling around pillars in the bar sculpted by a recognized Greek-Cypriot artist; the ornate iron doors of the lift that were stolen but "could have made fine museum pieces"; the hotel's coat of arms featuring a griffin to symbolize Nicosia after an archaeological find, etched into the glass of the hotel's wooden-framed doors, shipped from Italy, and also shaped into a floor mosaic that still graces the entrance floor. The mosaic is still visible but largely unnoticed while the doors were taken out after the hotel's closure and transported to a company-owned building across the road, along with other movables, to be protected there until things normalized. Instead, the building was burnt down in the course of the violence, and the valuables were lost forever. And lastly, the deputy-director's old accounting machine, a "huge thing, where you put cards and punched." The valuation/devaluation economy involved in this processes oscillates between different ways of accepting loss. Thus, even though the losses of particular items are mourned within a frame of normality, other losses are not—some things simply degrade, others are destroyed in fire, stolen, broken, painted over. These losses are instead subsumed under the collective sense of loss of the hotel and the abnormal conditions under which it occurred. Consequently, they are subjected not to mourning, but melancholia.

The reduction of the hotel from singularly prime property to dilapidated army barracks is the grand frame within which smaller-scale regressions from property to junk are understood. The loss of the hotel as a whole—as business enterprise, communal *topos*, and territorial location—is often a feature of Greek-Cypriot ethnocentric narratives of a prewar past. Major newspapers have run features on the hotel's past along these lines over the years. And many Nicosians have shared fond memories of the hotel with me bracketing out the conflict around it every single time. This is a cultivated affect of loss that builds on the knowledge that the hotel's ownership belongs to the Greek-Cypriot archbishopric, for example, but is oblivious to the fact that that purchase was prompted by ethnic antagonism. It builds on the memories of carefree celebration among co-ethnics while oblivious to politics that saw the erection of the eight-story high Saray Hotel in northern Nicosia as a Turkish-Cypriot rival enterprise. The economy on which the losses of Ledra Palace are evaluated lays bare the topological register on which the political, the affective, and the financial are imbricated. And it consequently points to the processes of silencing that supplement this imbrication.

FIGURE 5.4. Impressions from Nicosia airport: bulleted window panes (background); passenger lounge area, control booths, and wall advertisements still visible (top left); fig tree growing into the terminal building, ceiling panes gutted (top right); surviving sign banning concierge tipping amid bird droppings on the floor (bottom left); attacked aircraft preserved on the runway (bottom right).

BIRD DROPPINGS

Dry, old, and crackling under our feet. It is the only sound to be heard on this tour of Nicosia airport. We are in the abandoned terminal building. Here there is no script, no stories of appropriation, management, upkeep, or humanitarianism. The inside of the building, generally inaccessible even to Nicosia airport tours that the United Nations also offers, seems an ultimate space of abjection. We don't speak on this tour because destruction and decay seem (deceptively) self-evident. There seems to be no script guiding this tour. Amid the droppings on the floor there is broken glass, parts of flayed paneling, exposed and rusted wire, decayed carpeting, torn flooring. There are broken billboards on the walls advertising tourist destinations, gutted lighting on the roof, half-surviving signs on booth shells announcing passport checks and hygienic controls. A placard stand instructs that tipping concierges is forbidden (see figure 5.4).

Nicosia International Airport (NIC) has not been listed on flight schedules since 1974, when Turkish planes bombed it when attacking the capital. The airport buildings and surrounding area are now controlled by UNFICYP, which houses its headquarters there—it is known as the UN Protected Area (UNPA). Since 2002, Greek- and Turkish-Cypriot leaders have held their negotiation meetings at UNPA, with assistance from UN advisers under a new additional mission to UNFICYP, the UN Good Offices. Part of the area is under British UN command as it is formally a UK-retained site under the 1960 Constitution (i.e., a space within the Republic of Cyprus, which the UK could use at will and take control of in the event of war [Constantinou and Richmond 2005, 69]). As a British UNFICYP officer put it, the UK has assigned this site for the use of the UN with a view to ceding it to the Cypriot state after an eventual settlement (interview, UNPA, July 13, 2011). These are arrangements of sovereignty that like the airport, remain outside the purview of daily experience. Elsewhere (Constantinou, Demetriou, and Hatay 2012), I have shown that the division of the city post-1974, which left the Nicosia airport in the Buffer Zone, also changed the mental maps of the city—what used to go under the toponym "airport area" has now been replaced by newer buildings: now the area is named after a private university, a car dealership, the National Cemetery.

The airport's modern terminal was inaugurated in 1968 on the former site of a RAF airport, established in Cyprus since 1930, which had been turned over to civilian use in 1948. Civilian and military uses had in fact coexisted on the site since 1939, when the main landing strip was built; civilian flights were stopped during WWII while military use ended in 1966. In 1956, the bombing by EOKA of a Dakota plane at the airport played a role in the colonial administration's decision to exile Makarios to the Seychelles. The airport, in one sense, developed in tandem with the two military processes that have defined European modernity: colonialism and WWII. With the inauguration of its new terminal in 1968, Nicosia International Airport entered modern aviation by thoroughly becoming a non-place. Designed by the German company Dorsch with experience in airports, boasting high-end mass catering in its restaurants and cafeterias, and furnished with rows of leather seating, it was an ideal transitory space for the emerging masses of travelers and curious passers-by on Sunday ice-cream excursions, who came specifically to marvel at this Cypriot feat. It could have been anywhere: in Europe, where design features are still seen in airports in Copenhagen and Stockholm; in the Middle East, where the same company undertook other airport projects; and anyplace where the passing traveler's gaze was invited to marvel at the technological advances of an internationalized era, away from localized specificities of time and space.

Not anymore. The gutted traffic-control room, the carpeting of bird droppings, the shattered glass around bulleted window panes, the ripped advertisement screens in the former check-in area, the flaking signs on pillars proclaiming health and export rules, and the fig tree growing inside the building amid the debris, are all signatures of Nicosia International Airport in its very specific singularity. So is the hollowed out hull of a Trident jet that flew its last Cyprus Airways passenger flight into the airport during the war before being attacked, and remains damaged on the side of the landing strip. These unique signs mark the shift from the transitoriness of traveling to the permanence of abandonment, from the globalization of design to the localization of ruination, from inclusion in the international space of sovereign independence to the exclusion of ceasefire buffer zones.

A violent emplacement of non-place seems to have taken shape in the Nicosia airport, which, in throwing it outside the city's spatial habitus, has rendered it abject. But it is abject in a different sense from any other place on the Buffer Zone. It is, like Ledra Palace, a place where the celebration of Cypriot modernity masks a difficult political coexistence, where grandeur obfuscated an incipient militarization of social and cultural life, where Greek- and Turkish-Cypriot co-presence did not amount to coexistence. Old pictures of the inauguration feature President Makarios without his Turkish-Cypriot vice president, at that point in 1968 heading a community largely displaced in enclaves; and in a nostalgic Web post, a Turkish-Cypriot pilot reminisces that "many Turkish Cypriots in those days used to venture out to the airport just to have a look at an airplane from Turkey and to boost their morale." The airport signalled opulence for Greek-Cypriots, escape or deliverance for Turkish-Cypriots. Like Ledra Palace, Nicosia airport marks the exclusions and militarizations that Greek-Cypriot subjectivity gains its coherence by rejecting. It is abject in the way Navaro-Yashin analyzes the abjection of the Green Line and inner city northern Nicosia for the constitution of Turkish-Cypriot subjectivity (2012, 47–50). But it is abject in other senses too. It marks out knowledge that is not foreclosed or denied, but not quite lucid either. It is an "abjection considered as invisible [i]n return for which citystate and knowledge can endure" (Kristeva 1982, 84).

Nicosia airport was heavily attacked by Turkish planes in July 1974 and was defended by the Greek-Cypriot National Guard with the help of Canadian UNFICYP forces. On July 22, 1974 a Noratlas military transport airplane was shot down by friendly fire when the National Guard mistook it for a Turkish aircraft. It caught fire and crashed nearby, killing all passengers except one who had managed to jump out in time. The plane had been carrying soldiers from Greece in an attempt to provide support to National Guard forces after the landing of Turkish troops two days earlier. The operation, code-named "Niki" [Victory] had originally included twenty Noratlas and ten Dakota planes, carrying equipment and 318 soldiers in total. Out of these, only fifteen Noratlases took off successfully, but two stopped in Rhodes after facing technical difficulties, while another returned without landing. Of the twelve remaining planes, the first two landed successfully, but the rest came under fire by the Greek-Cypriot forces. The story of operation Niki is often commemorated in August newspaper features on the war, on TV and on the Internet. It is a story that speaks about the unpreparedness of the fighting corps, of the chaos of war, of valiant defense, and of support by Greece.

Less discussed has been the fate of the crashed plane—until recently. The National Cemetery was erected at the spot where the plane had fallen. It is the resting place of Greek and Greek-Cypriot soldiers who died in 1974 and the site of most war-related commemorative events. Among the rows of gravesites that line the Cemetery, one encounters the names of those whose remains are buried in individual graves, the names of those who died but whose remains are awaiting identification, names of those who were only properly buried (i.e., post-identification) decades after the war, and empty graves too, awaiting identified remains—such cenotaphs in fact make up about half of all the graves (figure 5.5). Overlooking these graves is the arch memorial to the most major of losses of 1974, a monument rising at the top of the hill on which the cemetery is built.

FIGURE 5.5. National Cemetery at Tymvos (Tumulus) near Nicosia airport: Lined-up graves (top), some with inscriptions making reference to year of death (1974), and year of DNA identification of the remains (e.g., 2014); some evidencing cleaning and tending (bottom right), others unnamed and presumably empty; a special plaque in the central memorial mound commemorates the soldiers killed in the Noratlas plane, buried at the site in 1974 (bottom left).

On that very spot, on July 27, 2015, a special ceremony marked the beginning of excavations to unearth the plane, which apparently had been buried at the site by the National Guard and the special Greek military forces based on Cyprus. That burial had somehow not been part of the media narratives on previous occasions, although many Greek-Cypriots had known where the plane was. Of the twenty-eight commandos and four crew members that it was carrying, the bodies of sixteen had been discovered after the attack outside the plane and were buried in individual graves at the cemetery, twelve of them having been identified at the time. The remaining fifteen bodies, believed to be inside the aircraft, became the object of a search during the 2015 excavation. A year later, on May 30, 2016, the Commissioner for Humanitarian Affairs announced that the initial work was over, having identified the remains of twenty-eight of the thirty-one dead. While the discovery of the plane was hailed by Greek and Cypriot officials as a step towards honoring the dead heroes, the circumstances under which the aircraft was buried and the memorial built on top hint at questions that were never raised and continue to be muted among Greek-Cypriots. In a special ceremony at the cemetery, the commissioner offered a "big apology, on behalf of the state, to the families of our heroes for the long delay in proceeding with the unearthing operations."[6] The apology also extended to the fact that the location of the plane and the bodies had been known but not acted upon—a point that received much less attention in the media. The Greek ambassador's statement that it is "perhaps pointless to point a finger of blame in such tragic moments, especially bearing in mind all that was happening at the time" was, by comparison, much better reported.

The National Cemetery excavation that took place in 2015 was probably prompted by a case brought against the Republic of Cyprus by the families of two dead commandoes at the ECtHR (*Tzilivaki and Others v. Cyprus*, application no. 23082/07), and which was declared inadmissible. The text of the case shows that the plane was buried on the day it fell, that some bodies were identified then and buried in separate graves, and that in 1979, the bodies were exhumed and returned to families for reburial. Following efforts to identify remains properly, underway since 1999, families were asked to provide DNA samples and to return the remains for identification, which, by 2006, were found to have been misidentified. Note that this identification process runs parallel but is not connected to the identifications carried out under the mandate of the Committee of Missing Persons, which investigates deaths connected to "inter-communal" incidents. By the time identifications were concluded, it transpired that in fact the families had been given remains of forty-two different individuals. Since 2003, the state had been assuring the families that the burial site of the plane would be excavated, which is also what was submitted to the ECtHR. In considering the obligation to excavate, the court argued that "regard must be had to the fair balance that has to be struck between the competing interests of the individual and of the community as a whole; and in both contexts the State enjoys a certain margin of appreciation" (ibid., 7). In this balance, the court accepted the government's point that "it was previously considered not appropriate to disturb the Memorial due to uncertainty of information, the possibility of interference with existing graves and the edifices on the site" (ibid., 8) and concurred that "a major excavation at a commemoration site" is a matter of a "sensitive nature" (ibid.). The crucial question of why the commemoration site was erected there specifically is in this case the essence of that "sensitive nature" and of its relevance to community vis-à-vis individual interests. And it is the question that the court does not ask.

There are significant and much wider questions here about knowledge: who knows what and to what extent things are known, verbalized, celebrated, or left unsaid? They are also questions of responsibility: who buried the plane and its passengers, how and why? Was the monument a memorial of knowledge or of silence? Did it exhibit or did it hide? In the answer "both" that these questions propel me, I encounter Kristeva's social and political abject: "verbalization has always been confronted with the 'ab-ject' that the phobic object is. Language learning takes place as an attempt to appropriate an oral 'object' that slips away and whose hallucination, necessarily deformed, threatens us from the outside" (1982, 41). Like in children, she continues,

> [t]he speech of the phobic adult is also characterized by extreme nim-
> bleness. But that vertiginous skill is as if void of meaning, traveling
> at top speed over an untouched and untouchable abyss, of which, on
> occasion, only the affect shows up, giving not a sign but a signal. It
> happens because language has then become a counterphobic object;
> it no longer plays the role of an element of miscarried introjection,

> capable, in the child's phobia, of revealing the anguish of original
> want. In analyzing those structures one is led to thread one's way
> through the meshes of the non-spoken in order to get at the meaning
> of such a strongly barricaded discourse. (ibid.)

We have always known the story of disaster of 1974; we have always discussed it. But in the same way we erected a memorial over the blunder we tried to hide, we have spoken this disaster over the abyss of what remained unacknowledged. In that abyss lie the minor losses that are ours, Other, or indeed, brotherly. The abject of Nicosia airport is the barricade of that discourse that the National Cemetery mumbles out. And indeed, we can now recognize in that nimble discourse the workings of performativity: in recognizing the unstable truth of conflict discourse, which I have been exploring up to now, in opening up that space of uncertainty in subjectivity, that subject can tread over the abyss of the abject. Knowledge here has a political function. Nimble discourse, in the guise of performative political rhetoric on loss, I would claim, attempts to un-know, it infantilizes.

Children, as we have seen, are important characters in conflict literature. The 2007 short film *Airport for Sale* (Farmakas) is an allegory for the Cyprus conflict, told through the attempts of six children, four Greek-Cypriots and two Turkish-Cypriots, to restore a clock that they clandestinely extract from the abandoned terminal of Nicosia airport. Their quest to have it fixed is quashed when an absent-minded watchmaker tells them this is not an autonomous machine, it is the appendage of a mother clock, which stopped at the time of the attack. Using Greek, English and Turkish, he explains:

> It's pretty, it's beautiful but it doesn't work. It is a slave clock. There
> used to be many of these around at some point. It could be possible to
> change the mechanism of this one too, but … Look here: This clock
> can only work if the boss-clock wants it to. The chief. *The master
> clock* [in English]. *Ana saat* [the mother-clock, in Turkish] [...] *when
> the master clock died, all the little slaves followed suit and well, time
> stopped* [in English]. (13:12–14:41)

The film is unremarkable within the genre of Cypriot division allegories. Its symbolism is well spelt out, and its political commentary rather softened. The central tension is between the innocence of children and the devastation they encounter, their hopes for restoring time and continuity and the cruel reality of machinations greater than their world. These are precisely the tropes that sketch out the Greek-Cypriot topography of loss: motherlands and fatherlands, networks of power, and innocent locals both naughty and afraid (like the children in the film), who play within the ruins and grow up to ignore them. In these terms, the film's dramatic climax, in the diagnosis that the ur-event is that time stopped, is indicative of the symbolism in that topography of loss: loss of place stands for loss of time see also Davis (2017b).

What Greek-Cypriots lost in the north is not simply home or property —it is a sense of integral subjecthood. Their identity, transformed through loss, has become part and parcel of who they are today, and the lament for places is often a lament for who they might have been in them. Nadia, as we see in chapter 3, laments her childhood in lamenting Famagusta. Nitsa, a fifty-five-year-old businesswoman explained to me her relation to Kyrenia: "You have to understand, it wasn't a place we occasionally went to. We were there every weekend during the winter and in the summer the whole three months of school holiday. It was the little streets on which we first flirted, the harbor we strolled along in the afternoon, Mare Monte beach." This discourse communicates the sense of generalized refugeehood I explored in previous chapters, but it also communicates the loss of time as abrupt caesura, the end of continuity, and a break with childhood and teenage years. This sense of loss provides the sensory framework that supports political rhetoric; it sets the ground for empathizing with the plight of actual refugees (following a logic of "we are all refugees"). But it also reinforces the innocence of that subjectivity, claiming loss as trauma not because of its magnitude but because it was not our fault.

On these political terms, I am suggesting that by contrast to such major topological losses (everything that is symbolized by the loss of Kyrenia), there is also an abject topology of loss that emanates from the Green Line, and is particularly dense in the scatographics of the droppings-covered airport terminal. Here, fault and knowledge are put in question and require a different discourse to speak them out. These children, in contrast to teenagers of times past, must point and lament a future from now on, not one that never came to be.

Alongside *Airport for Sale*, a number of artistic and architectural studies have used these images of the airport as abject to envision a postconflict condition (Siandou 2012). As part of an exhibition dedicated to the airport, entitled *Uncovered*, an art project cleaned off a row of lounge seats and transferred them for exhibition elsewhere in the Buffer Zone, along one of Nicosia's crossing points; another reinvigorated its presence in the current age by building a mimetic website for it, with deceptively searchable flight schedules; another collected and restored objects from the ruins (Şenova and Paraskevaidou 2011). Such projects acknowledge what goes unsaid. Staple rhetoric on the topographics of loss typically concentrates on archimages of cultural heritage: churches that were looted and left to ruin through the passage of time in the north and mosques similarly abandoned in the south. These once holy places feature extensively in official publications that draw on the image of desecration brought about by the filth of animals and birds that have been allowed to lodge in these spaces as a sign of the Other's barbarism. Opposite these sites stands the airport, a monument of secular modernity, incipient conflict, and contested sovereignty. In the airport, as in Ledra Palace, loss is not quite that. A number of Greek-Cypriots have reasoned on account of both places, that it is better they are under UN control, as their strategic value was too high to cede to the Turks. But if these Buffer Zone sites are not quite losses they are in fact double losses for the art initiatives that feature them—they are both lost and not mourned.

And if, in the process of abjection, Ledra Palace has been discursively rehabilitated as a site of reconciliation and the symbol of peaceseeking, the airport remains outside this process. It is a space where speech is yet to return, symbolism yet to restore subjective identity. It sits "at the crossroads of phobia, obsession and perversion" (Kristeva, 1982:, 45). The process waiting to happen in this "topology of catastrophe" (ibid., 9) is the passage from *Oedipus Rex* to *Oedipus at Colonus* as Kristeva would say:

> The locale has changed ... a transformation of political laws [from tyranny to democracy] actually took place between the writing of the two plays.... In opposition to the sovereign Oedipus, overcome, destroyed, shattered through and within opprobrium, we have here an Oedipus who is *not king*, in other words an Oedipus who is a subject, who proclaims his innocence. (ibid., 86)

That is an innocence that comes after knowledge and not one that clings to childhood. And that is perhaps the process that is timidly beginning to take place as hurriedly buried planes, teeming with bones, are unearthed. Essentially, I would argue, these are claims to knowledge, and socially, claims to a nonsovereign subjectivity. In these imbrications between the affective, the legal, and the topological, we can now begin to examine crevices where other claims and other subjects become caught.

FIGURE SII.1. Imbrications on the Green Line: Destroyed roof in Nicosia's Buffer Zone.

II CREVICES

From the Refugee-Citizen to the Abject Refugee

FURTHER NOTES ON COUNTER-CONDUCT, JUSTICE, AND SOVEREIGNTY

Another sign on the streets of Nicosia: "'everyone has the right to a citizenship'—UN. Why do we spend a lifetime in statelessness?" The question was scrawled on a banner and hung on the railings outside the presidential palace in Nicosia, in the summer of 2017. It marked the spot where two stateless Kurds from Syria staged a hunger-strike protest. They were part of a larger group of protesters, who had petitioned the government at different points for naturalization, having lived in the Republic for different periods, ten years in some cases. Members of their families and some of their children had been naturalized. Their own applications were rejected on various grounds including "failure to integrate, indicated by lack of knowledge of the Greek language by members of the family." Migrant rights organizations and political parties supporting their plight called for a march on the Ministry of the Interior, citing falsehoods in the rejection letter (about linguistic competence, lengths of legal stay, and others), vindictiveness arising from the protest and punitive instrumentalization of family members' linguistic abilities.

A crowd of about fifty or so activists and other Kurds in a similar position gathered at the park, alongside foreign and local camera crews. A delegation was formed to deliver the demand and was received by a high-ranking official at the ministry. They returned without a positive message: the strikers were asked to leave the park; they were creating a bad image outside the presidential palace. The erroneous grounds on which their claims were rejected were repeated. They were also told their actions were "ungrateful." The Republic, the official finally clarified, extended citizenship to people who were "useful" to it. The Cypriots in the delegation left the meeting scandalized, relating the comments back with an air of mockery. The refugees were demoralized but unsurprised. But they were told not to worry—the case would be taken further through other channels. A week or so later, they were informed that their cases were being reexamined, and the hunger strike ended, but the protest continued.

Earlier hunger strikes had ended with naturalization applications being approved. These protests had been effective in changing a policy that up to then largely restricted naturalization to Western citizens. Both protests expose the predicament of 1951 Convention refugees in Cyprus, who face limitations even under this privileged status of recognition as refugees, as well as the predicament of being effectively barred from claiming a life beyond refugeehood. Having analyzed the imbrications through which the refugee-citizen emerges in Cypriot governmentality, the chapters in this section turn to the analysis of those specific sites of imbrication that dislodge the refugee-citizen subjectivity, and where other, minor, subjectivities become lodged. I call these "crevices," similar to those points on a roof formed by the alignment or misalignment of tiles where possibilities for shelter and calamity exist: debris collects, nests are built, animals burrow, leaks begin. In such a crevice, where refugeehood is located outside citizenship, refugee protesters can take a government to task for violating UN law, cognizant of the fact that the violation of UN resolutions are key claims in the Cyprus cause against enemy-state Turkey. And refugee-rights activists can deride notions of useful citizens, exposing the fact that such use is measured financially, as when the Republic extends citizenship to investors who are in large part of Russian and Chinese origin.[1] This is a crevice in which refugees gain a voice.

But what does this use of the body on strike and the self-infliction of hunger entail? Situated at the limit of counter-conduct and its circumscription, a crevice is seldom a comfortable place. The imbrication of law and affect is a risky place. Under the 1951 Convention, the refugee is constructed affectively as a fearful subject: "fear of persecution" is the main claim to status and the criterion to be assessed is its "well-foundedness." It is an assessment, critical law has argued, whereby disqualification looms no matter what; in British court cases studied, being too fearful undermines well-foundedness, being not fearful enough undermines fear (Douzinas and Warrington 1991). In the end, what is established is the "dissymmetry between the addressees of the law (subjects, citizens, the nation) and those others, its secondary addressees, who should be aware however of its effects" (ibid., 132). In the judgment of "well-founded fear of persecution," is a "well-founded fear of justice," which substitutes the morality of justice with its administration through process and norms. Extending these insights here, we could claim that the failure to recognize the refugee as a potential citizen is an extension of the failure to recognize the refugee in the first place, a failure that persists even after the granting of refugee status. In the UK cases Douzinas and Warrington discuss, a fear of justice is exhibited in the turning away from moral responsibility when refugee claims in the UK are rejected on procedural grounds. In Cyprus, a parallel pertains in administrative claims regarding evidence of language knowledge.

As we saw in section one, for the case of refugee-citizens, the seeming privilege that attends refugeehood works to disguise the abjection, which envelops it. Cognizant of this abjection, the claim of stateless refugees to Cypriot citizenship is a claim to the status of "not being refugee," a claim articulated and deconstructed in Arendt's famous essay *We Refugees* (1943). "We don't like to be called 'refugees,'" she says. Refugees are "those of us who have been so unfortunate as to arrive in a new country without means" (111). That lack of means forms the basis of a degrading humanitarian economy whereby benefits translate into privilege and become the means through which the state comes to demand gratitude. Morality of justice is exchanged for morality of humanitarian assistance under a mechanism that strips people of political subjectivity. However, this is not yet the mechanism that produces bare life in the Agambenian sense of the Musselmann (1998, 44). The refugee subjectivity that Arendt describes, not being quite bare life, is a condition that claims presence through "a dangerous readiness for death":

> although death lost its horror for us, we became neither willing nor capable to risk our lives for a cause. Instead of fighting . . . refugees have got used to wishing death to friends or relatives . . . finally many of us end by wishing that we, too, could be saved some trouble, and act accordingly. (1943, 112)

This is the political excess that resists bare life and reclaims biopower as the last vestige of itself.

In recent years, bodily acts such as hunger strikes, suturing of mouths and eyes, burning finger tips to make finger printing impossible, and making bodily pain a public site, have been read as "abject acts of citizenship

[that] force us to ask fundamental questions about . . . *our* politics as *human beings* . . . about our responsibility as privileged beings in participating in and continuing such systems of oppression" (Rygiel 2010, 203). Such acts are instances of counter-conduct to a biopower staked on the silent refugee figure, to whom political life is foreclosed. They are acts that recover the counter-conduct that refugee recognition precludes. But such biopower remains contingent. Its force arises from someone seeing, hearing, and recognizing— someone on the other side of the law (subjects, citizens, the nation) who can take to task "the fear of justice." The media, politicians, and activist movements are not merely amplifiers of refugee voices; they are the apparatus that enable audibility and visibility—within other exchange logics tied to the "illegality industry" (Andersson 2014). Indeed, I would suggest that the shift from the refugeehood paradigm to alternative bases for migration discussions, exemplified by a focus on autonomous migration (Tazzioli 2015; Andersson 2014; Mezzadra 2013; Papadopoulos and Tsianos 2013; Walters 2006) are attempts to recover political subjectivity by arresting the process that turns law into norm (chapter 4; Foucault 1990). In doing so, they question the precepts of legal governmentality and its effect of substituting justice by sovereignty.

But the conundrum of refugee political subjectivity remains. Its negotiation orders the self-administration of Sahrawi refugee camps in southwest Algeria (Fiddian-Qasmiyeh 2011) and Palestinian refugee camps in Syria, Jordan, and Lebanon (Martin 2015; Farah 2009; Peteet 2005). UNHCR and the law it represents administers increasing numbers of camps where refugees, asylum seekers, autonomous migrants, and other persons of interest are held on the way to Europe and on the way to autonomous camps such as Calais (including in various forms after the dismantling of the Jungle) and squats in Athens and elsewhere. What is entailed here are the extremes and replications of uneven power, which are surfacing forcefully now in the coupling of humanitarianism and security within and outside the camp, en route, and, as the Cypriot protest shows, after recognition. For a rescue organization to be able to operate on the Greek island of Lesvos today, part of its work entails contact with authorities and the passing on of information when boat sightings are done. Autonomous camps mount resistance, but still do so in the shadow of these power extremities, susceptible to violent evictions, attacks, and legal assaults. On the other end, this coupling is also spawning, not aberrantly I think, far-right European patrols off Algeria that rescue migrants and refugees and return them to the coast they departed from.[2]

The recovery of political subjectivity from within the extremes of these power dynamics and after attempts to shift the refugeehood paradigm, I want to suggest, entails a return to counter-conduct through the prism of the everyday I introduced in the notes of section 1. What are the contours of the everyday that circumscribe such counter-conduct and how are those limits contested? The everyday I turn to in section 2 is an everyday in flux, framed by processes of European integration and disintegration, wars in the region, clashing discourses of security, inversions of notions such as truth, assistance, and safety, and proliferating emergencies. It is a moment of flux in which, as Foucault reminds us through the examples of Anabaptism, Cold War dissidence, Luther, the English Revolution, and women's questions (more in Demetriou 2016), counter-conduct acquires socio-historical dimensions.

But it is not only to this flux that we must attend. We need to keep in perspective the genealogical dimension of refugee counter-conduct as examined in previous chapters. The performative emphasis that laid the foundations for refugee counter-conduct is relevant to what takes place in crevices today. And what takes place in crevices today is also related to what has taken place there historically. This is why I attend to both past and current crevices in this section. The first such crevice (chapter 6) is formed at the interstices of local and international refugeehood. The Cypriot refugee, I have shown, is one that resists, does not forget, struggles, etc. The refugee-in-one's-own-country schema enables this. This is why it should not be seen as legal misnomer but instead a double injury. And in that move, the responsibility of the state is taken away. Refugeehood under the 1951 Convention poses the question of state protection and state responsibility. The Republic of Cyprus has excelled in the first by providing early relief and fairly good housing in a planned manner post-1974—with help from the USAID. But in doing that, it skirted the responsibility question in two ways. First, concerning that protection which was not provided and that rendered some Cypriots as persons of concern to UNHCR in earlier times. Second, concerning the complicity in the breakdown of structures that led to the displacement of refugees of 1974 so that no other state but their own is responsible for protecting these refugees. And in return for that refugee-citizen status, the state has claimed an allegiance in struggle. This allegiance still undergirds the protection of refugees today, including 1951 Convention refugees. An echo of that exchange can be heard in the call of stateless Kurds to the Republic to respect UN laws (they are, after all, also struggling against the common enemy Turkey). As is seen in chapter 6, it can be discerned in other acts and policies too.

At the same time, in making orientation in such antagonistic terms a praised status, the state has had to ensure that this status is passed down and continues in perpetuity (i.e., through the generations and via refugee cards, which symbolize ongoing needs and ongoing trauma). A work on time is involved here, which happens governmentally through work on the family. And that has also entailed a passing down of the script that in being exaggerated and inflated risks jarring with experience and therefore spawning other political affects: critique, questioning, ridicule, apathy. Echoes of the work of this apparatus are heard in the counter-conduct of refugees who already have a voice. I thus return to refugee-citizens in chapter 7, to examine the implications of the generational transfer of refugeehood. So the leap of counter-conduct required here is not about gaining voice or presence, for the stage is already set for that. The leap required is about stepping out of the script and indeed questioning it.

Passing down refugeehood through the generations, in as far as it implicates the family, also implicates gender difference. Women have struggled differently in refugeehood, as indicated by the Women Walk Home movement that spurred the *Loizidou v. Turkey* case. And they have also raised different types of refugees in the next generation, whereby the passing down of refugee cards became the privilege of refugee fathers but not mothers. These differing roles open up questions of family in refugeehood, reminding us, as recent discussions foreground too, that refugee status is not about individuals but about families also. It is from this perspective not surprising that Kurdish refugees are being penalized for language competencies of family members. Many questions about the implication of family notions in refugeehood are indeed coming to the fore now, through increased scrutiny of trends that indicate far more willingness by states to grant subsidiary protection rather than refugee protection under the terms of the 1951 Convention system. The major difference in the quality of protection between the two is the possibility of family reunification, afforded only under the latter.

Family, in this sense, can be seen to work as a mechanism whereby an exceptional status (subsidiary protection) may replace the state's legal obligations (to recognize refugees). In this way, not only political life, but social life too, in the intimate domain of family, becomes a luxury reserved on this side of citizenship. And the morality of that decision is relegated to the normative and the administrative rather than to justice—in that move that we can now recognize as "fear of justice." The problem of family, chapter 7 shows, is not a problem of appearance or disappearance, but a problem of when and how the politicization and depoliticization of family life takes place. Families have always been political (Ferguson 2012)—the question is who gets to decide the terms in which they are so. Alongside the legal viewpoint, I also employ a historical take on the crevices formed around such politicizations of family. And I show how these have too often been violent places for women.

And I end the exploration of crevices with that ur-point in the time and place of Cypriot imbrications, the appearance of the refugee enemy. I take my cue in this from work on enemy properties (Yasmin 2015; Üngör and Lohr 2014; Bakonyi 2010; Neocleous, 2006) and particularly in Cyprus (Erdal Ilican 2011), which has shown how the concept is entrenched within processes that give rise to the caesuras of law and the resurgence of sovereignty in the exception. The site of the exception that founds refugee subjectivity in Cyprus is, the chapter shows, historically and materially, the enemy refugee. And this brings us back to abjection, citizenship, and the fear of justice—here as simultaneous, complementary, and indeed necessary processes in the imbrication of law, affect, and territory.

SIX   MINOR OTHERS

OTHER REFUGEES

If one searches the appellation "refugee" (*prósfiyes*) instead of "displaced" (*ekto-pisthéndes*) in Republic of Cyprus law, one mostly encounters the subjects of international protection under the terms of the 1951 Convention. This indicates a clear separation in lawmakers' minds about the difference between "our" refugees and "international" refugees.[1] Cyprus acceded to the 1951 Convention in 1963 and to its 1967 Protocol in 1968. Apart from the laws translating these documents, "refugees" reappear in this international protection sense again in 2000, with the Law regarding Refugees (6[1]/2000). At this point, Cyprus was in the final phase of negotiations for EU accession, a process that entailed bringing local legislation into line with European Union laws and directives, the *acquis communautaire*. Subsequent amendments to this law explicitly transposed EU directives on the procedures determining refugee status and protection. Yet even though international law and local perceptions may describe two different conceptual categories even in the minds of Cypriot lawmakers, their distinction and correspondence has often taken (even for other lawmakers) an imbricated form—both structured and uncertain. It is at those interstices that governmental practice has gained its force as subjectivizing apparatus. It is at these interstices that categories, gradations, and assessments of refugeehood are mobilized in ways that spawn new gradations that in turn govern other lives. The terms under which new and old refugees are "let live" are related. These relations allow the structures of imbrication to develop and endure.

Emin's story is indicative. His family migrated to Turkey from Bulgaria to escape the pressures of the Zhivkov regime shortly prior to its collapse in 1989. Emin barely remembers this move, or the one to northern

Cyprus, which followed, incentivized by Turkish policy to increase the population of ethnic Turks there. Since early 1975, the Turkish government has provided incentives for Turkish nationals to settle in northern Cyprus. Different schemes were implemented at different times, originally targeting agriculture and the rural areas. For the Republic, these policies have been viewed as the ultimate war crime, and over the years the population of settlers has come to symbolize the most repugnant Other in the north. The adversarial terms in which these policies have been mired point to a central concern with sovereignty. The policies are a central pillar of the state's attempt to create population through the physical transfer of bodies, which enable and consolidate territorial sovereignty, cleansing previous presences, and creating *terra nullius* through property reallocation (Kaufmann 1998; Connor 2005; Banner 2005; Öktem 2008; Zuriek, Lyon and Abu-Laban 2011; Erdal Ilican 2011). The example of Emin's settlement shows how this technique of population control also crosscuts and utilizes humanitarianism: people fleeing discrimination in one state are rendered the instruments of another state's claims to territory and sovereignty. This approach has also been applied to other cases of settlement in Cyprus from Turkey, whereby transferred populations had been rendered displaced through development projects, such as dam construction, or through conflict, in the case of people belonging to Turkey's own Other populations (Kurds and people from the region of Hatay, annexed by Turkey from Syria in 1939). Far from eschewing the question of agency in the implementation of such policies, I am arguing that in their rejection of being oppressed, people are subjectivized in other ways as they are dejected from one kind of population and incorporated into another. The social contract here entails that one regains the right to be counted as a political agent if one accepts their specific (physical and political) emplacement within the state's particular configurations.

And so this is how Emin grew up in northern Nicosia, attended school, and got a job as a manual laborer. When arrested for a minor offence, he was given a deportation sentence because he was not a citizen of the (self-declared and internationally unrecognized, as Greek-Cypriot politicians always remark) state of the Turkish Republic of Northern Cyprus. His family had not gone through the naturalization process yet; by the time they did, Emin was an adult, and they discovered they had lost the right to extend citizenship to him. That meant he could not exchange his deportation sentence for a fine or imprisonment. Emin returned to stay with extended family in Bulgaria but became depressed in the new and unfamiliar environment, especially after apprehending how few work options were open to him there.

But then, he realized he could return to Cyprus via the south, where Bulgarians, as EU citizens since 2007, had residence and work rights. The evening Emin arrived in Larnaca airport he was picked up by his Turkish-Cypriot childhood friends and partied his return to the island. He had come "home." He began searching for work in the south, made contact with his family who could now cross to visit him, and rented a room in a house where migrants lodged. Speaking no Greek or English, he failed to secure jobs, and soon discovered that his Turkish was frowned upon in the south. He also found it difficult to adjust to the filth in the house—the mattress had bugs, he told me, the sink was piled with unwashed dishes for days, cockroaches roamed, the bathroom and toilet were hardly usable. Within two months of his arrival, and without any prospects for work or better living conditions, he left for Bulgaria again, to the unwelcoming family he had partied his freedom from.

Emin had found himself in southern Nicosia pining for the loss of access to his house and family in a way that might well have resembled the words of the South Asian waiter I introduced in the beginning of this book. In a geography aligned with the specific discourse on loss I have been analyzing in the first section, Emin's longing for his home in the north seems as misaligned as the pining of that Asian waiter on the other side of the line. Emin had used EU law to circumvent the penalties imposed by law in northern Cyprus, just as the waiter had used the same law to move to the north and circumvent restrictions imposed by laws in the south. Like the waiter, Emin had little investment in the Cyprus conflict up to that point, and he had never before become conscious of how the border might restrict or enable his own movement. But he became engulfed in the conflict the moment he was forced to become mobile.

"Forced migration" might be the wrong term here in a technical sense, but it is nevertheless a term that speaks, in its very misrepresentation of ideas about origins and stability that it implies, to the situation of becoming lodged in the crevices of legal, social, and political structures, which under other conditions one might simply glide over, like rainwater. Forced out of his home in the north because of his lack of citizenship, and in possession of another citizenship, ironically of much greater currency in a global context, Emin goes against the current of the hegemonic imaginary of refugeehood: that people move out of autocratic and /or illegitimate states to more democratic and developed societies with greater legitimacy on the world stage. Emin's case illustrates the Eurocentrism that plagues the 1951 Convention and the concepts of forced migration that arise from that: concepts that in their implementation construct Europe as a prima facie safe haven when it is primarily "events occurring in Europe" and secondarily "Europe and elsewhere" (Art. 1 §B1a, B1b) that scandalized the international community enough after WWII to sign a Convention in which fourteen of twenty-four signatures are European. A EU passport that should have made Emin a world citizen instead imprisoned him in spaces that were not home. And it did so because home was mired in the international politics of sovereignty and its (non)recognition that constitute the Cyprus problem. Imbrication may entail traps as well as leakages.

A BORDER UNDER ERASURE

How are these crevices formed, between the layers of affect, territory, and law? In 2004, when Cyprus joined the EU, a special caveat was added to the Treaty of Accession intended to regulate the spatio-political abnormality. Protocol 10 clarifies that "[t]he application of the acquis shall be suspended in those areas of the Republic of Cyprus in which the Government of the Republic of Cyprus does not exercise effective control" (Article 1). As mentioned in chapter 4, the formulation of "effective control" is part of the legal discourse that the Republic has been using since the 1970s to refer to the postwar situation, which it called "abnormal," "unstable," "out of sync." The transposition of this discourse onto the EU level marks a double abnormality: it transposes legislation in the opposite direction to what normally is the case in the EU by making national law part of European; and second, it extends this particular reading of abnormality across the island. Protocol 10 in effect leaves the north in a state of legal suspension, within the EU as a territory, but without EU laws. In turn it announces a border under erasure as marking the limits of that territory. Through Protocol 10, the Green Line becomes a boundary that without being a border, is the EU's easternmost limit; it is a Line controlled on one side by Turkish military authorities, who are not recognized as a governmental structure but are internationally recognized and held accountable as occupation troops. And on the other side, it is controlled by indigenous authorities (the Republic) that do have an internationally recognized governmental structure but which do not recognize what they guard as a state border and therefore do not monitor it quite as such (but monitor it nevertheless). Green (2018) has called this a "one-sided border." My argument is that what is at stake is not the difference between one side or another, but the complicated ways in which this common ontology under erasure becomes shared. This is what imbrication prompts us to think about. The pervasiveness of this abnormality of the Cypriot Green Line is clear in all political discourse on the island and imbricates migration-related discourse too. And since 2004, it also implicates the EU.[2]

Exemplary of the way in which the abnormality of border governance conflates the governmentality of the Cyprus conflict with the governmentality of immigration are the occasional presentations by the Cypriot Ministry of Foreign Affairs of the problem of illegal immigration as Ankara's ploy to flood the Republic of Cyprus with migrants and jam the entire state mechanism. In 2009, the president of the Republic stated that "Turkey... illegally ... controls 54%–58% of the north-eastern coast of the Republic of Cyprus, which ... is a place of embarkation of illegal immigrants" (*Cyprus News Agency* June 19, 2009). Such claims have not been wasted on the far right, in parliament as of May 2016 (see also Katsourides 2013), who have further argued that Turkey's ultimate aim in sending migrants to the south is to Islamize and Turkify the whole of the island, via a reading that ties the two identities together. Echoing at least part of these concerns, the EU parliamentary Committee on Civil Liberties, Justice, and Home Affairs (LIBE) reported in 2008 that

> [t]he Green Line has evolved into a very serious problem regarding illegal immigration [which the Council and Commission should address] ... in the ongoing negotiations with regard to Turkey's accession ... [lest it leads] to a situation that is unmanageable, from a demographic, political as well as financial point of view. (DV\736332EN: 10)

Penned much before the eruption of the war in Syria, and the humanitarian crisis that prompted new EU measures in 2015, these words seem to be a foretelling of the situation that unfolded on the Greek-Turkish coast seven years later. They are also uncannily similar to the harsh statements pronounced by the European Commission on Turkey's failure to abide by the bilateral statement of March 18, 2016. Highly criticized by human rights advocates,[3] the document, which is a statement and not an agreement and, therefore, without any legal binding force whatsoever, is premised not on law but on the moral authority of Europe to decide who stays in Turkey, who is returned, and who is relocated.[4] Under the statement, all irregular migrants crossing after that date (including rejected asylum seekers) are to be returned from the Greek islands to Turkey. The EU in turn funds a "Facility for Refugees in Turkey" with 3 billion euros initially, and with a prospect for doubling that amount later, and resettles a Syrian from Turkey in a member state "'for every Syrian being returned to Turkey from Greek islands ... taking into account the UN Vulnerability Criteria" (Press Release 144/2016). When the implementation of the statement faltered (how does a statement become implemented, indeed?) on Turkey's insistence that the EU lifts immediately visa restrictions for Turkish nationals (also mentioned in the statement but without concrete commitments spelled out), the president of the EU Commission fell back on the argument of moral superiority, accusing Turkey for lack of diplomacy. This exchange agreement repeats a structure of exchanging cash for border controls, described most recently by Andersson (2014) for the case of Spain and Senegal. What I see prefigured in the LIBE statement on Cyprus back in 2008 is the leveraging of a moral authority on the given of European superiority backed by financial gestures that bolster that superiority. This moral authority, which enables a legally vacuous statement to be treated as all-important governmental instrument, has been established on the back of previous discourses, of which the LIBE statement is but a small example. This is the significance of a genealogical analysis to the exception that we are seeing unfolding today.

Thus, I am suggesting that the two situations, in 2015 and 2008, reveal a continuity in the European governmentality of migration, despite the dramatic changes to the context in which this migration takes place. They are based on the same understanding and priorities regarding migration, refugee protection, border security, and Turkey's position vis-à-vis these issues. As these understandings play out post-2015, it is the Aegean border and not the Cypriot Green Line that is the focus of attention as a weak spot. Notably, through this recent crisis, surprisingly few refugees had sought protection in Cyprus until 2018. And in one exceptional case of a sea rescue by a cruise ship in September 2014 off Cyprus's southern coast, 280 Syrian survivors of 345 people rescued had initially refused to disembark on the island, demanding their first point of entry be a different location in Europe (*AFP* September 25, 2014). Similarly in 2015, 114 Syrian refugees who disembarked on the British

Sovereign Base Area (SBA) of Akrotiri were reluctant to file claims with the Republic (*The Guardian* 21/10/2015). Much earlier, in 1998, six families of refugees had arrived in the SBA of Dhekelia and had been refused processing of their claims by the UK government. It was argued that although sovereign, SBAs were not British soil. The families have lived on the base since, resisting examination by Cypriot authorities, until 2017, when the UK High Court annulled the original decision and ordered that their claims be processed as if they were in the UK.[5] These very same understandings about protection and security as found only in Europe proper and not its periphery, inform the decisions that those subjected to them make and elicit actions that inflect Europe, refuge, and victimhood.

It is this governmentality that produces crevices in the Green Line. In becoming a border policed but not recognized, the Green Line is not merely a topographical register of loss, as I suggest in chapter 5. It is now a pocketed terrain over which Asian migrants and Bulgarian Turks can cross, clandestinely or not, and in crossing find themselves barred from what they have come to know as home in Cyprus. And it is also ultimately a terrain cut off from Europe proper where those without a home find it difficult to imagine making one.

POLICING AND CARE

A large part of what makes Cyprus unwelcoming to international refugees has to do with the inflection of conflict governmentality onto policies of protection. This starts at the Green Line. In policing, the definitions used to categorize migrants are largely determined by the existence of the Buffer Zone, and this in turn affects the rights afforded to them. In the statements of the government representatives quoted previously, there is a consistent labeling of irregular crossers from the north as "illegal migrants" (*lathrometanástes*), who then become asylum seekers if they apply for refugee protection. This appears to imply that there are two strands of asylum seekers—those who come from the north with relative ease and are "illegal immigrants," and those who come directly to the south and face more barriers in the process, who are more readily called "asylum seekers" or, since 2015, "refugees." This categorization implies that those who come via the Green Line are less genuine as claimants of refugee protection—they are, in a sense, more "illegal." If some asylum seekers are automatically classified as illegal migrants, it is questionable whether they are granted equal access to the asylum process. It is as if crossing the Green Line becomes a prima facie reason for rejecting refugee protection or subsidiary protection.

The police annual report for 2007 quoted a figure of 7,770 "illegal migrants," which came to the unit's attention, but this number, it was noted, also included "asylum seekers from the occupied territories [*etités asílu apó ta katehómena*]" (Cyprus Police Force 2008: appendix J). This categorization remained in place until 2015.[6] The category of "asylum seekers from the occupied areas" appears in more or less the same location in successive Annual Reports (2008,appendix H; 2009, appendix E; 2010, appendix E; 2011, appendix F; 2012, 27). It also appears in summary statistics on migration for the period 2013–2015. Furthermore, in the 2009 (51) and 2010 (30) reports, special sections are devoted to comparative statistics of asylum seekers from the free and occupied areas, noting the drop in the latter as an achievement. The criminalization of crossing is underscored further in the 2011 annual police report, which includes general crossing statistics, and not just those related to illegal migration. These crossings are categorized as "Greek Cypriots to the occupied areas / Turkish Cypriots to the free areas / entry not allowed / arrested" (appendix B).

Taken together, these categories mark out the Green Line as a site of criminality well beyond the scope of visa-regulated travel. Cypriots crossing to the other side are tainted by this criminality of the border, as they come to flank the columns of those arrested. In the mentality of policing, governability is about ensuring that everyone is counted and in place, vis-à-vis the border. The categories of police reports trace the development of a disciplinary apparatus that takes the Green Line as a site of calibration and measures illegality across it, first by reference to migrants, then to refugees, and finally to Cypriots. It corresponds well to the development of biometrics and travel policies that Rygiel (2010) traces from techniques that target terrorists to ones that evaluate the whole of the population against the binary of compliance and its absence. And it offers a particularly fertile ground for the development of far right discourse (see also Ellinas, 2010) that calibrates external and internal enemies across the Green Line. Indeed, as Katsourides suggests (2013), the development of far right discourse in Cyprus over the last century stretches back to hegemonic discourses on *enosis*, so that its *re*appearance today takes shape within and is bolstered by similarities with discourses of the mainstream right and the Church. In other words, the Green Line is the *topos* that normalizes extremism and founds the violence against multiple others (migrants, refugees, Turkish-Cypriots, Greek-Cypriot crossers) that the policing I described above begins to legitimize.

To Rancière, who sees the process of democratic subjectivation as beginning with police, the logic of police is the power that adheres to those who rule. This power, he says, "has to rely on a supplementary quality common to both rulers and to the ruled. Power must become political" (2010, 53). The police, he writes contra Althusser, is not so much the interpellatory device that hails citizens to order but the one that urges them on from public space, telling them that "there's nothing to see here" (ibid., 37). This function inaugurates the democratic paradox in inserting the question between power and the political, showing that the "very ground for the power of ruling is that there is no ground at all" (ibid., 50). Reading this against the Cyprus data suggests that the governmentality of policing the Green Line as a locus of loss is a matter of a melancholic rather than a productive emergence of the political. By linking crossing and criminality, policing encourages people to move on, away from and not across the Green Line. It suggests that there is nothing to see here. The subjectivation spurred on by guarding this space and moving people along it is a process that does not invite pondering over the lost ground of power. A good citizen, who need not be interpellated by statistics, is one who does not cross, does not probe experientially into the narrative of loss that the Green Line exudes. But this is a policing stifled by the whimsicalities of nationalist affect and normative aporias.

It creates gradations of legitimacy that are inflected by the Green Line not just on account of Cypriots and foreigners but across categories of foreignness too. Kurds, for example, may be seen as more legitimate asylum claimants than other Turks, rendering their "illegal" crossing of the Green Line somehow less illegal than the crossing of Turks from the north. At the other end, the free movement of Bulgarian Turks, many of whom, like Emin, may well be considered settlers, creates paradoxical situations that put the rigidity of local positions into question. In 2007, the special adviser to the president expressed an equivocal position when Bulgaria entered the EU. Queried by journalists on the status of Bulgarian Turks living in the north, who would now be able to cross freely, he said:

As Bulgarian citizens, they are considered, as from the 1st January 2007, to be EU citizens, with the rights and responsibilities this entails. Their right as European citizens, to move freely to the areas controlled by the State, does not, of course, annul the enforcement and application of the relevant laws of the Republic of Cyprus, as long as these laws are harmonized with the *acquis communautaire*. On the basis of these laws, the persons in question have committed the offence of illegal entry and stay in the Republic and may have possibly violated the property rights of displaced Greek-Cypriots. Bulgarian Turks (*Turkovúlghari*) who live in the occupied areas, can rightfully pass to the areas controlled by the Government of the Republic of Cyprus. But they cannot be absolutely certain that they will not be criminally prosecuted for their illegal entry and stay in the Republic of Cyprus. (PIO, 5/1/07)

At a time when the property litigation reviewed in the chapter 4 was at its peak, with the *Apostolides v. Orams* case having set a precedent for prosecuting non-Cypriots on property violations, this statement carried particular weight. It suggested that whereas Bugarian Turks could not be arrested for entering the Republic on crossing the Buffer Zone, they could be arrested and indeed prosecuted for living in a Greek-Cypriot property, in some cases for years prior to their otherwise lawful crossing to the south.

I would read this statement as a sovereignty claim against the EU's exceptionalization of this particular group of settlers who would be the prime targets of sanctions had they not been European citizens. But it appears to be a claim of questionable applicability, a claim that targets individual persons, persons who are informed that they are at risk of prosecution on a case-by-case basis. If the opposite of refugee determination could be legally formulated, this might be a starting point. A destination country is here extending not protection but persecution based on individual circumstance. The tensions and contestations around the 1951 Convention are playing out here vis-à-vis EU laws regulating freedom of movement, work, and settlement. Arguably, an unintended effect of policy laundering could also be discerned, whereby EU laws that enable settlement are legitimizing what other instruments (such as Article 49 of the Fourth Geneva Convention) might have termed a "war crime"—as the Republic maintains. At the same time, this means that targets of discrimination are rendered agents of war crimes, then subjects of European rights, before again being targeted for prosecution.

Emin and his family are candidates par excellence for this type of prosecution. Yet he was never arrested in the Republic for having lived in the north and possibly having violated Greek-Cypriot property rights—nor was his visiting family when they crossed to see him. Indeed, one may ask how it might have been possible for checkpoint guards to know whether or not they lived in Greek-Cypriot property. In the utterance of this possibility of arrest therefore, there is yet once more a performance of sovereignty. The force here is illocutionary (Austin 1962, 94–108) in as far as it demands that Bulgarian Turks do not cross to the south; and perlocutionary in as far as its unstated consequence is to deter some people from crossing, mostly Turkish-Cypriots. In announcing its powers to arrest, the state is becoming the decision-maker on the Schmittian exception. The practically impossible case-specific prosecution that it describes is, in its solely verbal pronouncement, an act of sovereignty.

In this sense, we might consider that the performativity of such sovereign speech acts as the opposite of Althusserian interpellation. The policeman's hail that Althusser speaks of (1970; also Butler 1997b) is meant to elicit an automatic response that stems from fear of arrest. And it does so for those who are most likely to be arrested, those who, as Althusser says, "have something on their conscience" (ibid.). Elsewhere (Demetriou 2013), I have suggested that this something need not be a legal infraction per se; it could also be a sense of vulnerability to the law, as when one is a minority subject. What the performative announcement does here is quite different but nevertheless an interesting counter-situation. The state is here saying, "I might be arresting you," but it is actually, in addressing its own public, suggesting this—"I might be arresting them." It does not expect Bulgarian Turks to hear the threat, and indeed, if I am to judge from Emin, neither do they hear it, nor are they interpellated by it. It is as though they are ushered on, Rancière-like, rather than being interpellated. And yet, an interpellatory remainder persists.

The subjects whom it interpellates are a different kind of minority; they are the subjects of that unrecognized Other, who could never properly be thought of as a sovereign. They are Turkish-Cypriots, who indeed heard this call of possible prosecutions on a case-by-case basis among the clamor of property litigation, and to a noticeable degree refrained from crossing the border around that time, fearing they would be sued for living in Greek-Cypriot homes. It is them who are the abjected subjects of this performative sovereignty as it announces its presence. But because it announces its presence via some other subjects (Bulgarian Turks), those other subjects become entangled in that terrain of the crevice where the performance of sovereignty and the interpellation of the state grind against each other. Abjection is constitutive of the crevices I examine.

Like Emin, many non-nationals in Cyprus experience such entanglement in the crevices of the Cyprus conflict. They are recognized refugees, asylum seekers, irregular and regular migrants. These categories, as we will see, call forth a concept of protection and state responsibility that jars with the staple image of the refugee as a national victim-subject. The result is that people become caught up in crevices of law and policy, which although designed on the premise of one set of ideas about the nation, is expected within a global system of protection to implement quite different techniques of statehood. This poses wider questions about the presumptions of international law—that refugees flee from conflict into safety—whereas in practice, in Cyprus as elsewhere, they often find themselves fleeing from one conflict situation into another.

BUREAUCRATS AS PEOPLE, AND VICE VERSA

Ronî is one of a few hundred Kurds who live in southern Cyprus. He came to the island from his hometown in Turkey in the mid-2000s in order to escape the possibility of further incarceration after he was released as part of a political prisoners' amnesty. He had been held in various prisons for the previous eight years for his part in the Kurdish independence movement and was tortured on a number of occasions. He initially went to northern Cyprus and after a few weeks crossed the Green Line clandestinely. He applied for asylum on arrival and was recognized as a refugee a few years later. Ronî took up EU-funded Greek language lessons, found work as an electrician, and soon managed to move out of the rundown hotel where he initially lodged. Looking back retrospectively in 2010, Ronî had little complaint on his treatment by the authorities:

> Bureaucracy is a problem in any state of the world ... that's the communist perspective; ... It's true; refugees (*mülteci*) do face problems here. But on the other hand you need to understand these people

(*halk*) too, who face their own problems. Their country has been divided in two; their heart is divided, just like our heart is divided in four parts [between the countries in which Kurdistan lies]. I understand this, and very well. What can you expect from these persons (*ınsanlar*)?

Ronî's approach to authorities is suggestive of the governmentality I have been examining, even as it projects a positive experience. It is an approach explicitly inflected via his political commitments to the Kurdish question. He readily sees the similarities between Cyprus and Kurdistan in a way that is compatible, if not quite identified with hegemonic Greek-Cypriot rhetoric. With the common enemy, Turkey, firmly implanted in the background, for Ronî, who has since his settlement in Nicosia socialized with left-wing activists, the main characteristic of this commonality is not nationalism but reunification. In this sense, Ronî seems acutely aware of the political terrain he treads in southern Cyprus. His quotation speaks of three categories of people: refugees, for which he used the Turkish *mültecı*; and *ınsanlar*, which would translate as "people" from the Turkish but in an individualized sense of persons; and *halk*, people in the communal sense—that is, the people of the country. As an explanation of his experience with the state, the first two are on opposing sides: himself as refugee on one side, individual bureaucrats (persons) on the other side. What bridges them is the mentality of community (*halk*), seen in the sense of a national cause. In other words, Ronî is suggesting, in the same breath that he has denied problems with authorities, that where these exist, they stem from the governmentality of conflict.

That governmentality orders the entire field of citizenship and its absence. At the end of 2015, there were 56,413 valid permits issued in the Republic for a variety of reasons: domestic work (18,549), foreign businesses (2,133), family members of Cypriot nationals (6,255), family reunification (1,683), long-term residents (217), students (2,703), visitors (5,459), trafficking victims (7), other "special" permits (5,459), and other "general" permits (7,840). Of these, 6,108 were issued under the category "international protection" (*dhiethnís prostasía*).[7] This category includes refugee status, humanitarian status, and subsidiary protection under the terms of the 1951 Convention and its 1967 Protocol, and the transpositions of EU directives on complementary protection.[8] Ronî's status is considered one of the most privileged among these categories, allowing him to live, work, and travel freely in the south. Many of the other categories come with restrictions, in law or in practice.[9] But as Roni readily recognizes, this privileged status arises from assumptions, on the part of bureaucrats who belong to the Greek-Cypriot people, about what constitutes a refugee.

Such individual bureaucrats read these numbers in particular ways. Speaking on a panel on "the demographic and migration problem in Cyprus" in December 2013, the director of the Civil Registry and Migration Department had this to say in conclusion to her presentation on the results of the 2011 census:

> In other words, roughly one in every four residents in the free areas of the Republic, which, subtracting the Turkish-Cypriots, number 772,000 approximately, is a non-Cypriot … a careful reading of the numbers leads to the conclusion … [that] in the Republic, the Greek-Cypriots, about 572,000 constitute a minority. … I reckon, therefore, that a demographic and migration policy must be planned and executed with targeted measures aiming at the protection and preservation of our ethnic identity and culture as well as the preservation of the population proportion (*plithizmiakí analoyía*) in Cyprus.[10]

The director's reference to "population proportion" is the major point on which her "careful reading of the numbers" turns. Even though this reference is not made explicit, it is one that most Greek-Cypriots would recognize as reference to the population proportions on which the Constitution of the Republic is founded—that is, the understanding that the citizens of the Republic of Cyprus are of two kinds, Greek-Cypriots and Turkish-Cypriots (Articles 1, 2, 3), who at the time the Constitution came into force in 1960, comprised 80 percent and 18 percent of the population, respectively. These proportions feature integrally in historical narratives of the conflict, often to emphasize the Greek-Cypriot claim to proportional representation, which in the nationalist script appears as the point of injustice: the Constitution gave a 30 percent stake to Turkish-Cypriots in the parliament, government, public service, and security forces (Articles 62, 123, 130) and 40 percent in the army and for an initial period the security forces too (Article 129, 130). It is this imbalance that a future settlement should redress. In a context where these representational provisions have been void since 1963, the main reason for the concern to keep the population proportions intact is therefore the ongoing (if often faltering) peace process. Diachronically, negotiations over a settlement have concerned the federal structure of the government as well as the amount of territory each federated state will control and hence the amount of land and properties expected to revert to Greek-Cypriot hands. These matters, which could impact the distribution of power, ethnically determined as it is, hinge on arguments about demographic data. This is why Turkish policies to populate the north by incentivizing Turkish nationals through land and property offers to settle there (Erdal Ilican 2011), have been such a sore point for Greek-Cypriot policy and are its first line of attack on the level of international diplomacy. And because state-sponsored alongside globalization-driven migration has inevitably altered these proportions, Greek-Cypriot politicians and diplomats often claim that they are fighting a difficult battle on the negotiating table, where they argue on the basis of facts, which are now outdated by four decades.

The last time this battle codified an outcome was appendix F of the Annan Plan's fifth version, which calls on the two sides to each prepare a list of forty-five thousand names of individuals who would gain federal citizenship upon enforcement of the plan. This number essentially refers to the number of settlers (i.e., non-Turkish-Cypriots, in the north) to whom the Greek-Cypriot side could accept extending citizenship (Greek-Cypriot discourse has presented them as "settlers who will stay"). And experts closely following the process have suggested, although not publicly, that this number essentially refers to a trade-off of migrants in the south for settlers in the north. Indeed, the last census before the Annan Plan was finalized, carried out in 2001, counted roughly 33,700 individuals who would have had a claim to freedom of work and residence in the Republic after enlargement, either as EU citizens or Cyprus-born foreigners (even though Cypriot citizenship is not strictly speaking based on *jus soli*, claims for naturalization based on birth and upbringing would be likely to succeed).[11] In other words, migration demographics would have been used as a yardstick to measure the extent of concessions that one could afford vis-à-vis the demands of the other side in the peace negotiation process. Furthermore, by not acknowledging this biopolitical logic publicly, one could afford to present such concessions as much more compromising than they might have been.

The EU-Turkey statement allowing Syrians migrants to be exchanged for refugees one for one between the two areas, readily springs to mind as a current example of how easily the demographic translation of people into numbers renders migrant bodies a site for performing a biopolitics of neglect—by which I mean biopolitics that dispense with their subjects as easily as they make them the focus of attention. In both of these cases, migrants, refugees, or foreigners waiting at the doors of citizenship, may be the focus of attention as far as treaties or peace plans are concerned—but it is well over their heads that interstate bargaining occurs. Thinking of this in the context of a different crisis in 2011, the global financial crisis, Saskia Sassen has asked why it is that "[w]e have an 'immigration crisis' every time we have a crisis about no matter what" (2011).[12] Her multiple answers suggest to her fundamental problems with immigration policy: how it is conceived, what it assumes, and how it is implemented. I would like to use my data from Cyprus to highlight the fact, also poignantly shown by Stevens for the US (2017b), that immigration policy is often not flawed in spite of itself but exactly because its performance is duplicitous.

This is often keenly felt and understood by those subjected to these governmentalities. In stark contrast to Ronî's sympathy for the work of bureaucrats who, after all, belong to "a people," Yakup had a different take on the intricacies of the Cyprus problem. Pondering the positive climate within which peace negotiations were conducted in the summer of 2015, creating hopes for an imminent agreement, he worried about his future. Yakup was a recognized Kurdish refugee like Ronî, in the south. Yakup feared that an agreement on the Cyprus issue would reunify the island and would allow his arrest. If the legal situation between the two sides normalized, he reasoned, the Turkish warrant still out for his arrest would be executed. We discussed the principles of refugee protection under the 1951 Convention that logically, I argued, would not have allowed the conclusion of an agreement that would put people at risk. He was not convinced. He did not believe that the Greek-Cypriot state and its bureaucrats, once in coexistence with Turkish-Cypriots and their administration tied to Turkey as it is, would any longer care to protect the freedom of people like him. In a situation of political flux, he seemed to be suggesting, bureaucrats who act as a people would be likely to align their practice to the priorities of the community—which could amount to cooperation just as easily as it previously amounted to ethnic enmity.

He was afraid in other words, of a bureaucracy which acts not mechanically as an Eichmann doing "a good job" in Arendt's celebrated treatise (1963), but indeed as a people who act politically, who want to reunite their country and who finally do so. In that apocalyptic moment, ethnicity would matter just as much as it does today, only that the privilege that goes with it would be reversed. "And even if the law does not allow them to send me back," Yakup ultimately asked, "who is to say that I will not be taken away in the middle of the night?" As I began to formulate a pacifying response, I thought back to activist friends in Athens, who had documented cases of abduction of Kurdish refugees in Greece and their transfer and imprisonment in Turkey. The border there is regulated by Schengen rules. I did not offer a response.

In the crevices between migration and the Cyprus conflict can lurk both the reach of the law and its suspension. And both can be equally frightful. And what seems homely in those crevices also comes with its own power structures. Bahar came to Cyprus as a student in the mid-2000s on a fake passport. She was fleeing her country, part of the former Soviet Union, where she was persecuted for her political activity for the rights of the Turkish minority, a group to which she belongs. She managed to make her way to Western Europe and apply for asylum there, only to be returned to Cyprus via the then-active Dublin II Directive.[13] She faced initial hostility, especially when the police interviewing her realized she spoke more Turkish than Russian; and she was detained. But she was eventually released, her claim examined, and she was given papers. One of the people who helped her was a Kurdish refugee, who knew the system and guided her through it. This intervention may have been critical. But it came at a cost. When they fell out and he became abusive, he reminded her that he made her who she was, that she could have been nothing without him—he meant she would not have been recognized as a refugee. From the things he said, this hurt the most.

In some sense, the bureaucratic sense, Bahar was indeed made a refugee by her Kurdish acquaintance. As a member of a Turkic minority group, she would not likely have fulfilled the criteria of bureaucrats acting as a people that implicate the Cyprus conflict in their interpretation of refugee protection. Yet in an unanticipated alliance with a fellow Turkish speaker, she was able to create refuge exactly in those crevices meant to deflect her. And then again, this refuge came at a cost, when that crevice was no longer homey. Within the ethnic logic that aligns the Cyprus conflict to refugeehood in the 1951 Convention sense, Bahar fell on the wrong side of the border, even if, paradoxically, she had not entered via the Green Line. But within that very same logic, individual agency could be utilized in unexpected ways. But in the multiple structures of power created in the process of inflecting refugee subjects across the Greco-Turkish dispute, individuals can come to subject each other. Agency can easily fall back onto state governmentality and become vocalized as the subjection demanded by an interpellated individual. How else can one demand recognition on the basis that "I made you [refugee]," if not via the demand that they be recognized as a hailing policeman's double?

MIGRATION ON THE LINE

The Green Line does not just inflect migration where it has a Turkish component, as in the cases of Ronî, Emin, Yakup, and Bahar. A Syrian refugee recognized much before war erupted in his country tells me of the battles he has had to fight, and the ongoing discrimination he experiences because of his Muslim faith. It renders him suspect, a proxy-Turk, he often feels. And it is not isolated individuals who draw this equation, and who may occasionally be found in bureaucratic posts. Off the southern coast in 2015, at the height of the war, following the floundering of a boat carrying Syrian migrants, the Minister of the Interior, speaking about an EU decision to allocate Syrian refugee quotas to member states, said that Cyprus would seek to take in three hundred refugees, preferably Orthodox Christians. And after being lambasted for blatant racism, he defended his stance explaining that this is because it would be easier for them to adjust to life in Cyprus.[14] The implied recognition that the Republic is inhospitable to Muslims, failed, by comparison to his original statements, to spark a debate about why this is so.

The Green Line inflects the experiences of non-Muslims too. The Asian waiter I met in the north is not exceptional in choosing to flee to the other side in order to remain in Cyprus or in the region. I also heard of a domestic worker who fled her employment due to exhausting conditions—one amid scores of similar stories of labor exploitation and abuse that researchers have been documenting for years (Agathangelou 2004; Trimikliniotis and Pantelides 2003). She resorted to crossing the Green Line, securing a work visa for Turkey and informing her relatives still in Cyprus that she had found much better conditions in Istanbul. Crossing the Green Line was also a measure of last resort for a Russian mother who, abused by her Greek-Cypriot husband and assured that no Cypriot court would give her custody of her children over a Cypriot national, left him and fled with the kids. Such stories abound, I found, among migrant communities who also learn to shape their strategies along that unspoken specter at the center of migration policy that is the Cyprus conflict.

After all, migrants have lived on the Green Line since the 1990s and their presence there has shaped Nicosia's development as a space of division, ruination, and then gentrification. Postwar, areas near the border were considered insecure and were left to wither, abjected like the spaces on the opposite side of the border that Navaro-Yashin talks about (2012). This made them cheap to rent and therefore attractive to migrant residents and businesses. The multicultural aspect of inner city Nicosia developed, in other words, because of the existence of the division. A 2004 survey of all households in the old within-the-walls city, carried out for the UN Operation for Project Services (UNOPS 2004) just at the point before the old town began gentrifying found that among 2,492 individuals surveyed, about half were Greek-Cypriots, the rest being Pontiac (16 percent), and nationals of India (7 percent), the Philippines (5 percent), Pakistan (4 percent), Russia (3 percent), Greece (3 percent), Sri Lanka (3 percent) and China (2 percent). The local elementary school (*Phaneromeni*) still boasts an exceptionally multicultural student body made up of over 90 percent foreign nationals and is one of the few schools island-wide to be classified as one of "educational priority"—meaning that targeted integration policies are designed and tested there. As the area has been gentrifying, in accelerated pace since the opening of a crossing point in 2008, it is becoming a gravitation center for various urban activist initiatives (Erdal Ilican 2013; 2017; Iliopoulou and Karathanasis, 2014).

Such division-inflected multiculturalism extends beyond the walls of Nicosia too. Social-housing estates, originally built to house Greek-Cypriot refugees in the capital's outskirts, are increasingly inhabited by migrants, a member of the Pancyprian Union of Refugees noted in an interview back in 2008. This was facilitated by policies providing ownership titles to Greek-Cypriot refugees. As the refugees moved out of their flats and into better accommodation, the new titles allowed them to rent the properties at affordable prices to migrants—and perhaps foreign refugees too. Territorially then, as much as in policy terms and on the affective level, the politics of the conflict is implicated in the landscape of migration. The topological imprint of refugeehood persists in spaces governmentalized as refugee *topoi* even as different populations of refugees come to inhabit them.

Kofinou camp registers this implication starkly. It is a reception center for asylum seekers, providing accommodation in prefab, one- or two-room houses, and some social services, to selected migrants who apply for refugee protection and whose claims are being examined. It is located four kilometers from the village of Kofinou in the southeastern district of Larnaca, two kilometers from the Menogeia detention center holding migrants who are due to be expelled, five kilometers from the ground center of a major TV satellite, and until 2013, less than a kilometer from the country's main abattoir. Monitoring organizations have referred to the location of the center as problematic in terms of effective access to Nicosia (forty kilometers away) and to opportunities for integration (KISA 2008; FWC 2015). Their complaints were attended by concerns over hygiene, overcrowding, quality of facilities, and working policies. Since those complaints, the centre has doubled its capacity, and although some facilities have been upgraded, problems persist.

But Kofinou is above all another site of territorial abjection. The asylum seekers it houses are not simply pushed away from governmental and public view, amid expellees in waiting, slaughtered animals and extraterrestrial communication lines. They are also emplaced in a space of past violence, where in November 1967, National Guard and police personnel attacked the Turkish-Cypriot village and its neighboring village of Ayios Theodoros and killed twenty-two people, at least three of them elderly civilians, the others presumably members of the TMT, while losing one of their own (Patrick 1976, 135–36). That event had been a turning point in the conflict, for having elicited the first clear threat of invasion by Turkey. It also resulted in the expulsion of EOKA leader Grivas from Cyprus (until his clandestine return in 1973 to direct an openly paramilitary force). And it caused Makarios to dramatically shift his discourse about what the Greek-Cypriot side should expect in the intercommunal negotiations from the "desirable" (*efktéo*) to the "feasible" (*efiktó*). After the division of 1974, the government settled Greek-Cypriot refugees in the now-abandoned Turkish-Cypriot village.

Sofia worked as a social worker at Kofinou Center and is familiar with the village down the hill. She spoke, in 2014, in desperation about the social conditions in both places. The community of Cypriot refugees in the village is highly impoverished, plagued by long-term unemployment, and at times trying social relations. The school, which children from the Reception Center also attend alongside village kids is a site of multiple challenges, where attainment is mired by the differing but equally disempowering structural conditions of the two societies and compounded by linguistic constraints. This stifled interaction between displaced Greek-Cypriots and foreign asylum seekers is paradigmatic of the structural conditions that determine refugeehood in Cyprus at the interstices of local and international interpretations. Kofinou is not a symbol or a metonym. It is the direct result of a governmentality built on the affective, legal, and territorial registration of loss on an ethnic matrix of which Turkish-Cypriots are the abject referent. And which on this abjection displaces the minor losses of impoverished others, even as it extends state care to them.

SEVEN UNHOMELY SUBJECTS

SANDBAGS HAVE TO BE SEWN

In the various war-photography collections from Cyprus that I have browsed over the years, two images have stood out (figure 7.1). One is from 1963. It features a group of women sewing. They are Turkish-Cypriots, and they are sewing sandbags presumably to be used in the defensive barricades set up around the enclaves. The other is in 1974; it shows a group of mostly women and children, of fair complexions, having drinks in front of a set of urinals—this caption says they are tourists caught in the crossfire and stranded in Ledra Palace Hotel. The two images offer different angles on the gendered impact of war. Both of the images are unsurprising. The first, providing a glimpse of women's assistance in the war effort is telling of a military division of labor that puts men in the trenches and women at home producing the material infrastructure to construct these trenches. It is a well-known aspect of women's history, repeated many times in modern warfare, when women have been given tasks away from combat but so relevant to it (Woollacott 1994; Summerfield 1998; Turpin 1998; de Pauw 2014). The second is an even more iconic image of victimization in war, where the victims are primarily women and children. In Greek, the single word *yinekópedha* (women-children) transmits, in humanitarian contexts, the sense of singularity in such subjectivity of victimhood.

The two pictures communicate part of the variability of minor losses I have been sketching throughout the book. The first image speaks of the losses of those who have been effaced by the greater losses of others around them: displaced Turkish-Cypriot women looking apprehensively at the lens as they contribute to the war effort. Bystanders are visible in the background, suggesting perhaps that the subjects, like in so many other aspects of the

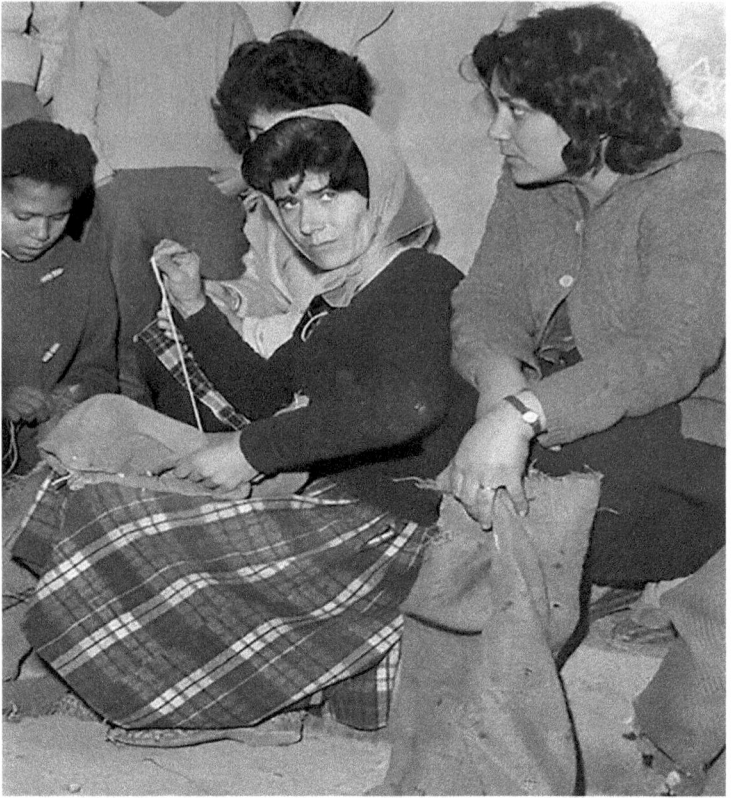

FIGURE 7.1. Turkish-Cypriot women sewing sandbags in December 1963, © AP images (top); tourists and nurse stranded in Ledra Palace Hotel in 1974, © Harry Dempster/Hulton Archive/Getty Images/Ideal Image (bottom).

conflict narrative, are aware of their performance in front of the lens. Even with such efforts to document women's contribution however, their agency remains largely bypassed. In Greek-Cypriot discourse, which has silenced Turkish-Cypriot displacement altogether, Turkish-Cypriot women are absent from 1960s history, apart from one case: the morally reprehensible figure of the woman killed along with her boyfriend in an infamous neighborhood in Nicosia in the early hours of December 21, 1963 and which sparked the clashes now recognized as the trigger of the tragedy that followed. In Turkish-Cypriot discourse, Turkish-Cypriot women become proxy-warriors, replicas of their male counterparts, signaling communal unity in the national cause.

The second image now, depicts the calibration of loss through the extremity of those nearly laughable losses at the opposite end of abjection: the losses of cosmopolitan visitors, placed across the spectrum from refugees (Nyers 2003), scared and inconvenienced by an unexpected war and waiting to be airlifted out. This absurdity and the effacement of other losses are related through the image of femininity.

In Cyprus, women's involvement in the war effort, rare as it is, extends normally to feeding and sheltering: in commemorative TV programs, mention is made of Greek-Cypriot women who hid soldiers at home, fed them, or helped them escape into safe territory as the Turkish army was advancing. These are big shifts that make heroes and victims mark out the crisis by assigning a different subject position to them. Amid the busts of heroes that grace the landscape, those of women are counted in single digits, most female figures being used generically to represent the country. From the EOKA days, stories are often told of women being used to smuggle ammunition or correspondence in fake pregnant bellies or grocery baskets past British soldiers, while the memoir of Elenitsa Seraphim-Loizou (1983 [2000]), the only woman to become area commander for EOKA, is a rare exception of female militant leadership. This role was allegedly connected to her former lowly profession as a hairdresser, which gave her little honor to protect, and "nothing to lose" from taking on a masculine role (Nayia Kamenou, personal communication)." Turkish-Cypriot women's efforts have similarly been acknowledged recently in sewing TMT caps and socks, working in the underground Bayrak radio station, and helping fighters. These were exceptional women, we are told, doing mundane female things. Socks and not sandbags are the products of their labor that history remembers.

The women sewing the sandbags however, do not seem exceptional. They are normal women in mundane everyday tasks, which have nevertheless been rendered exceptional, surpassing mundane tasks of care. The first image is strange not in itself, but as an image of the conflict. The strangeness of the second image is perhaps more plain to see. Here, the conflict is part of the frame—it is indexed by the urinals in the background, a brunette in white who is presumably a staff nurse, and the chair on which the drinks tray sits, a chair turned table. This image is strange because it depicts an unfamiliar view of conflict: not the guns, the soldiers, or people fleeing or being taken captive. It depicts people not visibly in panic (as seen in the images of women screaming in despair, mentioned in chapter 3). It depicts people nevertheless unnerved and in need of stiff drinks, the empty bottle of what seems to be a strong alcohol sitting in the tray.

In Barthesian terms, the puncta of the images, the sandbags in one and urinals in the other, create the "blind fields" (Barthes 1981, 56–57) that allow a reading beyond the graphically obvious—they allow an expansive, as Barthes would say, interpretation of the conflict (ibid., 45). Death, in these images, lurks hidden in the background of these seemingly mundane ways of coping with militarized lives. It is not as readily read as it is in the sight of tanks, guns, military uniforms, parachutes, hands behind heads, and mouths open in screams that prop up public perceptions of the conflict on both sides. I want to suggest that these puncta "prick" (ibid., 47) because they speak of that wound that carries the conflict beyond that moment of fighting and loss of life. They speak of those other minor losses incurred as the conflict is normalized and made part of daily life. In the very transgressions that these puncta depict— women sewing not dowry items but military equipment or women resting in the wrong toilets—something much more penetrating is being depicted of the Cyprus conflict. It is the fact that it has governmentally maneuvered women, as Enloe puts it (2000) into positions that facilitate the militarization of life in general and render it "homey." It is this work that this chapter explores. Such maneuvering, I argue, steers women into crevices that determine their roles, their political subjectivity, and the terms of their agency. As other scholars have noted, it makes citizenship, "despite claims to universality . . . patriarchal and restrictive of women's full and equal participation as citizens" (Rygiel 2010, 38).

The focus of this chapter is the range of gender-based exclusions arising from the governance of refugeehood in Cyprus. The military conflict left more men than women dead, but it is the women who have been tasked with the work of mourning. According to the Pancyprian Association of Parents and Relatives of Undeclared Prisoners and Missing Persons, of the 1,619 missing Greek-Cypriots (a number that as chapter 2 shows has been put in question), only 116 are women.[1] And of the five hundred missing Turkish-Cypriots listed by the Ministry of the Interior, ninety-nine are women, and eighty-one of those have "disappeared" in the mass killings of the three villages of Aloa, Maratha, and Sandallar on August 14, 1974 (see chapter 2). Among the coup dead, which the same Ministry counts, six are women among sixteen civilians and ninety-eight total deaths.

For all the literature on the Cyprus conflict, the numbers of Cypriot refugees are not broken down by gender. Yet the impact of displacement has had a gendered aspect from the beginning. On Greek-Cypriot refugees, Zetter noted in 1994 that women's roles in displacement shifted as communities were dispersed and relations of trust and exchange, otherwise dependent on women's work, were severed (1994, 316–17). The PIO report of 1974, which esti-mates there were 191,259 Greek-Cypriot refugees, allocates them into a rough figure of forty thousand families (1974, 50), in most of which women's earning capacity would have to increase or take a leading role. Loizos's ethnographic film study *Sophia and her People* (1985) of refugees surviving displacement, which takes the story of a refugee woman leading the wider family in a suc-cessful bakery business, provides another indication of changing gender roles. Among Turkish-Cypriots, where the militarization of life and confinement to camps was longer, such shifts might have occurred earlier but could also have been less accentuated. And yet, in the public imagery on both sides, it has not been empowerment but the victimization of women that has maintained the discourse. Recall that it was initially a woman-and-child pair that depicted the refugee victim on the relief-fund stamp.

This is unsurprising in the history of refugeehood. Today, ref-ugees come under focus as victims of humanitarian intervention particularly through the images of young women, pregnant women, and mothers with children. These conditions, calibrated under "vulnerability criteria" are also ones prioritized for relocation in the 2016 EU-Turkey statement, constituting single young men as the least likely population to be protected. Women's role in migration-related decisions, even when they are not the ones leaving, is yet to be properly analyzed. The women-as-victims frame (rather than women as decision-makers) is particularly resilient to subversion and contributes to what Hyndman and Giles (2011) have termed the "feminization of asylum." This refers to the separation of refugees into gendered categories and the concomitant governmentality of their movement and immobility, which has been in place since the beginning of processes of externalization of European borders. Prior to the appearance of migrant women in dinghies off the Greek coast in 2015, or pregnant asylum seekers in Ireland (Luibhéid 2013), this feminization meant their confinement to camps outside the EU and the viewing of males who crossed the frontier as warriors. And on its opposite end, the same feminization is leading global policy makers to announce "women, peace and security" as areas of priority that seeks to place women at the front line of the War on Terror, making them responsible for raising sons who will not become terrorists (Ní Aoláin 2016).

In places such as Cyprus, where refugeehood is a permanent status that persists postconflict or in protracted conflict, or indeed Palestine, where as Salih writes (2017), women register conflict temporality on their bodies, questions about the reconstruction of life—social, political, infrastructural, and affective—open up. These questions require that women's labor be specifically taken into account, in ways that determine their agency. I am arguing here that the processes of women's visibility, empowerment, and disempowerment work on a continuum between conflict, refugeehood, and migration. To take a gendered perspective on the everyday of postconflict subjectivity, therefore, under the terms suggested in the introduction to section I, is to look across this continuum in a genealogical way. Indeed, could we not see the main demands of the three waves of feminism as being intimately tied to postconflict subjectivities and conditions? When the vote was finally granted to women in the aftermath of WWI and due to lack of voting men?[2] And when the demands of the second feminist wave for social rights were answered in conjunction with women's entry to the labor force during and after WWII?[3] Or when the recognition of identity pluralities of ethnicity and sexuality came to the fore after the breakdown of the dichotomic separation of the Cold War?[4] The postconflict formation of subjectivity in Cyprus can be seen within such a field of rights claiming and rights granting between genders, circumscribed by relations of power but also succeeding in shifting them, ever so slightly. Refugee women are the first category to exemplify this.

WE CANNOT ALL BE REFUGEES

In May 2004, the Republic's High Court quashed an appeal to consider the constitutionality of the interpretation of the category "displaced person" by government officials (*Vrountou v. Republic,* case 436/2003). The decision cites two Ministerial Council decisions—one from September 1974, the other from April 1995, in which successively, "displaced person" is held to refer to those who lost access to their permanent residence as a result of the Turkish invasion and, in 1995, to those who lost property in the occupied areas. A third instrument, at the center of the appeal, is a circular from September 1975 from the Director of the Care and Rehabilitation of Displaced Persons Service. This circular instructs officials at the Service to consider displaced a non-displaced wife, "who is registered on her husband's displacement card" as well as his children, but not the non-displaced husband or their children of a displaced wife "who cannot be considered displaced" (ibid.). A "refugee card" as it is better known, provides its bearers access to housing and other benefits, as well as registration in the voting catalogues of the districts from which they have been displaced. In recent years, and as a result of this case, refugee cards have been separated from "certifications of displaced status," the first providing access to benefits, the other regulating voting localities.

The court decision also tells us that this circular was related to and approved by the Ministerial Council in April 1994 (i.e., nineteen years after it was issued). Reconsidering the validity of such approval in their April 1995 meeting, the same council further explained that despite repeated requests to include the families of refugee mothers in the interpretation of "displaced," such an expansion of the term could not be approved because (a) the real percentages of the displaced will be altered; (b) according to a relevant estimate by the Statistics and Research Department, the percentage of displaced people in that case would eventually rise to 80 percent of the whole population of Cyprus; and (c) there will be a disproportional rise in the voters registered in occupied districts, and this would affect the parliamentary seats apportioned to each electoral district (ibid.). Having presented these facts, the Court finally deemed that to decide on the constitutionality of the policies resulting from these decisions would be tantamount to calling for new legislation and thus acting as a constitutional monitor, a role that it interprets as outside its jurisdiction: "such an undertaking would be academic," the Court states (ibid.).

In reconstructing in this section the terrains across which the differential policies on refugee women have been shaped, I want to keep in mind the performative aspects of the discourse on loss that I have been emphasizing throughout the book. Specifically in this ruling, I want to suggest that the Ministerial Council's 1995 reasoning on displaced demographics, as well as the Court's shirking from the academic exercise of monitoring constitutional application through the design of new laws, communicate similar takes on governmentality. On the one hand, the Ministerial Council, speaking in the context whereby a new generation of children are coming of age in refugee settlements and seeking a continuation of their refugee benefits (primarily consisting of housing schemes), recognizes that the rhetoric of "generalized refugeehood" can be just that—rhetoric. The 80 percent projection is presented as a way of making obvious the ludicrousness of the suggestion that "we are all refugees"—a suggestion that this precise generation of children had been hearing on a daily basis. Radical as Dimitris's deconstruction of this rhetoric (chapter 4) may be, the Ministerial Council seems to agree with him.

At the very same moment, the vagueness of such a projection cannot but itself be read as rhetorical. At this short performative moment, rhetoric is announced as performance, and that announcement is unmistakably performative too. And in conjunction with that rhetorical flair, it is also being recognized that the reason we cannot all be refugees, the truth of the matter, is callously political: that Kyrenia and Famagusta (in its major part) can be maintained only as minor representative units in parliament and cannot be given a decisive say over the futures of free areas such as Nicosia, Limassol, or Paphos, just because refugee descendants live there. Under current laws, Kyrenia district has three seats in parliament and Famagusta eleven (including the areas not occupied) out of a total of fifty-six. In the municipal elections of 2016, around thirty thousand voters were registered in occupied areas of a total of 430,000.[5] A massive increase to these balances might mean that refugee representatives in parliament and local administration no longer focus mainly on policies around remembrance, the negotiation of return, and performatives around the conflict, as these "occupied municipalities" currently do, but might potentially also design policy across the political spectrum. In this sense, refugee motherhood becomes a platform for articulating the biopolitical power structures of refugeehood. The Supreme Court, on the other hand, endorses this biopower, declaring a lack of law, but proclaiming itself not sovereign enough to ameliorate this lack. The gap awaiting exceptional decisions is announced but not filled. A sovereign remains silent.

But I also want to suggest that despite the candid explanation of the Ministerial Council, there is still something not articulated in the performance of recognizing that we cannot all be refugees. This is the almost facile argument that the state cannot sustain housing provisions to 80 percent of the population. But even though this can be widely understood to constitute an imagined point (d) of the Council's considerations, it remains unarticulated. The inability of the state to care for its subjects is more difficult to verbalize than the cold politics of vested interests in parliamentary seats. The state, in other words, would rather appear invested in party and local politics than seem unable to provide benefits. This is the biopolitical conundrum at the heart of the discourse of refugeehood, which the gender question, in the many forms examined in this chapter, raises. Through the figure of refugee mothers, the generality of loss is undermined as practice and maintained as rhetoric. Biopower is asserted in the inability to care and in the exclusive and unquestioned power to name and categorize—(i.e., to create population). This is how the state performs.

The next stage of this legal case takes place in Strasbourg. There, the ECtHR ruled, in January 2016 (Case no. 33631/06) that there had been discriminatory treatment in the dispersal of housing assistance between the children of displaced men and those of displaced women and awarded to the daughter-claimant of such a displaced woman the equivalent of the housing assistance she had been refused in 2003, adjusted for inflation, and in addition to legal expenses and 4,000 euro for non-pecuniary damage. While the total sum of 32,000 euro is far off the 130,000 euro claimed by the applicant, the major point of the case lies in the Court's holistic assessment of the gender sensitivity of the housing benefit scheme for displaced persons:

> Finally, it is particularly striking that the scheme continued on the basis of this difference in treatment until 2013, nearly forty years after it was first introduced. The fact the scheme persisted for so long, and yet continued to be based solely on traditional family roles as understood in 1974, means that the State must be taken to have exceeded any margin of appreciation it enjoyed in this field. (ibid., §80)

The case has been widely hailed as an instance of democratic rectification, by gender organizations, equality bodies, and parties and politicians in the Republic. The Movement of Refugee and Displaced Mothers in particular, founded in 2005 on this specific cause, noted that the decision was one important step in the struggle for equality, which also includes the right to register the children of displaced women on the occupied electoral districts. After all, the Movement noted, the rights to housing benefits that have now been restored, are in any case inaccessible at the moment (in 2015, when the ECtHR decision was first announced) because of the moratoria imposed on a range of benefits in the context of the financial crisis. The president of the Movement herself, had had her own application at the ECtHR declared inadmissible a month later (November 2015, case no. 43331/09) on the basis of being out of time, since it was lodged with the ECtHR three years after the Supreme Court rejected her case on a similar basis to that of *Vrountou v. Republic*. Still, based on this decision, the Movement of refugee mothers has lodged new legal cases on behalf of other members.

At first glance this legal trajectory traces positive developments in the field of gender equality in Cypriot refugeehood. But I also want to suggest that it hints at a much more uncertain story about difficult subjectivities. The refugee women who sought housing rights embarked on a long legal process that is structurally related to the consolidation of a gender equality movement across Europe and in Cyprus. This is indicated by the Court's argument that "the advancement of gender equality is today a major goal in the member states of the Council of Europe and very weighty reasons would have to be put forward before such a difference in treatment could be regarded as compatible with the Convention in Cyprus" (ibid., §75). In Cyprus, the recognition that refugee mothers sought resonated with local NGOs and the Ombudsman's Equality Body, which welcomed the decision. But exactly on these counts, the governmental biopolitics in which female refugeehood is grounded, provide pause for thinking.

Much as the ECtHR seems to express chagrin at the state of affairs in Cyprus, the non-pecuniary damages of four thousand euros to an untrained eye at least, appear to belittle the emphasis given to the lack of "weighty reasons" that the government is chastised for. Even though the claimant had not provided valuations of such damage, she had provided an estimate of 112,000 euros for the loss she had suffered due to the fact that the denial of benefits in 2003 rendered her unable to benefit from the property boom in her area in the years intervening until her case was lodged. These valuations were rejected outright and evidently not considered as an effect of the discrimination in question, which non-pecuniary damage might redress.

Second, on the level of Cypriot gender politics, the plight of refugee mothers exposes a blind spot of the more general rhetoric on the Cyprus conflict and its losses that mires the discourse on rights. The Movement of refugee mothers has been successful, to the extent that it has, largely because it has employed a rhetoric in compliance with the hegemonic discourse on the conflict. The scandal over the discrimination against refugee mothers, the argument goes, is that the state discriminates against the very same people that should be recognized as mothers of the nation, as victims par excellence, as women who have struggled for the preservation of the state and the return of all refugees. In a letter to the president of the parliament on the occasion of a discussion of laws pertaining to voting rights in 2014, the Movement notes:

> We object to the endorsement of the Law regarding the election of members of the EU parliament, which grants the right to Turkish-Cypriots living in the occupied areas to vote . . . at the same moment at which you deny to matrilineal refugees the right to vote and be voted for in their places of origin.[6]

The letter goes on to highlight that Turkish-Cypriots live in a pseudo-state, do not pay taxes to the Republic, usurp our properties, litter Pendadhaktylos Mountain, and destroy our cultural heritage. The force of its argument hinges on the fact that while Turkish-Cypriot votes will have an impact on electoral results in the EU elections, refugee votes should be used to mitigate this impact presumably by selecting candidates who would highlight even more than they currently do, the plight of Greek-Cypriot victim populations. Thus, the critique against the state is mounted on the premise that the Movement's cause is a purer form of patriotism than the patriotism currently exhibited by the state.

In other words, what the story of these difficult subjects shows, is that the success of their counter-conduct is directly related to the ability of biopower to engulf critique while continuing to decide who gets a roof over their head and who does not, which victim discourse is to be celebrated and which to be quashed. This conundrum is not unique to Cyprus. Feminist literature has often found it difficult to articulate the views of nationalist women, and peace activism has often provided a better frame for exploring feminist dissent (Cockburn 1998; 2004; McWilliams 1995; Enloe 1989; Werbner 1999; Weber 2006). But the maneuvering of women via nationalism has also produced complications in liberal understandings of postconflict transitions, which critical studies have acknowledged (Aretxaga 1997; Helms 2003; 2013).

The case of matrilineal claims to refugeehood, which I have presented in this section, speaks to these difficulties. It highlights the challenge of intersectionality by showing how the frame of patriarchy creates inequalities across the social spectrum, adversely affecting all women and a good number of men too; but at the same time it also creates a terrain of fault lines across which feminist alliances are difficult, and often impossible. To reread Crenshaw's metaphor then (1989), from a different point of focus, intersectionality does not only tell us that marginalized women are doubly in danger of discrimination (as when they stand at an intersection). If seen from the point of view of victimhood already in place and not appearing to an integral subject as a possible threat (the woman who has been hit at the intersection and not just the woman standing there), once victimization occurs, the terrain of that intersection makes it all that more difficult to remedy (an ambulance is unlikely to come, from either direction). This is also pertinent to the treatment of gendered violence in conflict, which I examine later. These are different kinds of crevices formed by the same layers of military territorial splits, affective dispositions of victimhood and legal apparatus of managing ethnic difference that in becoming imbricated, form stress and breaking points. And in being different crevices they exert more manageable stresses on the structure, allowing it to endure despite its flaws. How exactly this has come to be is what I turn to next.

POSTCOLONIAL WOMEN

Sandbags have had to be sewn, literally and metaphorically, throughout the last seven decades. But the terms on which this work was carried out was determined by a military power order, which had little time for the subjects that actually carried it out. Over the two generations that have grown up immersed in the Cyprus conflict, postcolonial development has drawn hard racial and class lines around women's identities. The social aspirations of a growing, privileged urban class separated Nicosian women, for example, from the political reality experienced by other women, of ongoing violence and spreading mili-tarization. Some of these women were the Turkish-Cypriots sewing sandbags in the enclaves; some were their Greek-Cypriot neighbors who saw them leave and perhaps protested, as my great aunt did, the looting that ensued; others did the looting themselves, like Packard saw in his rounds with the Joint Force; still others, such as Arpik, moved in the opposite direction (i.e., out of Turkish-Cypriot enclaves), to be displaced in ways yet to be recognized. Women's expe-riences, at once engulfed by the conflict's general social dynamics and different, in bigger and smaller ways, from the men's, comprised the major and minor losses I have thus far been describing. But to look at them here particularly as a case of minor loss is to call attention specifically to the techniques through which all of the minor losses I have been talking about become engrained as little shifts throughout society—and as thus omnipresent also become unseen.

In the economically modernizing yet morally conservative and eth-nically cleansed society that was evolving post-independence, some women were expected to proceed as if nothing were amiss—sew their dowries or have them sewn, or cope with auxiliary tasks that paramilitaries weaved into their daily chores (Vassiliadou 1997; Agathangelou 2000; Cockburn 2004; Derya 2009; Hadjipavlou 2010). In the Nicosia suburb where I grew up, near the set-tlement of Omorphita where Turkish-Cypriots attempted to mount a resistance campaign after December 21, 1963, and were heavily attacked in the following days, the brutal killings of civilians—numbers unconfirmed in relevant lit-erature—were known. The images of a paramilitary leader Nicos Sampson posing on widely circulated photographs triumphantly waving the captured and disgraced Turkish flag as he led hundreds of hostages to captivity, loomed large in memories. His role in that event was also thought to have been among the key credentials that later propelled Sampson to the role of president in the coup of 1974. This knowledge made for furtive and resentful talk at home, talk of men demanding coffees from Greek-Cypriot housewives in the area after "they had done their day's job and were tired—how were we to know then what jobs these were?" my mother occasionally asked, recalling the moment she had been the teenage daughter of such a housewife.

Women's multiple roles as producers of the nation, transmitters of its culture, and participants in its modernization (Anthias 1989), were crafted on variable economic and ethnic registers, but crafted all the same. Silences, obfuscated by hegemonic rhetoric on the conflict, interwove intersectionally

(Crenshaw 1989) along categories of class, gender, and ethnicity. Societies on both sides have developed semblances of peace within the conflict. In earlier work on Ledra Palace (Demetriou 2012), I argued that the hotel offered a stage for Greek-Cypriot men and women to model their idealized roles as postcolonial subjects. In its opulent surroundings, ladies sipped tea and cocktails, danced, gossiped, admired art exhibitions, and played tennis, on a par with men (only the men discussed politics); but these surroundings were made opulent through the labor of Turkish-Cypriot chambermaids whose position in the social hierarchy was never a concern to their beneficiaries; later, this same lack of concern made possible the exploitation of migrant domestic and sex labor (Agathangelou 2004; Güven-Lisaniler et al. 2005).

In later years, when violence came into plain sight, Cypriot women, erstwhile vehicles of national modernity, were spotlighted as the victims of the aggression, in those graphic images from 1974, which emanated from the (again silenced) underbelly of that nationalism-modernity nexus. Later still, much of the conceptualization of peace in Cyprus has been built on this gendered division of political labor—with high-level political negotiation and civil society reconciliation standing at opposite ends of masculine-feminine views of conflict resolution (successive negotiation teams having included, up to the latest round, only one woman, on the Greek-Cypriot side). People involved in reconciliation activities post-1974 were effeminized, mostly seen as naïve but also presented in more sinister discourse as traitors. These understandings have coalesced around the rhetoric that issues of gender equality that might undermine national unity should not be prioritized at this juncture (Vassiliadou 2002; Neu 2010)—"this" having a diachronic duration as reference to the Cyprus conflict as an ongoing priority. As such, it was replaced only in the early 2010s by the reference to economic crisis that was now being prioritized over everything else, including gender. And if women's questions were deprioritized in this order, matters of sexuality were simply repelled with hostility (Kamenou 2012). One of the feminist reconciliation groups I have been involved in since 2009, the Gender Advisory Team (GAT), has approached officials on several occasions, asking for incorporation of feminist structures in the federal settlement: gendered power sharing, social justice institutions, disbanding of armies, residence-based and not ethnicity-based rights of citizenship, federal and peace-oriented education structures, truth-and-reconciliation mechanisms, meaningful incorporation of women in the transitional economy of development (Demetriou and Hadjipavlou 2014; 2016; 2018). "No one wants to spend eighteen months in the military," a Greek-Cypriot official countered our call for reversing the culture of militarism, "but we cannot forget that there is an invasion and occupation opposite us and forty thousand troops ensuring it." Those very same forty thousand Turkish troops represent the "Turkish guarantee," which Turkish-Cypriot officials are similarly reluctant to dispense with. What such reactions to the radicality of GAT's positions share is an ultimate admission that the governmentality of negotiations is a governmentality of conflict, not reconciliation.

Feminist explorations of these orders in Cyprus (Cockburn 2004; Vassiliadou 2002, 2004; Güven-Lisaniler and Bhatti 2005; Güven-Lisaniler 2006; Agathangelou 1997, 2004; Hadjipavlou 2010) show how militarism produced a hypermasculinized national imaginary, where the political hegemonic form of manhood was bolstered by a second, military hegemonic form. The first controlled the endless standoff between the two polities, the second downgraded the violence perpetrated by the ethnic self into a strategy of communal defense. The aggression was always on the part of the ethnic other, the defense, sometimes silenced and sometimes extolled, always of the self. Rape, for example, is often projected as a salient image of the barbarity of the Turkish army in 1974 in Greek-Cypriot discourse, while the sexual assault that Greek-Cypriot policemen inflicted, according to Turkish-Cypriot discourse, on their women at enclave border crossings during the 1960s is silenced. Unsurprisingly, on both sides, the needs of the women victims of such military tactics have largely remained unaddressed by the patriarchal discourse that privatized individual trauma in the interest of honor (Vassiliadou 2002; Agathangelou 2000; Roussou 1986).

Two generations of women have thus grown up on the two sides of the Green Line, haunted by images of the violence wreaked by the enemy and oblivious to the violence perpetrated by their own fathers and uncles; they have walked along sandbagged alleys in fear of transgressing the border, but they themselves or their mothers have sewn the sandbags together; they have been taught to fear the militant other side, but to seek protection in their own state's military, which still compulsorily recruits their sons and partners; they have battled to articulate feminism and even harder to articulate antimilitarism. Take the example of the Turkish-Cypriot left parliamentarian Doğuş Derya, who articulated the issue of war rapes; when she took her parliamentary oath on August 12, 2013, she declared that she would work for the benefit of

> everyone living in Cyprus, irrespectively of language, religion, race, birthplace, class, age, physical ability, gender, or sexual orientation, to create an environment of fairness and equality, to replace the culture of conflict and violence with that of peace and reconciliation, while staying committed to the principles of democracy, social welfare, human rights and freedoms, and to establish a federal Cypriot state.

Her words were resisted, shouted over, and ultimately stopped. The parliamentary session was halted mid-oath, live broadcasts went silent, questions of treason raised, and she reappeared, reading the normal oath. This was the first of such public reformulations of constitutional tenets that could conceivably be seen in a federal arrangement. And it threatened the narrative of homogeneous communities in struggle.

The inevitably flawed homogenization achieved by the division has made Cypriot minority women even less visible in public life, their difference marked as a liability to the national unity on which the two state discourses were staked. Recall Annie who lived in the Buffer Zone, Metin's Greek-Cypriot girlfriend who saw her brother killed as a warning against her sexual choices. There were similarly women who stayed in their homes as these became engulfed by military camps in the north, and others who married across the divide; who did ordinary things as women, but exceptional things as citizens in a conflict context. Migrant women also became marginalized within the postwar structures, as citizenship has come to be used as a political demographic tool against the enemy. The case of Turkish settler women in the north comes readily to mind, but recall also Bahar's example whose access to refugee protection was mediated by the patriarchal norms guiding Schmittian determinations of who might be a refugee friend who a refugee enemy.

In a context where the Cyprus conflict trumps all other serious social issues such as women's rights, racism, and exploitation, everyday claims often do become exceptional. Among such everyday claims, marital choices are a prime example. Paragraph 7 of Article 2 of the Republic's Constitution reads:

> (a) a married woman shall belong to the Community to which her husband belongs.

(b) a male or female child under the age of twenty-one who is not married shall belong to the Community to which his or her father belongs, or, if the father is unknown and he or she has not been adopted, to the Community to which his or her mother belongs.

Thus defining, via the logic of patriarchy, women as the property of men, law has come to mediate ethnicity and family life. Interethnic marriages were effectively prohibited under the above provisions. The moment such marriages took place, they were no longer *inter*ethnic: Article 2.7 rendered the wife a co-ethnic of her husband. Prior to the introduction of civil marriage in 1990 (Law 21/1990), their performance necessitated a religious ceremony in the Greek-Cypriot case (and thus conversion), or registration by the defunct Turkish-Cypriot communal chamber. Initially, civil marriages were confined to the Greek-Cypriot community (21/1990, Art. 2), later broadened to all "adherents of Orthodox Christianity, irrespective of citizenship or ethnicity" (Law 28[I]/1994, Art. 2), a specification later deleted (Law 93[1]/1994). Even then, Turkish-Cypriots were effectively prohibited from marrying, interethnically or otherwise, in the Republic. An ECtHR case concluded in 2001, indicated that "Section 34 of the Marriage Law provides: 'The provisions of this Law shall not apply to any marriage in which either of the parties is a Turk professing the Moslem faith'" (*Kemal Selim v. Cyprus,* Application No. 47293/99). Subsequently, and via explicit reference to the case, Greek-Cypriot lawmakers extended civil marriage rights to the Turkish-Cypriot community (Law 46[1]/2002). This application of family law is only one indication of how the conflict enters the domestic sphere. Another case, *Modinos v. Cyprus* (ECtHR application no. 15070/89), which resulted in a begrudging decriminalization of homosexuality, gave cause for public discussions over the importance of heterosexual masculinity to the national cause (Kamenou 2012, 153–56). Similar arguments were also aired in 2015, as a civil partnership law (184[1]/2015) was being passed.

These examples show how a hegemonic understanding of the conflict has "rendered invisible major processes and relations that have produced violence, oppression, and exploitation" (Agathangelou 1997, 49). This invisibility is not necessarily tantamount to denial, but rather brings about the normalization of relations, specifically unequal gender relations. It makes them seem as if outside the sphere of ethnic politics, and makes them accepted without question, exactly because they are "non-political" (ibid., 74). One impact of this is the lack of "gender awareness . . . [and] a feminist understanding of the social organization of men and women's lives in a patriarchal system," documented by Hadjipavlou for women across ethnic communities in Cyprus (2004, 70). Within this frame claims to exclusivist ownership of the trauma of conflict determines who has the right to speak, and these claims are contested in terms that exclude women as actors and certain feminist issues as illegitimate. Gender is thus part and parcel of the devices of subjectification developed around the notion of the conflict. As we have seen, not only interethnic marriages, but also less extraordinary marital choices, such as those of Greek-Cypriot refugee women, are subject to biopolitical mediation that stems from the conflict and which positions their progeny in specific ways vis-à-vis the conflict and vis-à-vis refugeehood.

MILITARISM AND UNRULY VICTIMS

Speaking in May 2016 after the suicide of a man who had used his military-issue gun to take his life, the Minister of the Interior announced the conclusion of an interministerial memorandum to allow the repossession of guns by the state where the owners are deemed to "exhibit violent behavior."[7] Between 2004 and 2015, 169 people were killed in homicides in the Republic. Of those, forty-four were women. Of the total, over a third were killed by firearms.[8] The disaggregated gender statistics do not correlate weapon types and social aspects of assault. Intimate-partner violence has only recently become a category of policing in Cyprus and appears only for 2011 and 2012 in international reporting (registering two-thirds and 60 percent of all homicides in the respective years). In the same period, 340 cases of rape were also recorded. The year of 2011 recorded one of the lowest homicide rates in the period. Yet in that very year, all of the women victims were killed by intimate partners or family members. Femicide does not always abate when other crimes do. But it does relate directly to a characteristic of Cypriot society, its militarism. In the course of the Minister's statement in 2016, he also commented on the difficulty of repossessing weapons, since "hunting guns alone amount to 80,000." Code-locking mechanisms had been discussed as a complementary measure.

What the Minister meant is that the number of military-issue guns is even more, since guns are credited to each of the recruits (mandatorily conscripted to the National Guard upon graduation from high school), who are tasked with keeping their guns at home and looking after them while they remain on reserve duty until age fifty. By contrast, women receive no state-sanctioned training in the use of guns and do not have access to them. It is therefore unsurprising that news reports of fatal incidents of domestic violence feature either a military-issue G3 or a hunting rifle as the weapon of assault. An incident from October 2013, when an estranged husband gunned down his wife and wounded his daughter before committing suicide, illustrates this situation. The scenario was repeated in June 2014 when a man killed his wife, daughter, and critically wounded his son, before also killing himself. In August 2014 it was a hunting rifle shot intentionally by an alienated husband, and in June 2013 one shot accidentally by a son joking with his mother.[9] In 2011, when a Cypriot man gunned down his foreign partner and killed her daughter, the media reported near graphic details of the assault but omitted to mention the type of weapon.

Access to the means of violence is only one way in which militarism disadvantages women in Cyprus. In doing so, militarism highlights women's important role as victims whom the male population are trained to protect. The minister's statement in 2016 marked a break in this sense with traditional discourse, which saw the use of guns in domestic violence incidents as aberrant and for many years refused to draw a systemic link. And this was not because the link was difficult to see, but exactly because it was obvious. After the 1974 war, the leader of the socialist party, who had also led a militia to protect Makarios against right-wing paramilitaries in the prewar years, declared that from now on "every house must become a fortress, every patriot a soldier."[10] It has remained a readily used maxim to speak of nationalist grandiosity and what it failed to deliver in Cyprus; not least in foreclosing the possibility of negotiating a peace that might allow refugees to return. It is another instance of the excesses of performance where the reconfiguring of homes into fortresses undermines the recovery of homes lost, which is the key goal in the first place. But for all the cynicism, it nevertheless guided a governmentality that turned homes into battlefields and men into potential family killers. If in Israel "every woman is an occupied territory" (Sharoni 1992), in Cyprus she is the soldier's handmaid. And when unruly, she turns into an enemy. The discourse of loss and refugeehood enables the proliferation of enemies, engulfing women in it.

The crevice carved out by the comprehensive territorialization of the military across the country and into every home spells out that necropolitical limit where the state decides who is killed—here in deciding who can do the killing. There is impunity involved here, and it takes the form of the Law on Firearms 38/1974. This law, published in the immediate aftermath of the invasion on August 30, 1974, exempts from the right to own arms people convicted of the following crimes: murder, rape, abduction, arson, high treason, robbery, rioting, rebellion, participation in an unlawful organization, premeditated or attempted murder, and other offences as decided by the Council of Minsters (Art. 14). Taking into consideration the ways in which the conflict unfolded until that point and the pervasive practice among Cypriot men to belong to "unlawful organizations," this caveat should have excluded the vast majority of the male population, and it would have amounted to disarmament. Provided that there were legal convictions of those found to have belonged to such unlawful organizations. These never materialized; Makarios, in a move that remains controversial to this day, declared in November of that year, prior to his return to the island, that no one would be prosecuted for the coup upon his resumption of duties. Who participated in the coup and in what capacity is, as we saw in chapter 2, a moot point: some names are known to some, but that knowledge is never articulated, passed on, or uttered in anything but muffled speech—it is a phobic object, as discussed in chapter 5.

The result is a structure whereby every male gun holder was also rendered the agent of sacrifice—the emphasis was not on *homines sacri* as lives that could be killed, but on the impunity of those who had done the killing and who could now continue owning and controlling the means of that lethal violence. The failure to convict, in other words, turned a punitive law into a law that sanctioned the killing that had gone before and the killing that might be done after. It is not only that murder statistics are not properly disaggregated today. The military does not record incidents of violence outside of military areas, even if its own apparatus is being used—and thus does not assess the policies surrounding the use of that apparatus outside of its territory of control. Such investigations come solely under police jurisdiction and thus become civil matters, even when it is a military trigger that has been pulled. The most recent act that Cyprus signed on the field of domestic violence, the Council of Europe's Convention on preventing and combating violence against women and domestic violence, signed in 2015, does not reference crime related to military equipment or implicating army reservists. In other words, in being civil matters, deaths by military-issued guns do not implicate the army in the goings on of family strife. Except that every home has a gun in the closet. Exactly because such killings are today seen as civil crimes and not political crimes, the crevice where women experience violence and death must be seen as one belonging to the necropolitical order. In this order, refugee mothers can verbalize great acrimony for the discrimination they have suffered from the state but do so on the conviction of their maternal role in upholding the nation and its pride. And in so doing, they confirm the rightful existence of those closeted guns.

Another set of crimes in which politicization has thwarted recognition is that of war rapes. Here, politicization has worked differently. Rape has been a widespread metonym for victimhood in Cyprus, on both sides. While Turkish-Cypriot discourse has presented Greek assaults through the image of women abused and raped by policemen as they exited or entered their enclaves, Greek-Cypriot discourse has dwelled on rapes of the Turkish army in 1974 and projected the whole country as in a victim state of having been raped. And yet, when questions about the rehabilitation of actual victims of war rapes were raised by feminist parliamentarians on both sides, alongside acknowledgments of the existence of Other victims, public opinion was scandalized. The Turkish-Cypriot parliamentarian Doğuş Derya, who swore on her own oath in 2013, raised the issue in 2014 and was castigated by colleagues and in social media for suggesting, "treasonously," that Turkish soldiers raped. Having brought the threats she received to court, she was asked, as she took the stand, to explain "who raped who in 1974": "men raped women," she replied.

When a Greek-Cypriot MP Skevi Koukouma took up the issue a year later, the debate was no less animated, if more effective in bringing about a policy shift. What she had denounced in parliament was the insistence of government officials tasked with scrutinizing the award of state benefits in a post-financial crisis environment, for women who had been receiving benefits for having "suffered" (rape) in the war, to provide evidence of such suffering. The crucial difference between the two positions is that the first raised the question in the course of claiming a shared pain while the latter concentrated

primarily on the failure of the state to provide thorough and dignified repa-
ration mechanisms to primarily Greek-Cypriot victims. Only once the public
debate had been exhausted on the question of the state did Greek-Cypriot
politicians suggest that Turkish-Cypriots may have also suffered likewise on
the other side.

Notably, it seems that the sensitive issue of military rapes was much
harder to discuss decades after the event than it had been at that time. A
renowned documentary on Greek-Cypriot suffering in 1974, appropriately
titled *Attila '74—The Rape of Cyprus* ends on a candid and painful description
by a woman of her multiple rapes by Turkish soldiers (Cacoyiannis 1974).
Interviews conducted by Maria Hadjipavlou in that year provide a number
of similar testimonies that seem to have been forthcoming at the time (1987:
249–53). By the 2010s, this has become one of the least discussed aspects of
loss. My own second- and third-hand knowledge of rapes in that period suggests that many took place in the context of other war atrocities against civilian
populations, including at the start of the military campaign. This suggests they
were a military tactic of terrorizing the population into flight and enabling
easier capture of the territory. Rape, and the threat of rape, was a technique of
enforcing displacement. And it might have also been a technique of enforcing
enclavement as well, as information about such atrocities deterred people in
the remote Karpasia peninsula from initially venturing through enemy bridge-
heads and into safety in the south. And in a number of villages near Karpasia
where people stayed for months after the war, the decision to move out was
enforced, some Turkish-Cypriots recount, by neighbors threatening to rape
their daughters and wives. Nadia's mother, recall from chapter 3, moved out
of Famagusta to save her daughters from such a fate.

Why were these accounts so much more forthcoming at the point
when they occurred than in the distance of time? The reason quite probably
lies in the social reception of the victims by their own communities after the
event. Hadjipavlou offers no interviews from rape victims during her major leg
of fieldwork, two years after the first set of such interviews was taken. But she
does relate stories of women who returned to husbands who filed for divorce,
of women who were booed out of refugee camps because "whores [were] not
welcome there," and of women who ended up in Nicosia brothels (ibid., 253).
Oftentimes, it had been other women who had done the booing, claiming to

be protecting their sons from disgrace. The Cypriot poet Pantelis Michanikos (1926–1979) wrote in 1975 in his collection *Deposition (Katáthesi)*:

> And what do you expect from people
> who had their women raped in front of their eyes
> and did not pull out their pocket knives.
> Without feeling
> then
> without feeling
> today too
> they simply ask
> for a divorce.
> Scoundrels like this
> cannot fight for anything.

It has repeatedly been noted that these rapes constituted the platform on which access to medical abortions was relaxed after 1974, with the agreement of the Church, otherwise an unwilling party to such a policy (ibid., 252; Vassiliadou 1997). Those military biopolitics are plainly clear to see in the relevant law. Published on November 15, 1974 (just as war pregnancies would begin to be visible, entering their second trimester during which procedures would still be safe), Law 59/1974 is an amending law touching three areas of the Criminal Code in the following order: (1) violence against others and intolerance; (2) wearing of army and police insignia without authorization; and (3) medical abortions. Under the law, abortions can take place by registered doctors and after relevant certification by police and the doctor, that the pregnancy is the result of rape and if not terminated "would seriously shake the social standing of the pregnant woman and that of her family" (§4b). Alternatively, they can also take place on the certification of two doctors that if the pregnancy were to continue serious physical or mental harm would befall the pregnant woman "or members of her family older than her" or that "the child born would suffer serious physical or mental abnormality" (§4c). In this sense, Greek-Cypriot lawmakers left no room to doubt, even though the events of 1974 are nowhere to be mentioned (and in stark contrast to other pieces of legislation passed at the time), that the bodies of women and men are now a terrain to be policed, sartorially and surgically. And by mentioning the two in the same breath, I would suggest that they are also shirking away from the abject raped body, articulating it only under the duress of time, and then again behind the screen of men's military uniforms. The policing is as governmental as it is social.

And it continues to operate in a post-conflict modality today. When an amendment to the Law was being discussed in February 2018, tabled by a crossparty coalition of women MPs and aiming to legalize all abortions up to twelve weeks into the pregnancy, the media concentrated on only one of the many arguments they had put forward: that pregnant teenagers need to be protected from resorting to termination treatments and drugs available in the occupied areas (RIK news, 26/02/2018). The liberation of women's bodies hinged on their proper emplacement on this side of the postconflict landscape.

THE WOMAN AT GROUND ZERO

Cemaliye is a theater play, written by Greek-Cypriot Constantia Soteriou and performed in 2016. It tells the story, a "herstory," of that zero point of the Cyprus conflict, when Greek-Cypriot policemen shot dead a Turkish-Cypriot man and a Turkish-Cypriot woman in the early hours of December 21, 1963. Cemaliye Emir Ali, or Cemaliye Emir Hüseyin, was a prostitute in the small inner-city Nicosia neighborhood of Taht-el-kale, a Turkish quarter left in the Greek part of the city. While I was growing up in a postwar environment that found it difficult to speak of events prior to 1974, but spoke incessantly of the losses of that fateful summer, Cemaliye appeared occasionally in discourse, as a nameless prostitute that gave credence to the argument that 1960s violence was a series of hapless affairs, a case of troubles exploited politically by Turkish state interests and their agents in the Turkish-Cypriot community. In Turkish-Cypriot discourse, Cemaliye's name is known, the profession effaced. Her martyr's grave in the cemetery is far less adorned that that of her male companion, a celebrated TMT fighter and security guard where she worked.[11] Scott Gibbons, who has written an unmistakably partial account of atrocities against Turkish-Cypriots in that period, describes her as "Jemaliye Emir, happy, good looking divorcee with few cares" (1997, 9). Unspoken or gilded over, her precarious condition is depoliticized on both sides.

Wrongly so, the play suggests. Those fatal machine-gun shots at point zero were fired because the enemy's profligacy could not be tolerated and had to be disciplined. And because Cemaliye and her partner, when asked to be so disciplined by giving their names to be recorded, refused to be placed on record. And because she, a woman, stood up and spoke back to the policemen, a Turkish-Cypriot friend who has researched her story tells me. What Neşe Yaşın finds scandalous about Cemaliye's death is that it was preventable. Not at the instant she was shot, as Greek-Cypriot readings of the event as mishap would have it, but for a long time following that moment. She tells me that Cemaliye crawled to the end of street several tens of meters away as she bled and that she called out for help to Greek- and Turkish-Cypriot neighbors as she did so. Nobody came to her rescue. Cemaliye's death, that zero point of the bloodshed, was the result of social dejection, communalized fear, and the terrorization that lurks at the juncture of gender and ethnic abjection. Her neighbors, and not the sovereign, decided that she could be killed with impunity. And thus, she died in that crevice etched between an ethnic enclave, sexual moralities, and emergency panics.

EIGHT **ENEMY REFUGEES**

WHEN IS A TURKISH-CYPRIOT NOT A "TURKISH-CYPRIOT"?

Up to now I have been arguing that Turkish-Cypriots are an abject specter in the imbricated Greek-Cypriot terrain of refugeehood. In this chapter, I take a closer look at the appearance of Turkish-Cypriots in Greek-Cypriot society and law. It is an ambivalent appearance, precarious and under erasure. Oftentimes the reality of Turkish-Cypriot presence jars with constructions of "Turkish-Cypriotness" in daily life and in law.

According to a Supreme Court decision from 1995, a Turkish-Cypriot resident of Pyla village—which borders the Buffer Zone and the British Sovereign Base Area of Dhekelia, but is largely under Republic of Cyprus administration—who had wanted to sell a plot of land, was wrongly categorized by the Land Registry Department as a "Turkish-Cypriot" (*Northgate Ltd v. Republic*, case no. 440/93, §2). That inverted-comma definition, the decision held, did not apply to this particular Turkish-Cypriot, who lived in areas under the control of the government and who had access to his property and the freedom to do as he liked with it. The law under which the Land Registry Department rejected the application (Law 139/1991) and annulled the sale reserves the other, scare-quote definition, for Turkish-Cypriots displaced from properties in the south and left without access to them or the means to make decisions regarding them. The Supreme Court thus recognized a gap between taken-for-granted definitions of Turkish-Cypriotness and legal ones. It chastised the department for not "undertaking the necessary research" to establish the validity of that legal definition in the specific case and its departure from the evident Turkish-Cypriotness of the person in question. And of course, in stating exactly that, the Court upheld the ethnic logic by which that latter Turkish-Cypriotness becomes "evident."

Governmentally, we might also see an interesting instance here of the Supreme Court chastising the department for bad faith in granting rights to Turkish-Cypriots. As the Court declares that not all Turkish-Cypriots are "Turkish-Cypriots," it exposes the gesture by which Greek-Cypriot lawmakers have regulated the constitutional rights of Turkish-Cypriots after the communal separation of 1974—and withheld them: that is, by equating individual people to the fate of the ethnic community they belong to. In this, they have assumed that all Turkish-Cypriots chose to live under their own authorities in the north, that they all chose to leave their properties behind, and that they were now definitively and totally absent from the Greek-Cypriot south, the free areas, in which the government exercised control. In other words, they came to read territory, "the areas under the control of the government," in ethnic terms, as territories from which Turkish-Cypriots had been cleansed.

The Supreme Court reminded the department that not all Turkish-Cypriots had left. Pyla is a well-known exception (Papadakis 1996). Because of the location of the village, within the SBAs and post-1974 partly also within the Buffer Zone, the Turkish-Cypriot inhabitants of this mixed village have lived under an administrative regime shared between the Republic, British SBA authorities, and the UN. These Turkish-Cypriots, have never been displaced, and so they have never lost rights in order to regain them, or in this instance in order to have them exercised through a proxy that the relevant law set up. That Law, 139/1991, tasked the Minister of the Interior with the custodianship of Turkish-Cypriot properties. As Custodian, the minister heads a committee consisting of representatives from across ministries, parties, farmers' associations, and the (Greek-Cypriot) Pancyprian Union of Refugees, which decides on the proper administration of Turkish-Cypriot properties. The custodianship includes decisions over who is given rights to live or work the property, decisions over the collection of income from it and decisions over its maintenance and improvement, as well as decisions regarding its demolition or sale provided these are the only profitable ways in which to manage it (Art. 6). These responsibilities are held to rest with the custodian (the minister) for as long as the unstable situation (*ékrithmi katástasi*) persists, which does not allow Turkish-Cypriots to travel to the areas under the control of the Republic and exercise their property rights.

The Republic's government is therefore tasked with the trusteeship of these properties, but this is in consultation with interest groups (farmers,

Greek-Cypriot refugees) that stand to gain from access to, as well as use and management of these properties. The inclusion of farmers and refugees among these groups alludes to the fact that the vacuum created by the displacement of Turkish-Cypriots was filled by the needs for housing and work of the Greek-Cypriot refugees and the rural poor. The law, in short, attests to a governmentality whereby the material losses of ethnic Others were mobilized to ameliorate the losses of "our own" refugees.[1] In its preamble, the Custodian Law also informs us that its goal is to formalize practices that were already in place and thus far regulated by administrative arrangements (*dhiikitikés diefthetísis*). The law formalizes the norm and in so doing recognizes its prior existence at its place.

The Supreme Court's decision, then, points to these legal and ethnic governmentalities of managing loss and identifies what it is that they take for granted (equivalence of individual identity and ethnic belonging). In doing so, it allows us to see the gaps they set up in that very process between the evident (Turkish-Cypriotness) and the normative ("Turkish-Cypriot"-ness). I argue that these gaps sustain the entire structure of loss, which I have been speaking about throughout this book. I show, over the next few pages, that the construction of Greek-Cypriot refugeehood is propped up against its main category of exclusion, Turkish-Cypriot refugees. Legal, affective, and material registers have been shown in earlier chapters to result, often inadvertently, in the exclusion of various other groups, caught in the crevices that this second part of the book has been examining. These registers have in fact been oriented against a very specific figure of the enemy: Turkish-Cypriots. The court decision examined here exposes the legal and social attitudes towards Turkish-Cypriots and the empty properties they have left behind over the course of the conflict, and it begins to speak about the relationship between the legal and the social in the specific biopolitical processes by which law is engulfed in the normative.

And as we have seen with other types of crevices, this structure also engulfs other subjects beyond those targeted expressly by the law. In one such case, the members of a migrant family applied for naturalization under separate applications lodged at different points in times. They were all approved. However, on becoming naturalized Cypriot citizens, some family members were assigned to the Turkish-Cypriot community under the presumption that since they were Muslims they should become "Turkish-Cypriots," while others were assigned to the Greek-Cypriot community. The latter has been the default practice in naturalizations since the division and the dissolution of the Turkish-Cypriot Communal Chamber in the 1960s, which would have been the body responsible for cultural and private affairs involving Turkish-Cypriots. When I asked a migration official years ago whether persons to be naturalized get to choose the community to which they will belong, he seemed surprised at the question. Why would someone prefer to be a subject without rights, he seemed to suggest; "No, people being naturalized are not asked." This relationship between the legal and the social, and the legal and the normative, is one from which, I argue, the figure of the enemy refugee (Turkish-Cypriots) is an absent presence.

In examining the ramifications of the legal term *tourkóplikti* in chapter 4, I argued that one of its main functions is to point to Turkish-Cypriots as absent figures in the structure of loss as constructed by Greek-Cypriot discourse. This absence is not value-free. It is a morally and affectively charged absence—the absence of an enemy. Murat Erdal Ilican has shown, in a study of property rights in the course of Cyprus's modern history, that the postdivision treatment of the properties of the displaced on both parts of the island harks back to British wartime legislation on "enemy properties" (2011, 174–211). Tracing this legislation to 1914 and World War II views on German properties, he argues that it ultimately enacted an equivalence between people and property. In the two societies that developed postdivision, he says,

> the feeling of loss and gain was part and parcel of daily life especially regarding property ownership. Whilst some lost, others benefited from the status quo either in political or economic terms, primarily by utilizing either directly or indirectly the "prisoner of war" condition that the vast amount of refugee properties had been subject to. (ibid., 210)

In the use and abuse of such enemy properties, he suggests, we can trace the treatment and mistreatment of the enemies themselves (ibid.). I am using this argument here as a starting point for arguing further that the mistreatment of that enemy, as seen in the abuse of their rights, is what reproduces and sustains the efficacy of loss in the making of community. And to do so, it has necessitated their absence. Turkish-Cypriots, and their equivalence to "Turkish-Cypriots," in other words, are the children in the closet whose necessary torture sustains the prosperity of Omelas in Le Guin's novel, so evocatively analyzed by Povinelli (2011, 1–45). These abject subjects determine the citizenship of all of us (Nyers 2003; Rygiel 2010). As enemy subjects they prefigure the exception that becomes a "permanent state of emergency" (Neocleous 2006) in the postconflict period. Citizenship, in other words, is governed within that space where the abject (enemy refugees) and the ideal (our refugees) mirror each other. But because neither abject nor ideal can ever exist absolutely, as we have seen, these figures of abjection and idealization are performative figures and the space between them is mired by tension and instability. It is a fragile space, like a tiled roof, with a hole in the center.

It is no coincidence, I would propose, that the carefully crafted definition of "displaced" (*ektopisthéndes*) that we have seen in much of the early legislation reviewed in chapter 4, is abandoned in favor of the word "refugees" (*prósfiyes*) in the Custodian of Turkish-Cypriot Properties Law and not another.[2] A refugee, article 2 of 139/91 tells us, is

> a person who, in the time immediately preceding the invasion had their normal residence or base or center of business activities in an area which, as a result of the invasion has been rendered inaccessible or affected and includes a person whose work or business, on account of the unstable situation, has been affected to such a degree as to render him [*sic*] unable to respond to their contractual obligations.

The entry of the word "refugee" into the Cypriot legal vocabulary is not simply an insertion of the social understandings of Greek-Cypriot refugeehood into the plane of law. It is also an expansion from the previous definition of "displaced," which regulates housing and welfare, into the plane of business and financial conduct (of refugees and farmers). It is on the precedent of this definition that Law 71[I] of 1994 then founds the Pancyprian Union of Refugees as the major body of their representation. And it is also, crucially, a gesture of adversarial discourse vis-à-vis Turkish-Cypriots. It is on the back of enemy refugees that Greek-Cypriot refugees come into their own as legal subjects and economically viable citizens.

WE ARE ALL GURBET

Pyla is not the only place in the south where Turkish-Cypriots live. Recall the UN's reporting of sixty-two Turkish-Cypriots having stayed in the south after the Third Vienna Agreement (chapter 2). The census of 1992 registers a mere 163 Turkish-Cypriots, and that of 2001 registers 360. In 2011 the census registered 1,128 Turkish-Cypriots living in the south. It also registered 1,405 individuals with Turkish as a mother tongue, but of whom 908 were Cypriots (another, or a separate, 188 individuals, registered Turkey as their country of origin). Of the 908 Turkish-speaking Cypriots, 342 were registered in Limassol and 153 in Nicosia, another 273 were registered in Larnaca district, where Pyla is located. It is unclear whether previous censuses counted Turkish-Cypriots in Pyla (e.g., among the 163 of the 1992 census, which would have been a rather low figure), or, like the Land Registry, considered them absent "Turkish-Cypriots." A Turkish-Cypriot friend who was visited by an official in the course of the 2001 census, joked that the official had no awareness of and no category in which to place a Cypriot who spoke Turkish. This is only a minor indication of how public perceptions, or lack of awareness, reflects a wider governmentality. In the event, those public perceptions may also come to assume a lack of tools that might in fact be there (if the 2001 counted 360 Turkish-Cypriots but not my interlocutor, the category must have existed somewhere in the questionnaire or entered retrospectively by more thorough officials). These are the workings of biopolitics that I turn to in this section.

Different groups of Turkish-Cypriots have been subject to differing governmental policies through the years. In the district of Nicosia, Turkish-Cypriots have mainly resided in the neighboring villages of Potamia and Dali, which they refused to leave after the war. This is the village where Martin Packard was told of interethnic debts that prevented Turkish-Cypriots from leaving (chapter 2). It is a possibility that reminds us that coexistence, having been celebrated as alive and well in Potamia and Dali, might also bear its own undercurrents of enforcement. In Limassol, Turkish-Cypriots have lived in the town's Turkish quarter after crossing from the north at various points since 1974, many surviving on government support in the form of housing and social welfare benefits.

Fevzi was showing me his tattooed knuckles as he introduced me to his wife and daughter. The tattoos spell out "Jesus," and he shows me the gold cross on his neck. The tattoo was done in prison, where he served a few months, I assume for petty crime. He converted there, became Christian, and was greatly helped by the Greek-Cypriot man who became his godfather and gave him the gold cross. It was November 2002 and we were in Limassol. Fevzi and his family were among the Turkish-Cypriots who had been crossing the Buffer Zone into the south clandestinely at that point, and reportedly in increasing numbers. The Care and Rehabilitation of Displaced Persons Service, a branch of which operated in the buildings attached to one of the neighborhood's two mosques, provided them with housing. *Mérimna*, [social] care, the short name for the department, was on everyone's lips at the time. And "everyone" was the community of Turkish-Cypriots who stood at the doors of the office daily trying to secure a house to stay, electricity to be connected, broken doors to be fixed. These were the concerns that Fevzi's wife spoke about as he prided over his religious conversion. If *mérimna* failed to care, he seemed to suggest, his godfather would.

Turgut, on the other hand, who lived across the street, had no tattoos, cross, or godfather. He depended on the three other Turkish-Cypriot men with whom he shared a house and was trying to lobby the *mérimna* office to give him a separate house. Turgut drew distinctions between himself and people like Fevzi. They were *gurbet*, gypsies. They were not Turkish-Cypriots. But he also drew distinctions between himself and the other Turkish-Cypriot men he lived with. They had come to the south to escape the authorities in the north—they would have been charged or arrested for minor and more serious offences. He had no such convictions or accusations. He had come to escape the military. He was better educated, found it easier to secure daily manual jobs, and could hope to live on his own, perhaps even without state-provided accommodation. But when he looked up available housing in the newspaper and called landlords, he was flatly told the apartments were gone. He suspected it was his broken Greek and that they did not want foreigners, or indeed Turkish-Cypriots. A property owner I called proved him right—the property was only for Cypriots, I should know he said. Turgut's housemate, who had been around the *mahalle* (neighborhood) for a few years by then, thought of his position differently. *Hepimiz gurbet'iz*, he said, with a resigned sigh—"we are all *gurbet*."

Gurbet, often used in Turkish to designate Roma people, is a term intimately tied to the idea of traveling. But unlike the English designation "travellers" tied to perceptions of ethnicity, *gurbet* traveling is not meant to be descriptive; it does not pretend to be merely a statement of fact. It is a mournful kind of traveling, a traveling away from home. *Gurbet* can often denote migration, as in when circumstances force one abroad in search of a living. In this forced migration sense, *gurbet* is a statement about refugeehood.

And as such, the lament that "we are all *gurbet*," takes us full circle back to the antipodal Greek-Cypriot discourse of generalized refugeehood. If for the state, enemy refugees are the abject mirrors of "own refugees," the experience of those abject subjects at the receiving end is the generality of *gurbet*-hood— the abject of generalized refugeehood. The care pleaded for and half-heartedly handed out to Roma individuals and Turkish-Cypriots reflects and inverts the discourse of loss I have been examining. And in doing so, it makes everyone, materially and biopolitically, a refugee. It prints the loss on the skin, as it assimilates from one unhomely identity (Turkish-Cypriot-ness) into another (Greek-Cypriot Christianity). And it implants it in falling wall plaster, exposed wire, broken windows.

In a housing assessment I was involved in among the Limassol Roma in 2010, we noted infrastructural problems such as broken plumbing, chronic failure to undertake basic improvements (broken doors and window panes), and other generally degraded conditions. Women also spoke about health problems of insomnia and irritability, and failures to communicate with authorities in order to address these—language and literacy were major factors in this communication failure. They also spoke of separations from husbands, and husbands' inability to work after labor injuries. They greatly valued their children's school education—mainly because it meant that children could guide them through the form filling requested by *mérimna* and negotiate the care of authorities. But they also spoke of tense relations with neighbors and perceived fears. One of the Greek-Cypriots in the area, I was told on the day, had turned a shotgun against them a few days before.

It was not surprising. The ombudsperson and other organizations had previously reported on the spate of intolerance seen at the neighborhood school. Greek-Cypriot parents had asked for Roma children to be educated separately. In July 2004, a few months after the Annan Plan referendum, a Roma teenager was stabbed to death in the Limassol harbor by a man declared to have been deranged (Trimikliniotis and Demetriou 2009, 247). The government spokesman at the time insisted that the crime was not politically motivated,[3] even though it was reported that the man had used nonsensical statements about Christian Orthodoxy while carrying it out. Two years earlier, during the course of fieldwork in Limassol's Turkish quarter, a cousin of mine living not far from the area had suggested that the desperate situation that I was describing, might have a positive side. "If the worst of these communities can coexist without killing each other," she had said, "maybe there is hope for reunification without violence." I had been bothered by her projection of my description as a negative evaluation of humanity ("the worst of each community"). But I understood what she had meant. I had been describing, that evening, the conversations I had had with Greek-Cypriot refugee women living in the *mahalle* who complained about the Turkish-Cypriot "scoundrels" and "filthy" Gypsies. Some of these women, it turned out, also had strong views about the rightfulness of the coup and resented Makarios's return in 1974. The worst, for my leftist cousin, stood for those extremities of political positioning and abject social status. The lumpenproletariat of both communities was divested and resentful—but also, perhaps, those petty and political criminals who escaped justice were coexisting in that open prison of the *mahalle*.

The situation in Limassol could indeed have stood well as a metaphor of imprisoned refugeehood: an Agambenian camp, where people strive to retain a position on this side of *bios*, and who deride the *Muselmänner* for having succumbed to bare life. That could be conversion, assimilation, a psychotic repetition of propaganda, or a dwelling on loss and what might have been had national aspirations succeeded. In refugeehood, it is as if bare life is never completely bare—it is always somehow draped in that rugged loss.

EXODUS

The Turkish-Cypriots of Limassol were, in the early 2000s and prior to the opening of the checkpoints, subjects who ironically lived a camped existence exactly because they attempted to escape another. Navaro-Yashin forcefully describes (2003; 2005; 2012) how Turkish-Cypriot informants spoke of their life in the north in terms of imprisonment: an "open prison," a "chicken pen." Many of the Turkish-Cypriots I had met in reconciliation meetings in Cyprus since the early 1990s said the same thing. The word *mándra*, common in Cypriot Greek and Turkish to describe an animal pen, as in the back of a rural house, loomed large in conversations about the north. And thus, it was even more disheartening when people such as Turgut exercised agency, refused to serve the military state, and ended back in another pen, abjected and unseen.

If the governmentality of loss required the absence of the Turkish-Cypriot subject from the Greek-Cypriot imaginary, the opening of the checkpoints, as explained in chapter 3, in April 2003, inserted a caesura in the processes that maintained this imaginary. Turkish-Cypriots took center stage in this. For one, the decision of the Turkish-Cypriot authorities to lift their ban on crossing, was largely seen to have been catalyzed by waves of mass protests begun in late 2002, as negotiations over the island's EU accession threatened to exclude them from membership of the Union. So by news time on January 14, 2003, Greek-Cypriots watched over fifty thousand Turkish-Cypriot protestors asking their leader to resign, leave the peace negotiations to someone who could deliver a settlement and render them European citizens, and take away the border keeping them from the Greek-Cypriot south. In an estimated population of 250,000 at that point, that number is huge. Considering that the eligibility criteria for voting in the Annan Plan referendums two years later registered only 150,000 as adult Turkish-Cypriots, that number of people who took to the streets is unprecedented.

The size of the demonstrations had visible effects on Greek-Cypriot discourse. The prejudicial views of Turkish-Cypriots the media had presented up to then subsided, and Turkish-Cypriots came to be seen as victims of a Turkey-bound regime that had been oppressing them. The border, up to then largely unnoticed, became a focal point of consideration, as each new demonstration became more oriented towards it. On December 26, 2002, Turkish-Cypriot authorities took special measures to seal all possible crossing points to the south and stationed army contingents (in addition to the police usually staffing the crossing points) along the Green Line in Nicosia (Demetriou and Vlachos 2007, 45).

This repressive approach gave way as progress in the peace negotiations stalled again. Earlier demonstrations, dating back to a bank collapse in 2000, had shown that repression only alienated people. "When they saw them beat elderly fathers and uncles [during those demonstrations], Turkish-Cypriots realized then that this police was not theirs," explained Mehmet, who had participated in both the 2000 and 2002 protests. His point echoed the oft-repeated claim that Turkish-Cypriots were encouraged to hail the Turkish army in 1974 as a deliverance force, only to realize in later years that it was occupying and oppressing them too.

Such discourse, which many Greek-Cypriots were hearing from their TV screens in 2003 for the first time after 1974, resonated well with the hegemonic rhetoric on the Cyprus conflict and its losses, which held that the problem was one of invasion and occupation of the northern part. So when the press started to reproduce stories from the Turkish-Cypriot media in March 2003, that the Turkish-Cypriot authorities were planning a package of measures to combat unemployment by allowing "free movement" and "lowering army service" in the north,[4] the government of the Republic drew up its own plans. Asked about a possible "mass arrival of Turkish-Cypriots," the Greek-Cypriot Minister of the Interior assured the media that even though it had "no data to justify or confirm such information," the government was fully prepared to face such a situation.[5] Recall that many Turkish-Cypriots I met in Limassol in 2002 had arrived only in the previous few months and years. The government soon announced "special measures in support of Turkish-Cypriots."[6] Having signed the EU Accession Treaty, the president of the Republic claimed that the purpose of the package was to "give out a message that there is hope for them [Turkish-Cypriots] to be able to share the commodities and benefits from Cyprus's accession" (PIO, 18/4/03). This was only three days before Turkish-Cypriot authorities announced their intention to lift crossing restrictions as of April 23, 2003. A decision that had appeared so thoroughly shocking was the result of indirectly concerted policies on both sides to respond to an expected mass exodus of Turkish-Cypriots from the north.[7]

What concerns me here is the formulation and implementation of these policies by the Greek-Cypriot authorities, which have, since 2003, spelled out the basis on which Turkish-Cypriots have been reincorporated by the Republic as subjects of the state. Whereas prior to 2003, the few Turkish-Cypriots who chose to live in the south could be largely discounted—in discourse, rhetoric, demography, and care, as previous sections showed—after this date their visibility on exactly these fields became important. At the same time, the ambivalence with which these policy measures have been implemented is a projection of the state's approach to Turkish-Cypriots not simply as minor, but as other, enemy subjects. In Nyers analysis of abject subjects (2003), he claims that the constitution of some citizens as potential terrorists (i.e., enemies), begins the process of rendering them abject subjects, which is the process of "unmaking" their citizenship (e.g., annulling their naturalizations, rendering them subject to arrest and detention using lower legal thresholds than used with other citizens, allowing surveillance on the same basis). Building on Nyers, Rygiel (2010) suggests that enemy and abject subjects are one, or at least that one slips into the other fairly easily. Being abject subjects enables the designation of "enemy combatant" to be applied in the context of the War on

Terror and the practices of detention and rendition to be executed. We could say that in the case of Turkish-Cypriots, it is an already "unmade" citizenship that is being rehabilitated, but on the same basis of abjection. Extending rights under a "measures" framework renders these rights always transferable back to the state, annullable at the call of the sovereign, and conditional on the exception. But I further suggest that this is not an easy slip (between enemy and abject). For Kristeva the abject is not the enemy; it is a haunting presence (1982). Something must happen for the shift between abject subject and enemy to be effected—and vice versa. That something is a fundamental reordering of the political: the shift from tyranny to democracy (Kristeva's *Oedipus Rex* to *Colonus*), the inauguration of the War on Terror, the opening of the checkpoints. Those are the events over which we need to trace political continuities.

In the imbricated structure of loss I have been sketching, Turkish-Cypriotness was not a structural point but the absence of one. It was the gap left by broken tiles. And because the stated purpose of a roofing structure is to be solid and allow no vulnerabilities, these gaps are more easily papered over than filled in in ways that might reposition wider areas in the structure. That papering over is the effect of syncopated policies that accommodate Turkish-Cypriots when they appear through the border. The package of measures put together in response to exodus is one example. The piecemeal change in legislation, allowing marriage rights and voting rights in response to decisions by ECtHR as seen in chapter 7 is another. Education is a third, a plane where mixed approaches have been adopted: in Pyla there is a communal school, in Limassol a school that offers Turkish and Romani language lessons, and elsewhere there are private tuition subsidies for the children of Turkish-Cypriots living in the south.

The issuing of passports, that inaugural gesture of citizenship, is indicative. Access to those passports was unequivocally a major concern in the demonstrations of 2002 to 2003. But it was access that was not entirely foreclosed up to that point. Turkish-Cypriots living or studying abroad could apply to Cypriot embassies and be issued such passports, after submitting Republic-issued identity documents either for themselves or their parents. It was a process that carried risks though, as at different times Turkish-Cypriot authorities had banned these passports and threatened their holders with prosecution. But it was the main route for securing access to "the Greek side" (*Rum tarafı*) not for its own sake, but for the global recognition that it offered and the travel, work, and migration opportunities that went with it. Having returned to the north after the opening of the checkpoints in 2003, Turgut summed up his feelings of ambivalence during a chance encounter at the border: "It's terrible," he said. "There is nothing here. I am going to come back. Your side is Europe, here there is nothing" (*sizin taraf Avrupa—burada hiç bir şey yok*). Turgut was articulating the inescapable precariousness of existence on either side as an Other subject.

In securing Republic of Cyprus passports, Turkish-Cypriots become EU citizens and gain rights as Cypriots; but the lack of equivalence with Greek-Cypriot citizenship is immediately apparent (or at least was until recently). The precarious status of the citizenship provided to Turkish-Cypriots by the Republic of Cyprus is printed on the passports they succeed in obtaining. For whereas passports issued to Greek-Cypriots have a ten-year validity span, the ones issued to Turkish-Cypriots are initially valid for two years, at the end of which their holders may apply for an extension which is granted, following "special checks" by the authorities, "at no extra charge," the registry officials readily explain. In 2003, many Turkish-Cypriots discovered that the process took considerably longer than it did for Greek-Cypriots. This was because, I was informed by workers in the Immigration Department, "no proper databases exist for Turkish-Cypriots and it takes time to gather the relevant information for each case." That information, I learned on a subsequent visit, is collected by the Central Intelligence Service, which is not normally involved in the issuing of Greek-Cypriot passports. Back in 2003, linguistic differences in the presentation of personal data could distinguish a Greek- from a Turkish-Cypriot passport. In current biometric passports, nothing, apart from one's name, signifies what kind of subject the holder is. As governmental instruments, passports indicate a shift from a sovereign governmentality that categorizes by pointing a finger, to a biopolitical one which studiously collects and condenses fingerprint and other knowledge away from public view.

Such shifts have occurred on other planes of policy as well, as the European integration process advanced in the years that followed 2004. The package of special measures of 2003 was the first comprehensive policy to be announced. Known as *métra ya tous Tourkokíprious* (measures for the Turkish-Cypriots), the document was adopted by the Ministerial Council on April 30, 2003—a week after the crossing points opened. The document makes persistent references to law: words, phrases, and titles such as "legality," "international law," the "acquis communautaire," the "European Court of Human Rights," "Cypriot legislation," "lawful," "official," and so on, are strewn throughout the text. The reason is made apparent in the preamble: "the measures cannot be interpreted as entailing the risk of recognizing the secessionist entity or its acknowledgment, or of assisting in any way the secessionist entity in the occupied areas" (preamble, §4). Turkish-Cypriot rights are granted on an individual basis and in a context of prevailing anxiety lest they end up amounting to state recognition of the north. It is a rare occasion where structures in the north are described as anything other than "the pseudo-state"—the only available designation in formal parlance for them. In their appearance inside a legal instrument such as policy measures that bind the Republic of Cyprus, authorities in the north are given substance (an entity) away from the realm of make-believe (pseudo) and delegitimized in substance as "secessionist."

The measures outlined in that document cover movement (people and goods), employment, cultural issues (participation in events, heritage, TV programs), humanitarian affairs, political and social rights, and local authority cooperation. Although many of the measures in fact leave room for further regulation—at the very least in order to shield the state from future accusation of discriminatory policy—with hindsight the document seems ambitious, taking into account the extent to which the measures have been implemented to date. Indeed, the inadequacy of implementation is implied by the appearance of additional documents announcing further measures that largely contain details regulating what seem to have been problematic areas (e.g., economic cooperation and crossing of vehicles for professional use).[8] This arguably relates back to the focus of governmental policy on law rather than practice. In other words, this package of measures seems to have been dictated by the need to set (legal) order over the chaos that was expected to result from the exodus of Turkish-Cypriots to the south following the accession of the Republic to the EU. The measures thus made rights that could not be denied (e.g., medical care, provision of citizenship documents) enforceable by removing the requirement that their holders be resident and pay taxes in the south. Other measures, such as the one envisioning the creation of an office under which "Turkish-Cypriot affairs" would be coordinated, or a measure encouraging the conclusion of agreements on mobile telephony, never materialized. Instead, the second, was taken up twelve years later by a Turkish-Cypriot leader voted in on a pro-peace ticket. After an extremely positive first meeting with his Greek-Cypriot counterpart, they together announced that they would pursue progress on the issue as part of their own, new, package of confidence-building measures (then, as before, the initiative failed to bear fruit).

The limited extent of success of the measures was plain to see from September 2003, when an assessment document was publicized. [9] Revealing a biopolitical take, the text emphasizes the successes through numbers. A table under the "social insurance" head shows a steady increase in the number of Turkish-Cypriots "who are contributors to the Social Insurance Fund" from 687 in April 2003 to 1,101 in September 2003, and a marginal increase in the beneficiaries, from 4,261 in April to 4,264 in September (this includes some former Turkish-Cypriot civil servants who apparently continued to receive pensions after the division). A column showing the "total" registers an increase from CYP 700,007 in April to CYP 741,778 in September, presumably being the amount of their contributions. Similarly, the Ministry of Health reports that "[t]he number of patients treated [in Government Medical Institutions] during September 2003, increased from 227, in April 2003, to 1060 or by 367%." This is exemplary of the construction of "Turkish-Cypriot influx" and its perceived exponential effect on resources. That baseline of 227 naturalizes a number that can by no means be considered a base for future projections—it can only represent Turkish-Cypriots who either lived in the south or, presumably having had identity documents before the opening of the Green Line, were eligible and crossed to receive treatment in the last week of April.[10]

In this demographic biopolitics the success of care is rendered quantifiable as Turkish-Cypriots are presented first and foremost as beneficiaries of support rather than active participants. In those early days, the measures were successful on two counts. On the one hand they were taken up by a number of Turkish-Cypriots who sought passports, work, and treatment in hospitals. On the other, they were also successful as performative work on the Greek-Cypriot public, who formulated, largely through media discourse, a concept of "Turkish-Cypriots" as competitors for benefits they were seen as unworthy of. And this view was exacerbated further by the panic of mass exodus and exponential rise that the numbers exuded. This perception put in motion its own dynamics, lowering the uptake of the measures and making it easier to scrap benefits such as health coverage under exceptional measures in the context of financial collapse in 2013. And yet even after the scrapping of most benefits, it is a discourse that persists, and features high on the agenda of nationalist parties, from the center to the far right. It is an argument that can easily be appealed to in a number of contexts, as the example of matrilineal refugee claims in chapter 7 has shown. And because of its easy uptake, it can be, and often is, bounced around every time the threat of an imminent peace agreement appears. And because of its elusive frequency, it is arguably a discounted factor in the rise of nationalism dominating the rearrangement of the political landscape in the parliamentary elections of 2016 (when three new, rejectionist parties entered parliament on tickets against an agreement, including the far right sister party of the Greek Golden Dawn). What goes under "care" puts in place the foundations on which intolerant discourse builds.

In the years that followed the implementation of the measures, Turkish-Cypriots have often reported discriminatory behavior in hospitals and various government departments, which is ultimately premised on the belief that Turkish-Cypriots receive without contributing. Ömer, who prided himself in 2006 for having two homes, one on each side of Nicosia, was concerned about attacks against Turkish-Cypriot-plated cars parked in the south (slashing their tires, or throwing eggs on the windscreen), which have not been thoroughly investigated. Such attacks have been going on since 2003 and intensifying in recent years. On May 15, 2016, when the Nicosia football team, aligned with the right, won the football cup, fans outside the club's headquarters attacked Turkish-Cypriot cars with sticks and chased one Turkist-Cypriot out of town. And on June 24, 2016, a Turkish-Cypriot-plated car was chased out of the beach and club resort of Ayia Napa, and eventually stopped and attacked as its passengers ran into nearby fields before they were also beaten. These were incidents reported widely in the media on both sides. Arif described how, in the same period, his own car was booed and banged by a passing group of men as he stopped at traffic lights in the center of Nicosia. He did not report it to the police, as he did not think much would come out of it. But he was now worried about crossing with his car to the south and bringing his children over. Even though there was an attempt to present the media-reported incidents as isolated, experience, shared on the personal level in domestic environments, shows they are nothing but.

It thus seems that on the level of the Republic's policy, the management of the Turkish-Cypriot population within the Republic is fraught with tension between the need to produce policy and the fear that implementing it might contradict national interests, which are of course understood as Greek-Cypriot interests. This is the tension that abjection had successfully managed until 2003. This tension now feeds into widely held ethnocentric biases, further undermining policy implementation but also fueling extremist action, legitimated by the belief that such integration policies are undeserved. Povinelli (2011) has suggested that endurance is a key mode in which the state in late liberalism abandons individuals in positions of disadvantage. Such endurance may be tested in the effort needed to get an engine running, a boat afloat, a washing machine working. Such materialities that hover between property and junk, I suggested in chapter 5, are especially pertinent to the endurance of Cyprus conflict structures. Here, more directly in line with Povinelli's argument, I want to suggest that endurance, in a situation where late liberalism is inflected by a peripheral position in global power dynamics and local conflict anxieties, proliferates upwards on the social scale. It is not only a matter of structural violence that renders ethnic and racial distinctions into class ones. It is also a matter of a structural violence that takes the overcoming of those distinctions, as when middle-class Turkish-Cypriots find themselves pursuing their middle-class affairs in the south, and returns them into ethnic antagonism. In 2016, the erosion of endurance can be seen in the fact that it is not the worst of the two communities that are coexisting uncomfortably, but a normal that is perpetually on the brink of effacement. What goes as care, on the part of the state, is actually a governmentality that measures and regulates, in the process putting in place the foundations on which intolerance discourse builds, when these measures are scrutinized by nationalist politicians and taken back, as in the case of health-care access withdrawn after the financial crisis. The work of endurance takes on from the duplicitous care that announces difference as a statistical category.

This precarious presence, unnoticed, discounted, surviving nevertheless, is symbolized in Nicosia's architecture. In southern Nicosia, economic prosperity and property development have resulted in shopping malls, high-rise office buildings, company headquarters behind all-glass façades, luxury apartment blocks designed by international architectural houses. In the decade after EU accession, and before the property crash that followed the financial crisis of 2013, the Nicosia skyline changed dramatically. But a specific set of buildings in central Nicosia, some of which occupy prime locations for development, have been preserved (figure 8.1). These properties belonged to Turkish-Cypriots, and as such had, since 1974, come under the control of the

FIGURE 8.1. Property development in Nicosia: "Enemy," Turkish-Cypriot, properties persist amid high-rises in southern Nicosia (top left); the opposite
in the north, where Greek-Cypriot properties are prime targets for
development purchases, like in the case of a luxury hotel standing
amid undeveloped properties in northern Nicosia (bottom right).

government, and since 1991, of the Custodian of Turkish-Cypriot properties. In other words, because the properties had been abandoned due to the conflict, their sale, and thus their destruction, was prevented. These buildings, until a few years ago largely unkempt and degraded, sat curiously among avant-garde commercial towers. Their presence spoke uneasily of their absentee owners and their effacement from postwar public life, in all the ways in which this chapter explored.

But in the last decade or so, these buildings were also developed. They were restored, maintained, and many given to use by government departments: the office of antiquities, the former ombudsperson's office. A number of the buildings are not owned by individuals, but by Muslim religious foundations administered by the Evkaf. As such, they were already being used prior to 1974 by non-Turkish-Cypriots. These users were categorized as *thésmii enikiastés* (institutional leaseholders), a category used by the Custodian Department for persons who remained the users of Turkish-Cypriot properties on the basis of rental agreements with the Evkaf or Turkish-Cypriot individuals. Such lease holders included embassies and Greek-Cypriots.

Thus, in spite of the destruction caused by the conflict, and in spite of the rendering of particular sites as Other (and less significant than one's own), these very processes of Othering, abandonment, and failure to achieve peace (e.g., through a negotiated solution ending the conflict)—which are all firmly based in the existence of the conflict—have resulted in the paradoxical situation of buildings being preserved. The buildings are metonyms of the imbricated roof structures this book is describing.

EMERGENT ORDERS

This chapter surveys some of the ways in which Turkish-Cypriots are not "Turkish-Cypriots" and vice versa. At stake in this nonidentity, I have claimed, is the entirety of that imbricated structure of loss that has concerned me throughout. And while the previous two chapters show how that structure has created crevices from which minor others can speak and act, the fact that the structure of loss has only left erasure in the place of Turkish-Cypriotness, means that for these enemy others, the crevices that exist are punctured, craterous. They are the places where the governmentality of ethnic binarism exploded the sovereign bomb of exception and declared that Turkish-Cypriots were no longer legal subjects—they could be only "Turkish-Cypriots," Greek-Cypriots, or nothing at all.

That explosive moment came on November 10, 1964, when the Supreme Court decided that a state of emergency existed in Cyprus, despite its not being declared (*Attorney General v. Mustafa Ibrahim and Others*). The Court had to consider whether to grant bail to four young Turkish-Cypriot men who had been arrested carrying rifles and bullets to a TMT-strongpoint in the Pendadhaktylos Mountain range. They had been charged with "preparing war or warlike undertaking." The Court rejected their defense attorney's appeal that it was not, under the terms of the Constitution, the right place to try them—they should have been tried by Turkish-Cypriot judges. Even though the Constitution had been amended without the consent of the Turkish-Cypriot political power-holders, as provided in it, the amendments that allowed a wholly Greek-Cypriot panel of judges to hear the case were deemed necessary under the circumstances. These were the same circumstances, the Court opined, that rendered it impossible to publish the said amendments to the legal process in Turkish in the *Official Gazette*. The decision effectively announced the state of emergency in the same breath that it also announced the absence of a sovereign. As one of the three sitting judges put it,

> the fact that in spite of what has been going on in Cyprus since December, 1963, no Proclamation of Emergency has been issued under Article 183, rather than indicating, contrary to glaring fact, that no such emergency exists, strongly indicates that the present emergency is one which could not be met within the express provisions of the Constitution. (ibid., Triantaphyllides)

This is emergency outside the normal parameters of emergency, so to speak. Formally speaking, the exceptional situation pertaining to Cypriot law since 1963 has appropriately been described as "law of necessity" and not "emergency," acknowledging the lack of law, even exceptional law, to regulate it. Drawing on law from France, Italy, Greece, and Germany, judges argued this point from different angles (e.g., by considering the practicalities of "transforming legal theory into living law") in the absence of the formal procedures that are meant to do so (ibid., Vassiliades); they discussed the political situation through appeals to the obvious as for example in this reasoning:

> There is ample material on record, to show the conditions prevailing in the Republic at the material time and the circumstances under which the respondents were arrested. Indeed anybody living in the Island since the 21st of December, 1963, must have had sufficient occasion, some way or another, to acquire knowledge of the warlike emergency, harassing the people of Cyprus, during the last, nearly ten months now. (ibid.)

They debated the representativeness of the Constitution: "the Constitution of the Republic was not made by a constituent assembly of the people of Cyprus" (ibid., Josephides); and they pondered the tension between law and society: "the present difficulties of the people of Cyprus, and of their Republic, originate to a considerable extent, in the sin of ignoring time and human nature in the making of our constitution ... [which] was, basically, made fixed and immovable ... law is made for man; and not man for the law" (ibid., Vassiliades). And at the very end, the Court decided that on the basis of demography, the unstated but explosive condition of emergency could be considered liveable for Turkish-Cypriots:

> Finally, considering the proportion of the Turkish citizens of the Republic to the total population and the present composition and powers of the Supreme Court established under Law 33, I do not think that it can be said that the intention of the legislature in enacting the said Law [of necessity], which was passed to meet an imperative and inevitable necessity, was in substance to abolish any of the constitutional safeguards of the Turkish community.

Having thus taken all legal ground under Turkish-Cypriot feet, the polity that emerged after 1964 could now restructure itself around those craters of Turkish-Cypriot absence.

It is on this basis that the various laws and policies with which I began this chapter have been building. The absenteeism of Turkish-Cypriots since 1964 has allowed the articulations of "refugee," affectively, topographically, and normatively, to reflect the ethnic singularity that undercuts the whole structure of loss. This absenteeism is effectively the equivalent of denationalization that Agamben sees as decisive in the emergence of bare life. Post-1964, and even more so post-1974, Turkish-Cypriots were denied all rights—from voting to marriage—that the Constitution extended to them as members of a communal group,. And it was not until appeals to the ECtHR that they got them back as individuals (*Aziz v. Cyprus*, 69949/01; *Selim v. Cyprus* 47293/99). We can thus trace a story between the recognition of an undeclared state of emergency in 1964, the Custodian law, and the ECtHR decisions. It is a story of how political life is stripped away, comes to be equated to property, and returns as existence outside community.

The existence of Turkish-Cypriots as "children in the closet," as Le Guin and Povinelli would put it, is known. But it is an unspoken knowledge. And it is this lack of speech that goes hand in hand with the knowledge that renders loss performative in all the ways I have described thus far. It is the refusal to speak that lends the performance its efficacy. In Povinelli's analysis, driving away from Omelas, as Le Guin offers in the end of her novel, is not an acceptable conclusion—it is a cop-out. In my analysis thus far, I have shown that dissensus and counter-conduct could perhaps be more acceptable conclusions. But the question posed by Turkish-Cypriot absences is this: what if in the end that dissensus is tied up with recognizing the unspoken and sustaining the entire structure through that very recognition? Perhaps this is what is symbolically entailed in seeing Omelas in the mirror: looking at the ideal in reverse, and recognizing its congruence to abjection is perhaps the only (if unstable) ground we have for counter-conduct.

Much of the critical literature on the War on Terror has provided excellent accounts, as mentioned earlier, for how citizenship is unmade (Nyers 2003; Rygiel 2010; but also Amoore 2006; Vaughan-Williams 2008; Noxolo and Huysmans 2009; Aradau, Huysmans, and Squire 2010). But if we are to ponder a possible post-War on Terror, we need to start formulating accounts of how citizenship, once unmade, is then *remade*. This is not an imaginary situation. Detainees have been released from Guantanamo. Rendition victims have received compensation. Refugee detention practices have been condemned in courts. The law, bent, laundered, contravened, and overridden, sometimes haunts the sovereign. But that does not necessarily mean that vindication triumphs. We know nothing of the lives rebuilt post-Guantanamo or post-rendition. How does that recovery of the ordinary, as Das would say, come about? What we have is glimpses of other wars and other conflicts. The Cypriot postconflict subject of refugeehood, idealized, abjected, and remade as self and enemy citizen gives us an idea of just how bleak the picture might be.

CONCLUSION

CHRISTMAS BOXES

It is a summer Wednesday in 2003 and UNFICYP is delivering humanitarian supplies to the enclaved of Rizokarpaso, center of Karpasia region. The Greek-Cypriot enclaved arrive on tractors and load them with gas bottles and foodstuffs. They are all women, elderly ones, in black dresses and headscarves that mourn the loss of family members. Elsewhere, this might have been an empowering image: rural, elderly, marginalized women steering big vehicles and bringing supplies home. Here, it is most likely a defense tactic. Frail women elicit less antagonism receiving goods to which their onlooking (Turkish) settler neighbors have no access. I am not told this, but I am told of strained relations between the two groups, widespread intimidation of the enclaved, and problems with Turkish-Cypriot authorities, primarily regarding schooling and various kinds of permissions and licenses, relating mainly to property rights. These are well-known problems, at the focus of the work of the Republic's parliamentary Committee on Refugees-Enclaved-Missing-Adversely Affected Persons. They have been the focus of campaigns targeting the international community and of ongoing UN monitoring.[1]

Sometime later, a settler girl tells me of her Greek-Cypriot friend in the village. She fondly remembers the dolls the friend gave her when they were little because she did not have any of her own. At Christmas time, such dolls were collected among other toys from schools in the south, and they were packed in ration boxes that made it to the enclaved on UNFICYP visits. They were items that connected Greek-Cypriot school kids to their lost brethren over the Line, the ones not lucky enough to be refugees. It had not occurred to any of us then that they would enter a gift economy that mitigated ethnic antagonism—and that they would end up in Turkish hands.

But this is the complex of performances through which people become subjects in postwar Cyprus. They perform friendship, humanitarianism, frailty, but also struggle, fear, enmity, and perseverance. In the performance, the line between truth and simulation does not exist. Survival undercuts a whole spectrum of activities. Survival is at stake because this is a culture of refugeehood, where life is predicated on an assumption of loss.

Less known have been better relations, maintained in another village in the area where enclaved Greek-Cypriots live. Years later, Savvas Liasi, the informal spokesperson of the Greek-Cypriots of Ayia Triada, tells me of good relations with Turkish neighbors—Turks who came from various Anatolian villages with a long Greek history, and who spoke Greek as a first language. They have tended fields together, maintained exchanges ritualistic and economic, ensured a social balance, which by 2017, Liasi could describe this way: "We have had no problem." There is stoic talk, though, of a missing son from the 1974 war, whom he buried only a few years ago, and a daughter, who having left at eighteen, could not return to visit for the next twenty years. She saw them only infrequently, she says, when visiting relatives in the south on her return trips from abroad, whenever her parents were given permission to cross for a few days—one at a time, her mother and father, to make sure someone stays in the house, lest it be listed as "abandoned" and assigned elsewhere. They probably waited in the queues Michel remembers seeing on his crossing to Kormakitis, in the opposite direction.

Enclavement, experienced indirectly, guides Toula Liasi's artwork, which centres around the notion of "home." Her art project *Rusted Evidence* is a series of photographs from installations she produced using materials in her parents' home: buckets, plates, tools, utensils, barrels, wire, fencing, and tomb crosses from the cemetery. They are objects that the enclaved have hung onto, she explains elsewhere in her work (Liasi 2016), because they have needed to stay rooted in their place, they have needed to keep as much "home" as they could through these objects. As an art critic has put it, "The enclaved built their own system attached to spaces and objects that belonged to them, which they had to maintain at all costs if they were to preserve the ownership/power in their own spaces" (Toumazis 2013).

Savvas Liasi has maintained good relations through patient work with authorities structures too: he coordinated village needs with UNFICYP, as for example in asking for olive oil "one time when conditions were hard and the olive trees did not produce." And in writing countless petitions, the Turkish word *dilekçe* (petition) featuring prominently in the description of his life over the years—to ask for permits, for extension of stays in the south, for improvements to the church, and so on. His hand puts an imaginary paper on the table as he describes this, and grabs an imaginary pen with which he mimics the writing he has been doing. The biopower of good relations bureaucratizes the body.

NOT A THEORY

In this book, my theoretical claim is that refugeehood is not an isolated condition but one that props up the whole structure of citizenship. As examined here, loss has been shown to determine understandings of the conflict in Cyprus. These understandings take affective, territorial, and legal forms. And these forms are inextricably connected to one another in what I described as an imbricated structure. The idiom of imbrication has been used to bring into relief a particular type of connection, one that is at once ordered and uncertain. An objection might be that imbrication is not a theory. My claim is precisely this: it is not a claim to theory that explains and perhaps also anticipates, but to an approach that helps us understand better how things come to be. In this sense, like Crenshaw's concept of intersectionality and Enloe's idea of maneuvering, imbrication offers a tool, a conceptual image, on the basis of which we can think through the concurrence of order and uncertainty.

The connections between affect, topology, and law that I explore are performed. Through the book I speak of performances in school contexts, in legal proceedings, on tours, in personal narratives, and in daily interactions. The performative, I have claimed, underlies the Cyprus conflict, it sets the basis upon which the layers of imbrication are spread out. Performativity is in this case more than the context for particular actions. It is a type of knowledge shared and unsaid, through which we know that the ways in which we are positioned vis-à-vis the conflict, the ways in which we speak about it and choose not to, partakes of an excess. Like in Butlerian drag, what makes the performance is this excess. "Politicians shout more than refugees," goes an oft-repeated phrase to describe this excess; it refers to the effervescent rhetoric about loss, passionate and trite at once, and often without substance in the material support it has to offer. But the issue is precisely that it is not confined to political rhetoric, to the stage. It is performed habitually—in school essays, in social media comments, in meal gatherings. And it is performed in the knowledge that it presents the impossible—like drag performs an ideal femininity that does not exist, in the performance of ideal refugeehood a pure victimhood can claim no responsibility and demand and expect full restoration. It hinges on an understanding of what Navaro-Yashin called the "as if"—that things may not be quite like that, but from where we stand it is best to say they are. And in the process, "what is" and "what is best" become inseparable. The "not quite" gets lost.

But also, this precise knowledge is why performativity can account for both conduct and counter-conduct; depending on where one stands. This has been the second part of my argument: that an imbricated layout should not be taken as the end schema of imbrication. The force of the image I am proposing arises both within the layers and in their crevices. Crevices exist in the interconnections between these layers of affect, topology, and law. They are the locations where subjects stand (or crouch, or lie wounded). And they thus determine how they perform. Dissensus is often the condition of these performances. It is spread throughout the structure and it underlies this knowledge of the performance. It carries the potential to disrupt. But it does not always disrupt. And it mostly does not. Performances arise in specific locations within the structure, and where they arise, account for the forms that dissensus takes. A legal battle, an irregular crossing, an alliance to help navigate the system, the formulation of a grievance, speaking back to a policeman: these are examples of counter-conduct arising from dissensus, acts that recognize the falsity of the "as if" and refuse it. And they also remind us that endurance is not only a property of the subject but of the structure too. Where people claim to be refugees "otherwise," where they counter the ways in which the state conducts them as refugee subjects, the aim is not necessarily, or even primarily, to dispense or explode the structure altogether. It is to pick at it, so that space is made for them too. And whereas this may leave holes here and there, or create instabilities, the structure endures despite it all. It endures in spite of but also through performances.

But it needs to be remembered that whatever happens in these crevices is not always an emancipatory struggle. Each act has its consequences. After all, the state also performs, and it also calls back its own performances. A better visualization of the structure then enables a better understanding of why performativity, dissensus, and counter-conduct are theories of subjectivation and not emancipation. An irregular crossing of the border may mean one stays on the island—but it does not mean job security, decent accommodation, or social acceptance. In fact, exactly because it is irregular all those other things are undermined. The border persists, and precarity increases. And this is arguably what a South Asian waiter is pining for.

Recent migration literature has pluralized the focus by turning to spaces such as detention centers, in gray spaces between inclusion and exclusion and of the law, on home communities of returnees and deportees, and in old and new diaspora and migrant communities. These multiple foci trace the multiple versions of success and failure in crossing borders. The account I am offering here presents a perspective from that gray area of not quite crossing. It looks at refugeehood not as a binary question, perhaps not even a question of the in-between (for that also stretches between two poles). Perhaps refugeehood, I suggest, should be seen as a multiple condition of being: at once succeeding and failing, performing and knowing, submitting and resisting.

RECONSIDERATIONS

Cyprus is a unique case study, it is often claimed. It is one of the longest-running conflicts in the world, it negotiates multiple sovereignty arrangements in ways that few places do, and it sits at the crossroads of three continents. Many of the examples I have offered in this book are unique too: displaced individuals with stories that do not comfortably sit with the general narrative, refugees of singular trajectories leading them here, migrants moving against the flow. I have used such uniqueness to show precisely the efficacy and limitations of a structure predicated on prescribed forms of refugeehood, which assumes it knows who refugees are, what they feel, from where they flee, and what they find. As a unique place, I have suggested, Cyprus is a destination of conflict and not peace for refugees.

But if we pause to think through this suggestion we begin to question Cyprus's uniqueness. One parameter that refugee protection has often taken for granted and which the ethnographic findings here question are that refugees flee from conflict settings into nonconflict environments. This has been shown in the book in various ways. But Cyprus is not the only location where this happens. In 2016 as these lines are penned, the first port of call for many

Syrian refugees, Turkey, is in turmoil with war in its eastern Kurdish provinces. Other countries in the region are only relatively more stable than Syria. Kenya, hosting the largest refugee camp until recently (Dadaab), has its own history of political violence and beleaguered economy. Tanzania, which is cited as an example of exceptional response to the refugee crisis in the Rwanda conflict and the country of Malkki's seminal study (1995), is beset by great poverty. Rwanda, a classic example of a postconflict society, had been hosting Congolese refugees since 1996 and Burundians since 2015. In fact, we have known that refugees flee from conflict into safety only in Europe.

Only that is also not true. It is not just that the prime examples of refugees that prompted the write-up of the 1951 Convention were European. And not only that today's migration can be traced back to colonial legacies in the "Eurafrica" encounter (Hansen and Jonsson 2014). More importantly, it is doubtful how far Europe can be taken as a nonconflict area today. As they landed on Greek shores, at least in the recent past, refugees landed in a mesh of policies informed by the antagonism with Turkey. Since February 2016, NATO ships have been patrolling the waters between the two countries, assisting both as well as FRONTEX to "tackle the refugee and migrant crisis."[2] These patrols, the Greek Minister of Defense has mentioned on several occasions since, provide an excellent opportunity for international observers to witness Turkish violations of Greek airspace, which has been a point of dispute since the 1990s (see also Madianou 2005). But they also implicate bilateral tension in an increasingly confrontational field between Turkey, the EU, and member states, where the crossings and readmissions of migrants, and possibly unrecognized refugees too, become a prop in belligerent performances. Like in November 2016, when Turkish Prime Minister Erdoğan threatened to "open the flood gates" into Europe to the three million refugees then in Turkey, should the EU continue to pass judgment on his crackdown of internal opposition following the attempted coup of July 2016 (*Independent*, 25/11/2016). Or in March 2015, when Greek Defense Minister, Panos Kammenos, threatened that "Greece will unleash a 'wave of millions of economic migrants' and jihadists on Europe unless the eurozone backs down on austerity demands" (*Telegraph*, 9/3/2015). The politics of conflict, Greco-Turkish, Euro-Turkish, or Greco-European, become entangled and are amplified on the backs of refugees and migrants.

In Spain, the Basque and Catalan issues inform reception policies in differing ways. In the wake of the August 17, 2017, attack in Barcelona, which killed fifteen, and amid tensions over the Catalan independence referendum that eventually took place on October 1, much discussion focused on an *El Pais* editorial that called on Catalan politicians to "wake up ... [from having] made the independence fantasy the sole issue on Catalonia's political agenda over the last few years" (18/8/17). Up to now, Catalonia had been hailed as an example of refugee reception, and often in disagreement with Madrid policy, while it was also reported that central police have allowed differential access to European police databases to Catalan and Basque police (denying the first and granting the other).[3] In Ireland, the legacy of conflict shapes policies of multiculturalism and integration. And it has become implicated in the Brexit negotiations as these are coming to focus on the fate of the Irish border, an erstwhile celebrated sign of the end of that conflict, now threatened with closure amid a discourse that prioritizes keeping migrants out of the UK.

These examples are at once exemplary of conflict legacies becoming folded into new conflicts but also indicative of the conflicts that envelop the West as a whole. For how legitimately can we indeed claim, that in countries of the West fighting a War on Terror for nearly two decades now, refugees are landing into peaceful environments? The British vote for Brexit and the spiraling racist crime comes to mind, alongside US President Donald Trump's continuing attempts, as of summer 2017, to institute an anti-Muslim travel ban, build a wall in the Mexican desert, and downplay a resurgence in white supremacy. These examples may continue to stupefy us, but they hold a collective lesson: that the West is being rendered a space of conflict for all of us, and that this is done on the back of refugee trajectories. The examples I have highlighted above are thus unique only if we uphold a flawed understanding of such refugee trajectories centered on the move from conflict to peace, and granting success in refugee recognition only where one is deemed worthy of such peace. Such understandings draw more from moral evaluation than lived experience.

The other parameter of refugee discourse I have questioned here is that international legal protection can be decontextualized from local social and legal concepts, and indeed local affective terrains. The crevices in which foreign refugees are caught as they navigate the terrain of refugeehood in Cyprus are all indications of the opposite. But indeed, so are pregnant refugees in Ireland (Luibhéid 2013). As Luibhéid argues, the history of Irish emigration and lack of early regulation of immigration has left asylum-seeking women stranded in irregularity for years and rendered them suspect for abusing the system when they became pregnant. A crevice here is carved by emigration history, itself related to the conflict, lengthy asylum processes, and cultural assumptions about race and sexuality. Another crevice catches Roma migrants in France (Nacu 2012). In 2010, France expelled Romanian and Bulgarian Roma in contravention of the EU's freedom of movement principle, effectively announcing the suspension of their rights as EU citizens—undoing their citizenship, in other words. Crevices, I would argue, exist for multiple other cases of refugee and migrant minorities. Such minorities are maneuvered and overlooked in the meeting of international and local law. Voutira's call (2003) for attention to ethnographic concepts dovetailing with 1951 Convention applications is as pertinent as ever.

Refugee status emerges in this study as anything but a unified sociolegal category. It is not only that local and international concepts jar; we have also seen how refugeehood appears and disappears under many guises in local law. The subjects of refugeehood are considered displaced, refugees, struck, injured; they are matrilineal and patrilineal refugees; they are refugee friends and refugee enemies; they are *gurbet*, *tourkóplikti*, *troglodytes*. Across these categories loss is accentuated, effaced, evaluated. Subjection becomes consistent as it also becomes differentiated.

And at the end of all this, the refugee label sticks. Refugee identity is not marked by temporariness but is exactly the opposite. It sets a status—one that is not overcome when one goes home but instead marks that home, that society, that community, as one that knows and feels refugeehood as a generalized condition. Refugeehood determines, in being its conceptual opposite, gradations of citizenship, but it is similarly a mode of being spread across a series of gradations. The two are not separate but in fact imbricated in one another.

The reconsideration of these parameters as I have argued here shows that refugeehood is an essential component of the ways in which citizenship is conceptualized and structured; it provides the means for establishing, maintaining, and reproducing discrimination, both in law, and in everyday life. And that ultimately, it affects a much wider group of people than those recognized under the "refugee" label. And that is why delimiting that label concerns us all. Better protection of the few, the legal argument often used to defend stringent differentiations between refugees and migrants, is a tool and not a goal. It has resulted in lower standards of protection for the few as well as the many. It is the crying call of hotspot processing in Greece, the conclusion of the EU-Turkey statement, special economic zones in Jordan.[4] It was also the call of refugee patriliny in Cyprus and the selective processing of Syrian applications for relocating Orthodox Christians to the island after 2015. The results of these techniques are fearful publics of natives and immigrants alike, living in insecurity that figures as a plague of our times. Ultimately, we are all dis-placed and longing for the homes we used to have, "just over there," across time and space.

These reconsiderations are pertinent now, when on a global scale multiple so-called refugee crises, of which the Syrian is only one, appear to expose such fundamental inabilities to create meaningful policies. The archaeological analysis of discourse I have undertaken here has highlighted for me the extent to which this crisis is predicated on previous failures to address the implication of global actors in local conflicts, discursive and otherwise. If this crisis is unprecedented, it is a curious response to fall back on well-rehearsed and failing, past practices. Only when we stop seeing refugeehood and citizenship as polar opposites can we begin to address refugeehood and conflict as a global condition, not one that divides the world into conflict and safe zones that are only seemingly so. Postconflict legacies are everywhere; this is after all the function of borders: to signify past conflict. It is this postconflict modality that sets the terms of citizenship as a condition after refugeehood. So the problem of refugeehood is ultimately a problem of managing multiple conflicts and of governing multiple losses.

NOTES

CHAPTER 1

1. See Navaro-Yashin (2012), Papadakis (2004), Dikomitis (2012), Erdal Ilican (2011), Julie Scott (1998), Sahin (2011), and Arslan (2008).

2. Descriptions of these official discourses are provided by Bryant (2012), Volkan (1979), Kizilyürek (2002), and Canefe (2002a and 2002b).

3. Thoughtful accounts of this ambivalence are presented in Navaro-Yashin (2012) and Erdal Ilican (2011).

4. Gordon, Isin, and Bagelman, November 13, 2015, OpenDemocracy: https://www.opendemocracy.net/can-europe-make-it/michel-foucault/rights-and-duties-of-international-citizenship.

5. Ibid.

6. Indicatively, Isin (2002; 2012), Soguk (1999), Ong (1999; 2003; 2006), Soysal (1994; 2015).

7. A lengthy examination of this is undertaken elsewhere (Demetriou 2016a).

8. Brenner (2000, 368), Surin and Hasty (1994, 22) are relevant among many others. More recent studies should also be noted, such as Roque et al. (2016) who follows Mbembe and Nuttall (2004), and Loughran (2016), which are attempting to engage more with the theoretical import of imbrication.

CHAPTER 2

1. This is all the more significant considering that these studies have come on the heels of many works that have asked how Greek- and Turkish-Cypriots came to be differentiated as identities, from variable points on the nationalist spectrum: from ethno-nationalist lenses (Kyrris 1969) to perspectives from critical

nationalism studies (Attalides 1979; Kizilyürek 1993; Bryant 2004; Nevzat 2005). More recent work has shown that property rights as configured during the transition to modern statehood have had a defining role in the formation of these identities as mutually exclusive (Erdal Ilican 2011).

2.   Crawshaw takes these numbers from "casualty lists," presumably of the colonial government. They stand in sharp contrast to lists appearing in propaganda flyers distributed by EOKA at the time (Papageorgiou 1984), counting for example seventy-five dead only in the month of November 1976 (70–73), a month in which Crawshaw lists 34 total casualties. Another attempt (Bonner 2007, 156) to count casualties across this three-year period lists them as 104 British servicemen, eighty-four Turkish-Cypriots, and 366 Greek-Cypriots, of which two hundred are killed by EOKA. Crawshaw seems to be discounting EOKA victims, EOKA flyers seem to be inflating the numbers, but definitive counts, even today, are impossible to ascertain.

3.   The name, of course, was borrowed from another British colonial border that came to signify the abolitionist divide at the heart of the American Civil War.

4.   See AKEL's student wing commentary: http://www.proodeftiki-athinas. gr/aristera/14-istoria/123-to-akel-kai-o-antiapoikiakos-agonas.html.

5.   See also Makarios Doushiotis's investigative historical work: (http:// www.makarios.eu/cgibin/ hweb?-A=718&-V=history) providing diverging numbers from Crawshaw (198 civilians and fourteen police).

6.   Slightly differentiated lists (containing 238 and 243 names in separate instances) are provided in a volume produced by the Council for the Historical Memory of the EOKA Struggle (SIMAE)—see Psillita-Ioannou (1996). It is interesting to note that this list contains the names of only three of the eight people killed in Gönyeli. Note also that EOKA issued a list of sixty-six "fallen heroes" (*pesóndes*) and nine heroes hanged, at the end of its struggle (Papageorgiou 1984, 286–7). To these it is noted, further unnamed individuals should be counted, of whom nine were killed accidentally in violent incidents, sixty-four were murdered by Turks, and fifty-eight were murdered by "Security Forces," presumably belonging to the British police and including Turkish auxiliary policemen.

7.   In everyday language, Green Line is often used interchangeably with Buffer Zone, even when referring to areas outside Nicosia.

8.   It is notable that the most cited source on these numbers classifies the casualties not by fate but by ethnicity only (Oberling 1982, 120), brushing over a

deeply political question about the governmentality of the missing, which became an important issue in later phases of the conflict.

9.   Murat Kanatli, in interview, December 2016.

10.   See http://www.cmp-cyprus.org/content/terms-reference-and-mandate and http://www.mfa.gov.cy/mfa/mfa2016.nsf/mfa10_en/mfa10_en?OpenDocument, last accessed May 20, 2018.

11.   See http://www.mfa.gov.cy/mfa/mfa2016.nsf/All/CE7EF41F2317E76EC2257F9C002D259E?OpenDocument, last accessed May 20, 2018.

12.   Hitchens's work on Cyprus (1997 [1983]), another classic in Cyprus conflict accounts, is an example of this binary. Framed as a critique to Crawshaw, it is meant to attack liberal Western perspectives that seek to lay blame on the Cypriots rather than the imperialism of NATO powers.

13.   Data from pronews.org and newsit.com.cy 25/10/2014 and Cyprus Mail 16/6/2011.

14.   See http://infognomonpolitics.blogspot.com.cy/2009/07/blog-post_6152.html and "https://peacekeeping.un.org/sites/default/files/statsbymissionincidenttype_4_12.pdf, last accessed May 20, 2018. Lindley reports six Greek-Cypriot and three Turkish-Cypriot killings between 1974 and 2002 (2007, 100).

15.   See Papadakis (1994) and Makriyianni (2007).

SECTION I

1.   See Constantinides and Papadakis (2014); Wells, Stylianou-Lambert and Philippou (2014).

2.   See https://www.artcentre.skotinos.com/cycle-of-protest, last accessed May 20, 2018.

3.   Papaeti (2010).

4.   https://elenaparpa.wordpress.com/.

CHAPTER 3

1.   See also Constantinou (2008) and Trimikliniotis (2010).

2.   For critical evaluations of such imagery, see Wells, Stylianou-Lambert, and Philippou (2014) and Stylianou-Lambert and Bounia (2012).

3.   http://www.cwb-international.org/, accessed 15/08/2017. See also Clare McMahan (2008), King (2013), and Peacock (2016).

4.   For example: http://www.nicosia.org.cy/en-GB/home/, last accessed May 20, 2018.

5.   Given the centrality of the play in the theorization of loss, it is actually surprising that a sustained analysis of the insights offered by the play and its various critical discussions has not been undertaken with regard to Cyprus, except in Sant Cassia's work on the missing persons (2005). For my purposes here, the most succinct treatment of the various relevant themes is Butler's feminist take (2002), which prefigures her interest in grievability.

6.   Return-visit itineraries prior to 2003 were often restricted by time-specific checks that did not allow travelers to make stops away from their designated routes.

CHAPTER 4

1.   http://www.moi.gov.cy/moi/CRMD/crmd.nsf/All/A2539464949A270FC 2257EA400386E48? OpenDocument, last accessed July 8, 2016.

2.   Erdal Ilican's (2011) exploration of geographical differences in the distribution of wealth and loss after 1974 is illuminating on this point, which has also been raised by other refugees, as evidenced in this and following chapters.

CHAPTER 5

1.   See https://unficyp.unmissions.org/sites/default/files/28_october_1999. pdf, last accessed May 20, 2018.

2.   See http://www.theguardian.com/theguardian/1999/jul/17/weekend7. weekend, last accessed May 20, 2018.

3.   See also the summary of the case filed by the soldiers' parents with the European Court of Human Rights, *Kallis and Androulla Panayi v. Turkey* (ECtHR, Application no. 45388/99).

4.   For insightful accounts of the movement see Erdal Ilican (2013; 2017).

5.   The history and cultural meanings associated with Ledra Palace Hotel have been explored elsewhere (Demetriou 2012; 2015). In those works, I had begun to think its materialities through loss, which I develop here.

6.   http://www.sigmalive.com/simerini/news/336093/ekleise-akomi-mia-p ligi-tis-eisvolis, last accessed May 20, 2018.

SECTION II

1.   The scheme, which came into effect in 2016, is outlined here: http://www.moi.gov.cy/ moi/moi.nsf/All/36DB428D50A58C00C2257C1B00218CAB, accessed August 23, 2017. It provides the possibility for naturalization to owners of property within the Republic of Cyprus worth over half a million euro who have invested over 2 million euro in the country.

2.   See http://www.infomigrants.net/en/post/4161/defend-europe-far-righ t-group-to-fend-off-migrants-in-mediterranean, accessed August 23, 2017.

CHAPTER 6

1.   Two notable exceptions are a law introducing special import taxes to create revenues for assistance to refugees in 1977 (Law 14/1977), amended multiple times right up to 2000, and the law setting up the Pancyprian Union of Refugees in October 1994 (Law 71[1]/1994) with amendments up to 2014. The slippage between formal law and public discourse (*ektopisthéndes / prósfiyes*) is evident in these secondary laws, for which perhaps the threshold of scrutiny was lower than primary law that regulates identification, rights, and benefits examined in chapter 4.

2.   In light of the Brexit referendum in 2016 (announced as these lines were penned), this situation gives pause to consider the wider politics in which affect often comes to determine law. Elsewhere (Demetriou 2016b) I have suggested that while Protocol 10 offers a precedent for extending the *acquis* to Scotland and Northern Ireland in the event that the UK eventually leaves the EU, the failure to take it up is more likely to result from EU punitive governmentalities than legal difficulties.

3.   See EU Commission's fact sheet (2016) and criticisms by the Migration Policy Institute (MPI 2016), Council of Europe's Commissioner for Human Rights (Muiznieks 2016), and Amnesty International (EUR 44/3825/2016).

4.   Consider a parallel in the field of the financial crisis. The legal vacuity surrounding EU governmentality of exception is one of the rallying calls of former Greek Minister of Finance, Yanis Varoufakis, who was scandalized to discover while in negotiation of the Greek austerity package that the all-important body overseeing the management of financial crisis in the EU, the Eurogroup, "does not exist in European law" (https://www.yanisvaroufakis.eu/2016/03/30/the-e

urogroup-made-simple/, accessed August 26, 2016). Instead, in Varoufakis's work (2015), this legal evacuation becomes comprehensible via a historical analysis of Germany's role in the geo-economics of US concerns—and, I would suggest, a role that also required and was built upon the peripheral status of countries such as, and indeed particularly, Greece.

5.   See *Cyprus Mail*, 27/5/17 at http://cyprus-mail.com/2017/05/27/unhcr-welcomes-uk-court-ruling-sba-refugees/, accessed August 31, 2017.

6.   The Aliens and Immigration Unit arrested 666 "illegal migrants" during the year, and it deported 2,892 persons. This and other reports mentioned accessible at http://www.police.gov.cy/ police/police.nsf/All/17DB9FEDE5B978C0 C2257F92002036E1/$file/YAM-greek.pdf, last accessed July 9, 2016.

7.   Civil Registry and Migration Department statistics: http://www.moi. gov.cy/moi/crmd/crmd.nsf/All/ 083980C0BA1B224AC2257EA4003861BA?Open-Document, accessed June 14, 2016.

8.   The differences between "subsidiary protection" and "humanitarian status" remain unclear and largely within the bounds of national instruments and laws, as an ECRE study notes (2009). The interpretation of the concepts and protection provided under them according to EU directives has been criticized in a number of studies (Gil-Bazo 2007; Hutton 2009; Errera 2010; Schuster 2011b).

9.   Domestic work visas, for example, carry specifications about where one lives, works, and whether one may change employment. Student visas restrict employment. Permits on the basis of marriage may come with social services monitoring. The protection of trafficking victims is dependent on their cooperation with the criminal investigation and requires that the victims' passports be held by the police.

10.   Shiakalli, December 12, 2013, available at https://www.youtube.com/watch?v= UF2xTOy1MI8&noredirect=1, accessed June 15, 2016.

11.   Census of Population report, 2001, vol. 4, page 19.

12.   http://citiesofmigration.ca/ezine_stories/unscrambling-the-immigration-argument-saskia-sassen/, last accessed May 20, 2018.

13.   Under this law, since revised into Dublin III (604/2013), asylum applications are examined by the authorities of the country of initial entry. This means that all applicants are returned from Western Europe to countries of the periphery, such as Greece, Italy, or Spain. This arrangement was heavily criticized both in academia (Samers 2004; Papadimitriou and Papageorgiou 2005; Broeders 2007;

Enenajor 2008; Alberti 2010; Schuster 2011a; 2011b) and in law (Mallia 2011; Stefanelli 2011; Moreno-Lax 2012).

14.   Reuters, September 7, 2015: http://www.reuters.com/article/us-europe-m igrants-cyprus-idUSKCN0R711220150907.

CHAPTER 7

1.   http://www.missing-cy.org/archive/missing_statistics.html, last accessed May 20, 2018.

2.   See for example Hicks (2013) and Karlan (2002).

3.   For example, MacLean (2002) and Eisenstein (2015).

4.   Here the critique concentrates around the question of capitalism's alliance with feminist positions—for example Fraser (2013) and Jaquette (2010).

5.   Data from http://www.ekloges.gov.cy/, accessed August 29, 2017.

6.   Available at http://www.mitrogonia.com/attachments/article/140/ Επιστολή στον πρόεδρο της βουλής.pdf, accessed July 10, 2016.

7.   See http://www.moi.gov.cy/moi/pio/pio2013.nsf/All F21E60DD32D15 A43C2257FB00049622A?OpenDocument&highlight=G3&L=G, accessed June 22, 2016.

8.   Counts from statistics of the United Nations Office for Drugs and Crime: https://data.unodc.org. Search was conducted on June 22, 2016.

9.   Data from www.philenews.com, www.sigmalive.com, and www.antliw o.com, and www.cyprustimes.com, accessed June 22, 2016.

10.   See http://www.lyssarides.com/speeches/23.shtml.

11.   http://www.yenicag.com.cy/ yenicag/2011/12/mezar-taslari-mi-eski-yazilar i-mi-yoksa-resmi-tarih-mi-yalan-soyler-murat-kanatli/.

CHAPTER 8

1.   For a detailed and penetrating analysis of policies regarding the management of properties belonging to the displaced, covering both sides of the island in a comparative perspective, see Erdal Ilican (2011).

2.   The refugee assistance law (14/1977) imposing special import taxes did not actually refer to "refugees" as persons but to "refugee assistance" (*prosfiyikí ebivárinsis*), using the word in the adjectival form.

3. http://www.domresearchcenter.com/news/cyprus/cypa35murder.html, last accessed May 20, 2018.

4. Yenidüzen 19/3/03; Kıbrıslı 19/3/03; Phileleftheros 20/3/03; Politis 20/3/03; Kıbrıslı, 20/3/03; Politis 21/3/03; Politis 23/3/03.

5. Haravgí, 27/3/03.

6. http://www.moa.gov.cy/MOI/pio/pio.nsf/ All/38504A03776B41BEC2 257E520028C85A?OpenDocument, last accessed June 27, 2016.

7. This point is further elaborated in Demetriou (2007).

8. PIO press release, April 30, 2003, no. 8: "Politikí tis Kivérnisis énanti ton Tourkokipríon (Dhésmi Métron)" [The Government's Policy regarding the Turkish-Cypriots (Package of Measures).

9. PIO press release, September 16, 2003, no. 11.

10. A more realistic baseline might have been to quadruple 227 into a monthly number of about nine hundred, making the four-month increase by September 17 percent and not 367.

CHAPTER 9

1. Examples include http://kypros.org/Cyprus_Problem/enclaves.html; UNSG reports (S/15812; S/15502; S/16596); UNHCHR reports (A/HRC/25/21 accessed May 20, 2018; A/HRC/22/51; A/HRC/31/21).

2. http://www.nato.int/nato_static_fl2014/assets/pdf/ pdf_2016_10/20161025_1610-factsheet-aegean-sea-eng.pdf, accessed August 31, 2017.

3. BBC *Barcelona Attacks: What could they mean for Catalan independence?* August 20, 2017, accessed at http://www.bbc.com/news/world-europ e-40990947 on August 31, 2017.

4. The latter proposed by Betts and Collier (2015) and critiqued in a number of venues (also Harake 2017).

BIBLIOGRAPHY

Aas, K.F. 2011. "'Crimmigrant' Bodies and Bona Fide Travelers: Surveillance, Citizenship and Global Governance." *Theoretical Criminology* 15 (3): 331–46.

Adorno, T., and M. Horkheimer. 1979. *Dialectic of Enlightenment*. Translated by John Cumming. London: Verso.

Agamben, G. 1998. *Homo Sacer: Sovereign Power and Bare Life*. Palo Alto: Stanford University Press.

———. 2005. *State of Exception*. Chicago: University of Chicago Press.

Agathangelou, A.M. 1997. "The Cypriot 'Ethnic' Conflict in the Production of Global Power." Ph.D. Dissertation, Political Science Department, Syracuse University

———. 2000. "Nationalist Narratives and (Dis) appearing Women: State-sanctioned Sexual Violence." *Canadian Women Studies* 19 (4): 12–21.

———. 2004. *The Global Political Economy of Sex: Desire, Violence, and Insecurity in Mediterranean Nation States*. New York: Palgrave Macmillan.

Alberti, G. 2010. "Across the Borders of Lesvos: The Gendering of Migrants' Detention in the Aegean." *Feminist Review* 94 (1): 138–47.

Allinson, J. 2015. "The Necropolitics of Drones." *International Political Sociology* 9 (2): 113–27.

Althusser, L. 2006. "Ideology and Ideological State Apparatuses (Notes towards an Investigation)." In Sharma, A. and A. Gupta (eds) *The Anthropology of the State: A Reader* 9 (1): 86–98.

Altinay, A.G. 2006. "In Search of Silenced Grandparents: Ottoman Armenian Survivors and Their (Muslim) Grandchildren. "In Kieser, H.-L. and E. Plozza (eds.), *Der Völkermord an den Armeniern, die Türkei und Europa (The Armenian Genocide, Turkey and Europe)*, Zürich: Chronos, 117–32.

——. 2014. "Gendered Silences, Gendered Memories: New Memory Work on Islamized Armenians in Turkey." *Eurozine* February 2014: 1–24.

Altinay, A.G., and F. Çetin. 2014. *The Grandchildren: The Hidden Legacy of "Lost" Armenians in Turkey*. London: Transaction.

Amoore, L. 2006. "Biometric Borders: Governing Mobilities in the War on Terror." *Political Geography* 25 (3): 336–51.

Andersson, R. 2014. *Illegality, Inc.: Clandestine Migration and the Business of Bordering Europe*.Berkeley: University of California Press.

Anthias, F. 1989. "Women and Nationalism in Cyprus." In Yuval-Davis, N. and F. Anthias (eds.) *Woman–Nation–State*. London: Macmillan, 150–67.

Aradau, C., J. Huysmans, and V. Squire. 2010. "Acts of European Citizenship: A Political Sociology of Mobility." *Journal of Common Market Studies* 48 (4): 945–65.

Arendt, H. 1994 [1943]. "We Refugees." In Robinson, M. (ed.) *Altogether Elsewhere: Writers on Exile*. London: Faber and Faber, 110–19

——. 1951 [1948]. *The Origins of Totalitarianism*. New York: Schocken Books.

——. 1963. *Eichmann in Jerusalem*. London: Penguin.

Aretxaga, B. 1997. *Shattering Silence: Women, Nationalism, and Political Subjectivity in Northern Ireland*. Princeton: Princeton University Press.

Arslan, Y. 2008. "The Fairy-tale Like Story of Cyprus in the Eyes of Turkish Cypriot Youth: Re-Memorizing the 'Past' as a Communication Tool between Generations." In İlter, T., NN. Kara, M. Atabey, Y. Arslan, and M. Orun (eds.) *Communication in Peace/Conflict in Communication*, Famagusta: EMU press, 281–88.

Attalides, M.A. 1979. *Cyprus: Nationalism and International Politics*. London: Macmillan.

Austin, J.L. 1975. *How to Do Things with Words*. Oxford: Oxford University Press.

Badiou, A. 2005. *Being and Event*. London: Continuum.

Bakonyi, J. 2010. "Between Protest, Revenge and Material Interests: A Phenomenological Analysis of Looting in the Somali War." *Disasters* 34 (2): 238–55.

Banner, S. 2005. "Why Terra Nullius? Anthropology and Property Law in Early Australia." *Law and History Review* 23 (1): 95–131.

Barthes, R. 1981. *Camera Lucida: Reflections on Photography*. London: Macmillan.

Bates, D.C. 2002. "Environmental Refugees? Classifying Human Migrations Caused by Environmental Change." *Population & Environment* 23 (5): 465–77.

Baudrillard, J., 1975. *The Mirror of Production*. St. Louis, MO: Telos Press.

Beekes, R.S. 2009. *Etymological Dictionary of Greek*. Leiden: Brill.

Benjamin, W. 1999 [1968]. *Illuminations*. London: Pimlico.

Betts, A., and P. Collier. 2015. "Help Refugees Help Themselves: Let Displaced Syrians Join the Labor Market." *Foreign Affairs* 94 (Nov/Dec): 84–92.

Bhabha, H.K. 1994. *The Location of Culture*. London: Routledge.

Bigo, D. 2006. "Globalized (In)security: The Field and the Ban-opticon." In Bigo, D. and A. Tsoukala (eds.) *Illiberal practices of liberal regimes: The (in) security games* Paris: L'Harmattan, 5–49.

Billig, M. 1995. *Banal Nationalism*. London: Sage.

Bloch, A., and L. Schuster. 2005. "At the Extremes of Exclusion: Deportation, Detention and Dispersal." *Ethnic and Racial Studies* 28 (3): 491–512.

Brenner, N. 2000. "The Urban Question: Reflections on Henri Lefebvre, Urban Theory and the Politics of Scale." *International Journal of Urban and Regional Research* 24 (2): 361–78.

Broeders, D. 2007. "The New Digital Borders of Europe: EU Databases and the Surveillance of Irregular Migrants." *International Sociology* 22 (1): 71–92.

Brown, W. 1995. *States of Injury: Power and Freedom in Late Modernity*. Princeton: Princeton University Press.

———. 2010. *Walled States, Waning Sovereignty*. Cambridge: MIT Press.

Brun, C. 2010. "Hospitality: Becoming 'IDPs' and 'Hosts' in Protracted Displacement." *Journal of Refugee Studies*, 23(3), 337–55.

Bryant, R. 2011. *The Past in Pieces: Belonging in the New Cyprus*. Philadelphia: University of Pennsylvania Press.

———. 2004. *Imagining the Modern: The Cultures of Nationalism in Cyprus*. London: I.B. Tauris.

Butler, J. 1993. *Bodies That Matter: On the Discursive Limits of Sex*. London: Routledge.

———. 1997a. *Excitable Speech: A Politics of the Performative*. Abingdon: Routledge.

———. 1997b. *The Psychic Life of Power: Theories in Subjection*. Palo Alto: Stanford University Press.

———. 2002. *Antigone's Claim: Kinship between Life and Death.* New York: Columbia University Press.

———. 2004. *Precarious Life: The Powers of Mourning and Violence.* New York: Verso.

———. 2011 [1990]. *Gender Trouble: Feminism and the Subversion of Identity.* London: Routledge.

———. 2016. *Frames of War: When Is Life Grievable?* New York: Verso.

Canefe, N. 2002a. "Refugees or Enemies? The Legacy of Population Displacements in Contemporary Turkish Cypriot Society." *South European Society and Politics* 7 (3): 1–28.

———. 2002b. "Turkish Nationalism and Ethno-Symbolic Analysis: The Rules of Exception." *Nations and Nationalism* 8 (2): 133–55.

Chandler, D., and J. Reid. 2018. 'Being in Being': Contesting the Ontopolitics of Indigeneity. *The European Legacy*, published online January 2018: 1–18.

Chatty, D., ed. 2010a. *Deterritorialized Youth: Sahrawi and Afghan Refugees at the Margins of the Middle East.* New York: Berghahn Books.

———. 2010b. *Displacement and Dispossession in the Modern Middle East.* New York: Cambridge University Press.

Christou, M. 2007. "The Language of Patriotism: Sacred History and Dangerous Memories." *British Journal of Sociology of Education* 28 (6): 709–22.

Clare McMahan, S. 2008. "Infinite Possibility: Clowning with Elderly People." *Care Management Journals* 9 (1): 19–24.

Cockburn, C. 1998. *The Space Between Us: Negotiating Gender and National Identities in Conflict.* London: Zed Books.

———. 2004. *The Line: Women, Partition and the Gender Order in Cyprus.* London: Zed Books.

Comaroff, J., and J.L. Comaroff. 2001. "Naturing the Nation: Aliens, Apocalypse, and the Postcolonial State." *Social Identities* 7 (2): 233–65.

Conlon, D. 2011a. "A Fractured Mosaic: Encounters with the Everyday amongst Refugee and Asylum Seeker Women." *Population, Space and Place* 17 (6): 714–26.

———. 2011b. "Waiting: Feminist Perspectives on the Spacings/Timings of Migrant (Im) mobility." *Gender, Place & Culture* 18 (3): 353–60.

Connor, M.C. 2005. *The Invention of Terra Nullius: Historical and Legal Fictions on the Foundation of Australia.* Paddington: Maclaey Press.

Constandinides, C., and Y. Papadakis, (eds.) 2014. *Cypriot Cinemas: Memory, Conflict, and Identity in the Margins of Europe.* London: Bloomsbury.

Constantinou, C.M. 1995. "Memoirs of the Lost: The Dead and the Missing in the Politics of Poetry." *The Cyprus Review* 7 (2): 59–73.

———. 2007. "Aporias of Identity: Bicommunalism, Hybridity and the Cyprus Problem." *Cooperation and Conflict* 42 (3): 247–70.

———. 2008. "On the Cypriot States of Exception." *International Political Sociology* 2 (2): 145–64.

Constantinou, C.M., O. Demetriou, and M. Hatay. 2012. "Conflicts and Uses of Cultural Heritage in Cyprus." *Journal of Balkan and Near Eastern Studies* 14 (2): 177–98.

Constantinou, C.M., and S.O. Opondo. 2016. "Engaging the 'Ungoverned': The Merging of Diplomacy, Defence and Development." *Cooperation and Conflict* 51 (3): 307–24.

Constantinou, C.M., and O.P. Richmond. 2005. "The Long Mile of Empire: Power, Legitimation and the UK Bases in Cyprus." *Mediterranean Politics*, 10 (1): 65–84.

Crawshaw, N. 1978. *The Cyprus Revolt: An Account of the Struggle for Union with Greece.* London: George Allen and Unwin.

Crenshaw, K. 1989. "Demarginalizing the Intersection of Race and Sex: A Black Feminist Critique of Antidiscrimination Doctrine, Feminist Theory and Antiracist Politics." *University of Chicago Legal Forum*: 139–68.

Dahlman, C., and G. Ó Tuathail. 2005a. "Broken Bosnia: The Localized Geopolitics of Displacement and Return in Two Bosnian Places." *Annals of the Association of American Geographers* 95 (3): 644–62.

———. 2005b. "The Legacy of Ethnic Cleansing: The International Community and the Returns Process in Post-Dayton Bosnia–Herzegovina" *Political Geography* 24 (5): 569–99.

Das, V. 1995. *Critical Events: An Anthropological Perspective on Contemporary India.* Oxford: Oxford University Press.

———. 2007. *Life and Words: Violence and the Descent into the Ordinary.* Berkeley: University of California Press.

Davis, E. A. 2017a. "'The Information Is Out There': Transparency, Responsibility, and the Missing in Cyprus." In *Competing Responsibilities: The*

Politics and Ethics of Contemporary Life, edited by S. Trnka and C. Trundle, 135–55. Durham, NC: Duke University Press.

Davis, E. A. 2017b. "Time Machines: The Matter of the Missing in Cyprus." In *Unfinished: The Anthropology of Becoming*, edited by J. Biehl and P. Locke, 217–42. Durham, NC: Duke University Press.

De Genova, N. 2013. "Spectacles of Migrant 'Illegality': The Scene of Exclusion, the Obscene of Inclusion." *Ethnic and Racial Studies* 36 (7): 1180–98.

Demetriou, O. 2006. "Freedom Square: The Unspoken Reunification of a Divided City." *HAGAR: Studies in Culture, Polity & Identities* 7 (1).

———. 2007. "To Cross or Not to Cross? Subjectivization and the Absent State in Cyprus." *Journal of the Royal Anthropological Institute* 13 (4): 987–1006.

———. 2008. "Reading the Paratexts of the Cyprus Conflict: Policy, Science, and the Pursuit Of 'Objectivity.'" *The Cyprus Review* 20 (1): 93–113.

———. 2012. "The Militarization of Opulence: Engendering a Conflict Heritage Site." *International Feminist Journal of Politics* 14 (1): 56–77.

———. 2013. *Capricious Borders: Minority, Population, and Counter-conduct between Greece and Turkey*. New York: Berghahn Books.

———. 2015. "Grand Ruins: Ledra Palace Hotel and the Rendering of 'Conflict' as Heritage in Cyprus." In *War and Cultural Heritage: Biographies of Place*, edited by M. L. Stig Sørensen and D. Viejo Rose, 183–207. Cambridge: Cambridge University Press.

———. 2016a. "Counter-conduct and the Everyday: Anthropological Engagements with Philosophy." *Global Society* 30 (2): 218–37.

———. 2016b. "Europe's Metacolonial Reckoning: Thinking Brexit at the Margins." *Social Anthropology* 24 (4): 478–502.

Demetriou, O., and R. Dimova. 2018. *The Political Materialities of Borders: New Theoretical Directions*. Manchester: Manchester University Press.

Demetriou, O., and M. Hadjipavlou. 2014. "A Feminist Position on Sharing Governmental Power and Forging Citizenship in Cyprus: Proposals for the Ongoing Peace Negotiations." *Feminist Review* 107 (1): 98–106.

———. 2016. "Engendering the Post-Liberal Peace in Cyprus: UNSC Resolution 1325 as a Tool." In *Post-Liberal Peace Transitions*, edited by O.P. Richmond and S. Pogodda, 83–104. Edinburgh: Edinburgh University Press.

———. 2018. "The Impact of Women's Activism on the Peace Negotiations in Cyprus." *Nationalism and Ethnic Politics* 24 (1): 50–65.

Demetriou, T., and S. Vlachos. 2007. *Betrayed Revolt*. Nicosia: Ekfrasi.

De Pauw, L.G. 2014. *Battle Cries and Lullabies: Women in War from Prehistory to the Present*. Norman, OK: University of Oklahoma Press.

Der Derian, J. 2000. "Virtuous War/Virtual Theory." *International Affairs* 76 (4): 771–88.

Derrida, J. 1976. *Of Grammatology*. Baltimore: Johns Hopkins University Press.

———. 2000. "Hostipitality." *Angelaki: Journal of Theoretical Humanities* 5 (3): 3–18.

———. 2001. *On Cosmopolitanism and Forgiveness*. London: Routledge.

Derya, D. 2009. "The Unwritten History of the Turkish-Cypriot Women's Movement." In *Paths to Gender: European Historical Perspectives on Women and Men*, edited by C. Salvaterra and B. Waaldijk, 141–52. Pisa: Plus-Pisa University Press.

Dikomitis, L. 2012. *Cyprus and Its Places of Desire: Cultures of Displacement among Greek and Turkish Cypriot Refugees*. I.B. Tauris.

Dillon, M., and J. Reid. 2009. *The Liberal Way of War: Killing to Make Life Live*. London: Routledge.

Douzinas, C., and R. Warrington. 1991. "'A Well-founded Fear of Justice': Law and Ethics in Postmodernity." *Law and Critique* 2 (2): 115–47.

Eisenstein, H. 2015. *Feminism Seduced: How Global Elites Use Women's Labor and Ideas to Exploit the World*. London: Routledge.

El-Hinnawi, Essam. 1985. *Environmental Refugees*. United Nations Environment Program.

Ellinas, A. 2010. *The Media and the Far Right in Western Europe: Playing the Nationalist Card*. Cambridge: Cambridge University Press.

Enenajor, A. 2008. "Rethinking Vulnerability: European Asylum Policy Harmonization and Unaccompanied Asylum Seeking Minors." *Childhoods Today* 2 (2): 1–24.

Enloe, C.H. 2014 [1989]. *Bananas, Beaches and Bases: Making Feminist Sense of International Politics*. Berkeley: University of California Press.

Enloe, C. 2000. *Maneuvers: The International Politics of Militarizing Women's Lives*. Berkeley: University of California Press.

Erdal Ilican, M. 2011. "The Making of Sovereignty through Changing Property/Land Rights and the Contestation of Authority in Cyprus." PhD diss., Oxford University Centre for the Environment: University of Oxford.

———. 2013. "The Occupy Buffer Zone Movement: Radicalism and Sovereignty in Cyprus." *The Cyprus Review* 25 (1): 55–80.

———. 2017. "Radicalising No-Man's Land." In *The Politics of Culture in Turkey, Greece & Cyprus: Performing the Left Since the Sixties*, edited by L. Karakatsanis and N. Papadogiannis, 249–69. Abingdon: Routledge.

Errera, R. 2010. "The CJEU and Subsidiary Protection: Reflections on Elgafaji— and After." *International Journal of Refugee Law* 23 (1): 93–112.

Evans, G. 2017. "Brexit Britain: Why We are All Postindustrial Now." *American Ethnologist*, 44 (2): 215–19.

Farah, R. 2009. "Refugee Camps in the Palestinian and Sahrawi National Liberation Movements: A Comparative Perspective." *Journal of Palestine Studies* 38 (2): 76–93.

Fassin, D., and R. Rechtman. 2009. *The Empire of Trauma. An Enquiry into the Conditions of Victimhood*. Princeton, NJ: Princeton University Press.

Ferguson, K., 2012. *All in the Family: On Community and Incommensurability*. Durham, NC: Duke University Press.

Fiddian-Qasmiyeh, E. 2011. "The Pragmatics of Performance: Putting 'Faith' in Aid in the Sahrawi Refugee Camps." *Journal of Refugee Studies* 24 (3): 533–47.

Foucault, M. 1990. *The History of Sexuality: An Introduction*. Vol. I. New York: Vintage.

———. 2004. *Society Must Be Defended*. London: Penguin

———. 2007. *Security, Territory and Population. (Lectures at the Collège de France 1977–1978)*. Basingstoke: Palgrave Macmillan.

———. 2008. "The Birth of Biopolitics." Lectures at the Collège de France, 1978– 1979. Basingstoke: Palgrave Macmillan.

———. 2010. "The Government of Self and Others." Lectures at the Collège de France, 1982–1983. Basingstoke: Palgrave Macmillan.

———. 2011. "The Courage of Truth: The Government of Self and Others II." Lectures at the Collège de France, 1983–1984). Basingstoke: Palgrave Macmillan.

Fraser, N. 2013. *Fortunes of Feminism: From State-managed Capitalism to Neoliberal Crisis*. London: Verso.

Freud, S. 2005. *On Murder, Mourning and Melancholia*. London: Penguin.

Geoghegan, P. 2008. "Beyond Orange and Green? The Awkwardness of Negotiating Difference in Northern Ireland." *Irish Studies Review* 16 (2): 173–94.

Gibbons, H.S. 1997. *The Genocide Files*. London: Charles Bravos.

Gibney, M.J. 2004. *The Ethics and Politics of Asylum: Liberal Democracy and the Response to Refugees.* Cambridge: Cambridge University Press.

Giddens, A. 1984. *The Constitution of Society: Outline of the Theory of Structuration.* Cambridge: Polity Press.

Gil-Bazo, M. T. 2007. "Refugee Status and Subsidiary Protection under EC Law: The Qualification Directive and the Right to Be Granted Asylum." In *Whose Freedom, Security and Justice? EU Immigration and Asylum Law and Policy,* edited by A. Baldaccini, E. Guild, and H. Toner, 219-64. Portland, OR: Hart Publishing.

Gonzalez-Ruibal, A. 2006. "The Past is Tomorrow. Towards an Archaeology of the Vanishing Present." *Norwegian Archaeological Review,* 39(2): 110–25.

———. 2008. "Time to Destroy: An Archaeology of Supermodernity." *Current Anthropology* 49 (2): 247–79.

Green, S. 2013. "Borders and the Relocation of Europe." *Annual Review of Anthropology* 42: 345–61.

———. 2018. "Lines, Traces and Tidemarks: Further Reflections on Forms of Border." In *The Political Materialities of Borders: New Theoretical Directions,* edited by O. Demetriou and R. Dimova. Manchester: Manchester University Press.

Grichting, A.K. 2009. "Thirdscapes. Ecological Planning and Human Reconciliation in Borderlands." *International Journal of Environmental, Cultural, Economic and Social Sustainability* 6 (5): 239–56.

Griffiths, M.B.E. 2014. "Who Is Who Now?: Truth, Trust and Identification in the British Asylum and Immigration Detention System." PhD diss., COMPAS: University of Oxford.

Güven-Lisaniler, F. 2006. Gender Equality in North Cyprus (Turkish Republic Of North Cyprus). *Quaderns de la Mediterrània* 7 (1): 133–40.

Güven-Lisaniler, F., and F. Bhatti. 2005. "Determinants of Female Labour Force Participation: A Study of North Cyprus." *Review of Social, Economic and Business Studies* 5/6 (1): 209–26.

Güven-Lisaniler, F., L. Rodriguez, and S. Uğural. 2005, "February. Migrant Sex Workers and State Regulation in North Cyprus." In *Women's Studies International Forum.* 28 (1): 79–91.

Hadjipavlou-Trigeorgis, M.C. 1987. "*Identity Conflict Resolution in Divided Societies: The Case of Cyprus.*" PhD diss. Comparative Social and Political Change: Boston University.

Hadjipavlou, M. 2004. *Women in the Cypriot Communities: Interpreting Women's Lives.* Nicosia: Printways.

———. 2010. *Women and Change in Cyprus: Feminisms and Gender in Conflict.* London: I.B. Tauris.

Hammond, L. 2004. *This Place Will Become Home: Refugee Repatriation to Ethiopia.* Ithaca, NY: Cornell University Press.

Hansen, P., and S. Jonsson. 2014. *Eurafrica: The Untold History of European Integration and Colonialism.* London: Bloomsbury.

Harake, N. 2017. 'Turning Refugees into Workers: Economic Experiments in Refugee Management' paper presented at the International Postgraduate Summer School *Cultures, Migrations, Borders,* July 10, 2017, Plomari, Lesvos.

Harrell-Bond, B.E. 1986. *Imposing Aid: Emergency Assistance to Refugees.* Oxford: Oxford University Press.

Hartmann, B. 2010. "Rethinking Climate Refugees and Climate Conflict: Rhetoric, Reality and the Politics of Policy Discourse." *Journal of International Development* 22 (2): 233–46.

Harvey, D. 2001. *Spaces of Capital: Towards a Critical Geography.* London: Routledge.

Hathaway, J.C. 2007a. "Forced Migration Studies: Could We Agree Just to 'Date'?" *Journal of Refugee Studies* 20 (3): 349–69.

———. 2007b. "Refugee Solutions, or Solutions to Refugeehood?" *Refuge: Canada's Journal on Refugees* 24 (2): 3–10.

Helms, E. 2003. "Women as Agents of Ethnic Reconciliation? Women's NGOs and International Intervention in Postwar Bosnia–Herzegovina." *Women's Studies International Forum* 26 (1): 15–33.

———. 2013. *Innocence and Victimhood: Gender, Nation, and Women's Activism in Postwar Bosnia-Herzegovina.* Madison: University of Wisconsin Press.

Herzfeld, M. 1997. *Cultural Intimacy: Social Poetics in the Nation-state.* London: Routledge.

Hicks, D.L. 2013. "War and the Political Zeitgeist: Evidence from the History of Female Suffrage." *European Journal of Political Economy* 31: 60–81.

Hitchens, C. 1997. *Hostage to History: Cyprus from the Ottomans to Kissinger.* London: Verso.

Hyndman, J., and W. Giles. 2011. "Waiting for What? The Feminization of Asylum in Protracted Situations." *Gender, Place & Culture* 18 (3): 361–79.

Iliopoulou, E., and P. Karathanasis. 2014. "Towards a Radical Politics: Grassroots Urban Activism in the Walled City of Nicosia." *The Cyprus Review* 26 (1): 169.

Isin, E.F. 2002. *Being Political: Genealogies of Citizenship*. Minneapolis: University of Minnesota Press.

———. 2004. "The Neurotic Citizen." *Citizenship Studies* 8 (3): 217–35.

———. 2008. *Theorizing Acts of Citizenship*. London: Palgrave Macmillan.

———. 2012. *Citizens without Frontiers*. London: Bloomsbury.

Isin, E.F., and G.M. Nielsen, eds. 2013. *Acts of Citizenship*. London: Zed Books.

Jansen, S., 2006. "The Privatisation of Home and Hope: Return, Reforms and the Foreign Intervention in Bosnia-Herzegovina." *Dialectical Anthropology* 30 (3): 177–99.

Jaquette, J. 2010. *Women and Power in Latin American Democracies*. Miami: Center for Hemispheric Policy, University of Miami.

Jeram, S. 2013. "Immigrants and the Basque Nation: Diversity as a New Marker of Identity." *Ethnic and Racial Studies* 36 (11): 1770–88.

Kamenou, N. 2012. *'Cyprus Is the Country of Heroes, Not of Homosexuals': Sexuality, Gender and Nationhood in Cyprus*. PhD diss., European Studies Department: King's College London, University of London.

Karlan, P.S. 2002. "Ballots and Bullets: The Exceptional History of the Right to Vote." *University of Cincinnatti Law Review* 71: 1345–72.

Katsourides, Y., 2013. "Determinants of Extreme Right Reappearance in Cyprus: The National Popular Front (ELAM), Golden Dawn's Sister Party." *South European Society and Politics*, 18 (4): 567–89.

Kaufmann, C.D. 1998. "When All Else Fails: Ethnic Population Transfers and Partitions in the Twentieth Century." *International Security* 23 (2): 120–56.

Keane, D. 2003. "The Environmental Causes and Consequences of Migration: A Search for the Meaning of Environmental Refugees." *Georgetown Enviromental Law Review* 16: 209–24.

Khalil, A. 2008. *Irregular Migration into and through the Occupied Palestinian Territory*. European University institute Robert Schuman Centre for Advanced Studies CARIM Analytic and Synthetic Notes No. 2008/79.

Kibreab, G. 1997. "Environmental Causes and Impact of Refugee Movements: A Critique of the Current Debate." *Disasters* 21 (1): 20–38.

King, B. 2013. "Carnivalesque Economies: Clowning and the Neoliberal Impasse." *Kritika Kultura* (21/22): 472–89.

Kızılyürek, N. 1993. "From Traditionalism to Nationalism and Beyond." *The Cyprus Review* 5 (2): 58–67.

———. 2002. *Milliyetçilik Kıskacında Kıbrıs* Istanbul: İletişim.

Koskenniemi, M., and P. Leino. 2002. "Fragmentation of International Law? Postmodern Anxieties." *Leiden Journal of International Law* 15 (3): 553–79.

Kristeva, J. 1982. *Powers of Horror: An Essay on Abjection.* New York: Columbia University Press.

Kyrris, C.P. 1969. Περί του Εξισλαμισμού Μέρους των εν Κύπρω Ηγετικών Τάξεων Κατά το 1570–1571 κ.ε., και Περί της Εθνικής Προελεύσεως της Μουσουλμανικής Κοινότητας της Νήσου [Concerning the Islamization of the Ruling Classes in Cyprus during 1570–1571 and after, About the Ethnic Origins of the Muslim Community of the Island]. *Morfosis* 24–25: 1–20.

Latour, B. 2005. *Reassembling the Social: An Introduction to Actor-Network-Theory.* Oxford: Oxford University Press.

Liasi, T. 2016. *Home and Identity: Art Education in Cyprus and Other Areas of Conflict.* Nicosia: Kailas Printers.

Lindley, D. 2007. *Promoting Peace with Information: Transparency as a Tool of Security Regimes.* Princeton, NJ: Princeton University Press.

Loizos, P. 1981. *The Heart Grown Bitter: A Chronicle of Cypriot War Refugees.* Cambridge: Cambridge University Press.

———. 2008a. *Iron in the Soul: Displacement, Livelihood and Health in Cyprus.* New York: Berghahn Books.

———. 2008b. "The Loss of Home." In *Struggles for Home: Violence, Hope and the Movement of People,* edited by S. Jansen and S. Löfving, 65–84. New York: Berghahn Books.

Loughran, K., 2016. Imbricated Spaces: The High Line, Urban Parks, and the Cultural Meaning of City and Nature. *Sociological Theory,* 34(4): 311–34.

Luibhéid, E. 2013. *Pregnant on Arrival: Making the Illegal Immigrant.* Minneapolis, MN: University of Minnesota Press.

Lynch, T. 2014. "'Nothing but Land': Women's Narratives, Gardens, and the Settler-Colonial Imaginary in the US West and Australian Outback." *Western American Literature* 48 (4): 374–99.

MacLean, N. 2002. "Postwar Women's History: The 'Second Wave' or the End of the Family Wage?" In *A Companion to Post-1945 America*, edited by J.C. Agnew and R. Rosenzweig, 235–59. Oxford: Blackwell.

Madianou, M. 2005. *Mediating the Nation: News, Audiences and the Politics of Identity*. London: University College London Press.

Makriyianni, C., 2007. "History, museums and national identity in a divided country: children's experience of museum education in Cyprus." PhD diss. Department of Education, University of Cambridge.

Malkki, L.H. 1995. "Refugees and Exile: From 'Refugee Studies' to the National Order of Things." *Annual Review of Anthropology* 24 (1): 495–523.

Mallia, P. 2011. "Case of MSS v. Belgium and Greece: A Catalyst in the Re-thinking of the Dublin II Regulation." *Refugee Survey Quarterly* 30 (3): 107–28.

Markides, D.W. 2001. *Cyprus 1957–1963: From Colonial Conflict to Constitutional Crisis: The Key Role of the Municipal Issue*. Minneapolis: University of Minnesota Press.

Martin, D. 2015. "From Spaces of Exception to 'Campscapes': Palestinian Refugee Camps and Informal Settlements in Beirut." *Political Geography* 44: 9–18.

Mavratsas, C.V. 1997. "The Ideological Contest between Greek-Cypriot Nationalism and Cypriotism 1974–1995: Politics, Social Memory and Identity." *Ethnic and Racial Studies* 20 (4): 717–37.

Mbembe, A. 2003. "Necropolitics." *Public Culture* 15 (1): 11–40.

Mbembé, J.A., and S. Nuttall. 2004. "Writing the World from an African Metropolis." *Public Culture* 16(3): 347–72.

McNamara, K.E. 2007. "Conceptualizing Discourses on Environmental Refugees at the United Nations." *Population and Environment* 29 (1): 12–24.

McVeigh, R., and B. Rolston. 2007. "From Good Friday to Good Relations: Sectarianism, Racism and the Northern Ireland State." *Race & Class* 48 (4): 1–23.

McWilliams, M. 1995. "Struggling for Peace and Justice: Reflections on Women's Activism in Northern Ireland." *Journal of Women's History* 7 (1): 13–39.

Mezzadra, S., and B. Neilson. 2013. *Border as Method, or, the Multiplication of Labor*. Durham, NC: Duke University Press.

Mitchell, T. 1991. *Colonising Egypt*. Berkeley: University of California Press.

———. 2002. *Rule of Experts: Egypt, Techno-politics, Modernity.* Berkeley: University of California Press.

Moloney, R. 2004. "Incompatible Reservations to Human Rights Treaties: Severability and the Problem of State Consent." *Melbourne Journal of International Law* 5: 155–68.

Moreno-Lax, V. 2012. "Dismantling the Dublin System: MSS v. Belgium and Greece." *European Journal of Migration and Law* 14 (1): 1–31.

Moriarty, E. 2005. "Telling Identity Stories: The Routinisation of Racialisation of Irishness." *Sociological Research Online* 10 (3).

Morton, S. 2014. "Sovereignty and Necropolitics at the Line of Control." *Journal of Postcolonial Writing* 50 (1): 19–30.

Mowbray, A. 2005. "The Creativity of the European Court of Human Rights." *Human Rights Law Review* 5 (1): 57–79.

Muižnieks, N. 2016. Reply for the British Authorities to the Memorandum on the Human Rights of Asylum Seekers and Immigrants in the United Kingdom, for The Commissioner for Human Rights, CommDH/GovRep. *The Council of Europe.*

Nacu, A. 2012. "From Silent Marginality to Spotlight Scapegoating? A Brief Case Study of France's Policy Towards the Roma." *Journal of Ethnic and Migration Studies* 38 (8): 1323–28.

Navaro-Yashin, Y. 2003. "'Life Is Dead Here': Sensing the Political in 'No Man's Land.'" *Anthropological Theory* 3 (1): 107–25.

———. 2007. "Make-believe Papers, Legal Forms and the Counterfeit: Affective Interactions between Documents and People in Britain and Cyprus." *Anthropological Theory* 7 (1): 79–98.

———. 2009. "Confinement and the Imagination: Sovereignty and Subjectivity in a Quasi-state." In *Sovereign Bodies: Citizens, Migrants, and States in the Postcolonial World,* edited by H.B. Hansen and F. Stepputat, 103–19. Princeton, NJ: Princeton University Press.

———. 2012. *The Make-believe Space: Affective Geography in a Postwar Polity.* Durham, NC: Duke University Press.

Neocleous, M. 2006. "The Problem with Normality: Taking Exception to 'Permanent Emergency.'" *Alternatives* 31 (2): 191–213.

Nevzat, A. 2005. *Nationalism amongst the Turks of Cyprus: The First Wave.* Oulu: Oulu University Press.

Ní Aoláin, F. 2016. "The 'War on Terror' and Extremism: Assessing the Relevance of the Women, Peace and Security Agenda." *International Affairs* 92 (2): 275–91.

Noxolo, P., and J. Huysmans. 2009. *Community, Citizenship, and the "War on Terror": Security and Insecurity.* London: Palgrave Macmillan.

Nyers, P. 2003. "Abject Cosmopolitanism: The Politics of Protection in the Anti-deportation Movement." *Third World Quarterly* 24 (6): 1069–93.

———. 2006. "The Accidental Citizen: Acts of Sovereignty and (un) making Citizenship." *Economy and Society* 35 (1): 22–41.

———. 2013. *Rethinking Refugees: Beyond State of Emergency.* London: Routledge.

Oberling, P. 1982. *The Road to Bellapais: The Turkish Cypriot Exodus to Northern Cyprus.* Boulder: Brooklyn College Studies on Society in Change.

Öktem, K. 2008. "The Nation's Imprint: Demographic Engineering and the Change of Toponymes in Republican Turkey." *European Journal of Turkish Studies.* 7 (1): 1–33.

Ong, A. 1999. *Flexible Citizenship: The Cultural Logics of Transnationality.* Durham, NC: Duke University Press.

———. 2003. *Buddha Is Hiding: Refugees, Citizenship, the New America.* Berkeley: University of California Press.

———. 2006. *Neoliberalism as Exception: Mutations in Citizenship and Sovereignty.* Durham, NC: Duke University Press.

Packard, M. 2008. *Getting It Wrong: Excerpts from a Cyprus Diary.* London: Author House.

Papadakis, Y. 1994. "The National Struggle Museums of a Divided City." *Ethnic and Racial Studies* 17 (3): 400–19.

———. 1996. "Pyla: A Mixed Borderline Village under UN Supervision in Cyprus." *International Journal on Minority and Group Rights* 4 (3/4): 353–72.

———. 1998. "Greek Cypriot Narratives of History and Collective Identity: Nationalism as a Contested Process." *American Ethnologist* 25 (2): 149–65.

———. 2005. *Echoes from the Dead Zone: Across the Cyprus Divide.* London: I.B. Tauris.

Papadimitriou, P. N., and I. F. Papageorgiou. 2005. "The New 'Dubliners': Implementation of European Council Regulation 343/2003 (Dublin-II) by the Greek Authorities." *Journal of Refugee Studies,* 18(3): 299–318.

Papadopoulos, D., and V.S. Tsianos. 2013. "After Citizenship: Autonomy of Migration, Organisational Ontology and Mobile Commons." *Citizenship Studies* 17 (2): 178–96.

Papaeti, A. 2010. "Trauma, Memory and Forgetting in Post-war Cyprus: The Case of Manoli . . . !" In *Trauma, Media, Art: New Perspectives*, edited by M. Broderick and A. Traverso, 132–44. Newcastle: Cambridge Scholars Publishing.

Papageorgiou, S. (ed.) 1984 [1961]. *Αρχείον των Παράνομων Εγγράφων του Κυπριακού Αγώνος 1955–1959 [Archive of Illegal Documents of the Cypriot Struggle 1955–1959]*. Nicosia: Epiphaniou.

Papataxiarchis, E. 2016. "Being 'There': At the Front Line of the 'European Refugee Crisis'-Part 1." *Anthropology Today* 32 (2): 5–9.

Paraskeva, C., and E. Meleagrou. 2013. "Homes From the Past: An Expiration Date for the Right to Respect for Home Under Article 8 of the European Convention on Human Rights." *Annuaire International des Droits de l'Homme* 7 (2012–2013): 845–77.

———. 2018. "Property Restitution Cases in the Context of the Cyprus Conflict." In *International Law and the Rights of those Displaced by Armed Conflict*, edited by E. Katselli. London: Routledge (forthcoming).

Patrick, R.A. 1976. *Political Geography and the Cyprus Conflict, 1963–1971*. PhD diss. Deptartnebt of Geography, Faculty of Environmental Studies, University of Waterloo.

Pattie, S.P. 1997. *Faith in History: Armenians Rebuilding Community*. Washington, DC: Smithsonian Institute Press.

Peacock, L. 2016. "Sending Laughter around the World." *Humor* 29 (2): 223–41.

Peteet, J.M. 2005. *Landscape of Hope and Despair: Palestinian Refugee Camps*. Philadelphia: University of Pennsylvania Press.

Phuong, C. 2000. "'Freely to Return': Reversing Ethnic Cleansing in Bosnia-Herzegovina." *Journal of Refugee Studies* 13 (2): 165–83.

Povinelli, E.A. 2011. *Economies of Abandonment: Social Belonging and Endurance in Late Liberalism*. Durham, NC: Duke University Press.

Psillita-Ioannou, P. 1996. *Οι Ηρωομάρτυρες της ΕΟΚΑ [The Martyred Heroes of EOKA]*. Nicosia: SIMAE.

Raijman, R., S. Schammah-Gesser, and A. Kemp. 2003. "International Migration, Domestic Work, and Care Work: Undocumented Latina Migrants in Israel." *Gender & Society* 17 (5): 727–49.

Ramm, C. 2006. "Assessing Transnational Re-negotiation in the Post-1974 Turkish Cypriot Community: 'Cyprus Donkeys,' 'Black Beards' and the 'EU Carrot.'" *Southeast European and Black Sea Studies* 6 (4): 523–42.

Rancière, J. 2010. *Dissensus: On Politics and Aesthetics.* London: Bloomsbury.

Richmond, O. 1994. "Peacekeeping and Peacemaking in Cyprus 1974–1994." *The Cyprus Review* 6 (2): 7–42.

Richmond, O., and J. Ker-Lindsay, (eds.) 2001. *The Work of the UN in Cyprus: Promoting Peace and Development.* London: Palgrave.

Roque, S., M. Mucavele, and N. Noronha, 2016. Subúrbios and cityness: exploring imbrications and urbanity in Maputo, Mozambique. *Journal of Southern African Studies* 42 (4): 643–58.

Roussou, M. 1986. "War in Cyprus: Patriarchy and the Penelope Myth." In *Caught Up in Conflict.* 25–44. London: Macmillan.

Rygiel, K. 2010. *Globalizing Citizenship.* Vancouver: University of British Columbia Press.

Şahin, S. 2011. "Open Borders, Closed Minds: The Discursive Construction of National Identity in North Cyprus." *Media, Culture & Society* 33 (4): 583–97.

Salih, R. 2017. "Bodies That Walk, Bodies That Talk, Bodies That Love: Palestinian Women Refugees, Affectivity, and the Politics of the Ordinary." *Antipode* 49 (3): 742–60.

Samers, M. 2004. "An Emerging Geopolitics of 'Illegal' Immigration in the European Union." *European Journal of Migration and Law* 6 (1): 27–45.

Sant Cassia, P. 2005. *Bodies of Evidence: Burial, Memory and the Recovery of Missing Persons in Cyprus.* Vol. 20. New York: Berghahn.

Sassen, S. 2011. *Cities in a World Economy.* London: Sage.

Schuster, L. 2003. *The Use and Abuse of Political Asylum in Britain and Germany.* London: Frank Cass.

———. 2005. "The Continuing Mobility of Migrants in Italy: Shifting between Places and Statuses." *Journal of Ethnic and Migration Studies* 31 (4): 757–74.

———. 2011a. "Dublin II and Eurodac: Examining the (un) intended (?) Consequences." *Gender, Place and Culture* 18 (3): 401–16.

———. 2011b. "Turning Refugees into 'Illegal Migrants': Afghan Asylum Seekers in Europe." *Ethnic and Racial Studies* 34 (8): 1392–407.

Scott, James. 1985. *Weapons of the Weak: Everyday Forms of Peasant Resistance.* New Haven: Yale University Press.

———. 1998. *Seeing Like a State: How Certain Schemes to Improve the Human Condition Have Failed.* New Haven: Yale University Press.

Scott, Julie. 1998. "Property Values: Ownership, Legitimacy and Land Markets in Northern Cyprus." In *Property Relations: Renewing the Anthropological Tradition,* 142–59.

Şenova, B., and P. Paraskevaidou (eds.). 2011. *Uncovered: Nicosia International Airport.* Nicosia: Proteas Press.

Seraphim-Loizou, E. 2000. *The Cyprus Liberation Struggle 1955–1959: Through the Eyes of a Woman EOKA Area Commander.* Nicosia: Philothei.

Sharoni, S. 1992. "Every Woman Is an Occupied Territory: The Politics of Militarism and Sexism and the Israeli-Palestinian Conflict." *Journal of Gender Studies* 1 (4): 447–62.

Siandou, E. 2012. *Entrapped Modernity: Nicosia International Airport.* Master's dissertation, Raymond Lemaire International Centre for Conservation, Katholike Universiteit Leuven.

Smith, C.A. 2013. "Strange Fruit: Brazil, Necropolitics, and the Transnational Resonance of Torture and Death." *Souls* 15 (3): 177–98.

Soguk, N. 1999. *States and Strangers: Refugees and Displacements of Statecraft.* Minneapolis: University of Minnesota Press.

Soysal, Y.N. 1994. *Limits of Citizenship: Migrants and Postnational Membership in Europe.* Chicago: University of Chicago Press.

———. 2015. "Mapping the Terrain of Transnationalization: Nation, Citizenship, and Region." In *Transnational Trajectories in East Asia: Nation, Citizenship, and Region,* edited by Y.N. Soysal, 1–13. London: Routledge.

Spyrou, S. 2006. "Constructing 'the Turk' as an Enemy: The Complexity of Stereotypes in Children's Everyday Worlds." *South European Society & Politics* 11 (1): 95–110.

Stefanelli, J.N. 2011. "Whose Rule of Law? An Analysis of the UK's Decision Not to Opt-In to the EU Asylum Procedures and Reception Conditions Directives." *International & Comparative Law Quarterly* 60 (4): 1055–64.

Stepputat, F., ed. 2014. *Governing the Dead: Sovereignty and the Politics of Dead Bodies*. Oxford: Oxford University Press.

Stevens, J. 2011. *States Without Nations: Citizenship for Mortals*. New York: Columbia University Press.

———. 2017a. Introduction. In *Citizenship in Question: Evidentiary Birthright and Statelessness*, edited by B.N. Lawrance and J. Stevens, 1–24. Durham: Duke University Press.

———. 2017b. "The Alien Who Is a Citizen." In *Citizenship in Question: Evidentiary Birthright and Statelessness*, edited by B.N. Lawrance and J. Stevens. Durham: Duke University Press.

Stig-Sørensen, M.L.S., and D. Viejo-Rose, (eds.) 2015. *War and Cultural Heritage*. Cambridge: Cambridge University Press.

Stylianou-Lambert, T., and A. Bounia. 2012. "War Museums and Photography." *Museum and Society* 10 (3): 183–96.

Summerfield, P. 1998. *Reconstructing Women's Wartime Lives: Discourse and Subjectivity in Oral Histories of the Second World War*. Manchester: Manchester University Press.

Surin, K., and J. Hasty. 1994. "'Reinventing a Physiology of Collective Liberation': Going 'beyond Marx' in the Marxism (s) of Negri, Guattari, and Deleuze." *Rethinking Marxism* 7 (2): 9–27.

Tahsin, A.H. 1999. "Geçmisten Gelecege: Bir Kıbrıs Hikayesi." Nicosia: Işık Kitabevi.

Taussig, M. 2003. "The Language of Flowers." *Critical Inquiry* 30 (1): 98–131.

Tazzioli, M. 2014. *Spaces of Governmentality*. Lanham, ND: Rowman & Littlefield.

Thrift, N. 2008. *Non-representational Theory: Space, Politics, Affect*. London: Routledge.

Toumazis, Y. 2013. "The Memory of Objects." In *Rusted Evidence* edited by T. Liasi. Nicosia: Chr. Nicolaou and Sons.

Trimikliniotis, N. 2010. *Η Διαλεκτική του Έθνους-Κράτους και το Καθεστώς της Εξαίρεσης* [The Nation-State Dialectics and the State of Exception]. Athens: Savvalas.

Trimikliniotis, N., and C. Demetriou. 2008. "Evaluating the Anti-discrimination Law in the Republic of Cyprus: A Critical Reflection." *The Cyprus Review* 20 (2): 79–116.

———. 2009. "The Cypriot Roma and the failure of education: Anti-discrimination and multiculturalism as a post-accession challenge."

In *The minorities of Cyprus: Development patterns and the identity of the internal-exclusion*, edited by A. Varnava, N. Coureas, and M. Elia, 241–64. Newcastle: Cambridge Scholars Publishing.

Trimikliniotis, N., and P. Pantelides. 2003. "Mapping Discriminatory Landscapes in Cyprus: Ethnic Discrimination in the Labour Market." *The Cyprus Review* 15 (1): 121–46.

Turpin, J. 1998. "Many Faces: Women Confronting War." In *The Women and War Reader*, edited by L.A. Lorentzen and J. Turpin, 3–18. New York: New York University Press.

Uludağ, S. 2005. *Oysters with their Missing Pearls*. Nicosia: IKME.

Üngör, U.Ü., and E. Lohr. 2014. "Economic Nationalism, Confiscation, and Genocide: A Comparison of the Ottoman and Russian Empires during World War I." *Journal of Modern European History* 12 (4): 500–22.

Valpy, F.E.J. 1828. *An Etymological Dictionary of the Latin Language*. London: Longman.

Vassiliadou, M. 2002. "Questioning Nationalism: The Patriarchal and National Struggles of Cypriot Women within a European Context." *European Journal of Women's Studies* 9 (4): 459–82.

———. 2004. "Women's Constructions of Women: On Entering the Front Door." *Journal of International Women's Studies* 5 (3): 53–67.

———. 1997. "'Herstory': The Missing Woman of Cyprus." *The Cyprus Review* 9 (1): 95–120.

Vaughan-Williams, N. 2008. "Borderwork beyond Inside/Outside? Frontex, the Citizen–detective and the War on Terror." *Space and Polity* 12 (1): 63–79.

Varoufakis, Y. 2015. *The Global Minotaur: America, Europe and the Future of the Global Economy*. London: Zed Books.

Volkan, V. 1979. *Cyprus-War and Adaptation: A Psychoanalytic History of Two Ethnic Groups in Conflict*. Charlottesville: University of Virginia Press.

Voutira, E. 2003a. "Refugees: whose term is it anyway? Emic and etic constructions of 'refugees' in Modern Greek." In *The Refugee Convention at Fifty: A View from Forced Migration Studies*, edited by A. Van Selm et al, 65–80. Lanham, MD: Lexington Books.

Vural, Y., and N. Peristianis. 2008. "Beyond Ethno-nationalism: Emerging Trends in Cypriot Politics after the Annan Plan." *Nations and Nationalism* 14 (1): 39–60.

Walters, W. 2006. "Rethinking Borders beyond the State." *Comparative European Politics* 4 (2–1): 141–59.

Weber, C. 2006. "Middle Eastern Modernities: Women, Gender, and Nation in Lebanon and Palestine." *Journal of Women's History* 18 (1): 203–11.

Weber, C.M. 2006. *Visions of Solidarity: US Peace Activists in Nicaragua from War to Women's Activism and Globalization.* Lanham, MD: Lexington Books.

Weizman, E. 2012. *Hollow Land: Israel's Architecture of Occupation.* London: Verso.

Wells, L., T. Stylianou-Lambert, and N. Philippou. 2014. *Photography and Cyprus: Time, Place and Identity.* London: I.B. Tauris.

Werbner, P. 1999. "Political Motherhood and the Feminisation of Citizenship: Women's Activisms and the Transformation of the Public Sphere." In *Women, citizenship and difference,* edited by N. Yuval-Davis and P. Werbner, 221–45. London: Zed Books.

Woollacott, A. 1994. *On Her Their Lives Depend: Munitions Workers in the Great War.* Berkeley: University of California Press.

Yakinthou, C. 2008. "The Quiet Deflation of Den Xehno? Changes in the Greek Cypriot Communal Narrative on the Missing Persons in Cyprus." *The Cyprus Review* 20 (1): 15–33.

Zapata-Barrero, R. 2010. "Dynamics of Diversity in Spain." In *The Multicultural Backlash: European Discourses, Politics and Practices,* edited by S. Vertovec and S. Wessendorf, 170–89. London: Routledge.

Zembylas, M. 2012. "Pedagogies of Strategic Empathy: Navigating through the Emotional Complexities of Anti-racism in Higher Education." *Teaching in Higher Education* 17(2): 113–25.

Zembylas, M., and C. McGlynn. 2012. "Discomforting Pedagogies: Emotional Tensions, Ethical Dilemmas and Transformative Possibilities." *British Educational Research Journal* 38 (1): 41–59.

Zetter, R. 1991. "Labelling Refugees: Forming and Transforming a Bureaucratic Identity." *Journal of Refugee Studies* 4 (1): 39–62.

———. 1994. "The Greek-Cypriot Refugees: Perceptions of Return under Conditions of Protracted Exile." *International Migration Review*: 307–22.

———. 2007. "More Labels, Fewer Refugees: Remaking the Refugee Label in an Era of Globalization." *Journal of Refugee Studies* 20 (2): 172–92.

Žižek, S. 2000. *The Ticklish Subject: The Absent Centre of Political Ontology*. London: Verso.

Zureik, E., D. Lyon, and Y. Abu-Laban, eds. 2011. *Surveillance and Control in Israel/Palestine: Population, Territory and Power*. London: Routledge.

INDEX

The letter *f* following a page number denotes a figure

www.ingramcontent.com/pod-product-compliance
Lightning Source LLC
Chambersburg PA
CBHW050342270326
41926CB00016B/3576